Utah: A People's History

A Bonneville Book

University of Utah Press
Salt Lake City
1987

Utah: A People's History

Dean L. May

Library of Congress Cataloging-in-Publication Data

May, Dean L.
Utah: a people's history.

   (Bonneville books)
   Bibliography: p.
   Includes index.
   1. Utah—History.   I. Title.
F826.M29 1987   979.2   87–17898
ISBN 0–87480–283–0
ISBN 0–87480–284–9 (pbk.)

Book Interior and Jacket Design: Scott Engen, Salt Lake City.

Cover Photograph: Harvesting salt on the Great Salt Lake in the 1870s or 1880s.
C. W. Carter photo, courtesy of the Church Archives, Church of Jesus Christ
of Latter-day Saints.

For Leonard, and all my friends and colleagues who miss the warm promise of the Arrington Spring

and

For Helen Zeese Papanikolas, who opens eyes and builds bridges

Contents

Illustrations

Preface

Haistory belongs to the people. Though there must be discourse among the scholars—fierce debates and exchanges on arcane topics in professional meetings and journals—the product, to justify our endeavor, must ultimately be accessible to all. It is out of this conviction that I welcomed in 1978 the opportunity proposed by the chairman of the University of Utah History Department, Richard Tompson, to help produce a television series on Utah history. In discussions with Stephen Hess and Helen Lacy of the University's Instructional Media Services, and Bruce Christensen and Fred Esplin of KUED, Channel 7, we concluded that the time was right for production of a new television history of the state.

Television, for good or ill, had become preeminently the people's medium. And Utah's history, as historian Helen Papanikolas has long aptly reminded us, is the history of many peoples. We thus agreed to call our effort "A People's History of Utah"—a name that does not trip off the tongue but says much in its multiple meanings.

We had two models. David E. Miller in the 1950s had pioneered the use of television in teaching Utah history. I carefully watched and took notes on each program of his series. Their content was fascinating. One did not mind that they were in black and white and produced almost entirely from his office desk, as he, on camera, reached up to focus the lens on photographs or maps that illustrated his points. But their great appeal, I concluded, came from the fact that this was clearly a personal interpretation and that the production process retained the flavor of his personality. His enthusiasm was engaging and contagious. Thanks especially to Fred Esplin, we concluded that the production should insofar as possible retain the intimacy that characterized the Miller series.

Production techniques had changed greatly since the 1950s. Color was now available, location filming more readily accomplished, and splendid models for public education through television were before us in such series as Jacob Bronowski's "The Ascent of Man" or Kenneth Clark's "Civilization." Though our resources were miniscule compared to those used by Bronowski and Clark, and our topic perhaps less sweeping, we concluded to use their work as a second model—keeping their techniques of production, as well as the intimate quality of David Miller's pioneering work before us. Thanks to a series of capable directors, associate directors, videographers, and engineers the series will shortly be completed and before the people, who will judge how appropriate our models were and how well we succeeded in approximating them.

I used the programs in my Utah History courses as they were completed. And though they held the interest of the students and worked well in the classroom, their impact seemed ephemeral. They could not readily be mulled over, underlined, and reviewed. The pace of presentation did not lend itself to reflection. I decided that it might be desirable to print a popular history of Utah that could be a companion volume to the TV series. Stephen Hess, who had become director of Media Services and the University of Utah Press, thought such a book might be an ideal candidate for the Bonneville Book series, and Peggy Lee, Editor-in-Chief at the Press, agreed. Their generous support has led to the production of what I no doubt wisely have refrained from calling "A People's History of Utah: the Book."

This history of Utah is thus, like the TV series, avowedly popular and personal. This will be seen in the suggested readings at the end of each chapter. I have consistently tried to choose readings that would be available to the general reader in a nearby library and would be interesting to such persons. Thus, a good many unpublished studies, rare books or manuscripts, and conceptually difficult books have not been cited, even when they are important to Utah history. Moreover, most of those that were chosen are among the studies and sources that have appealed to me personally and thus helped in my efforts to understand the complex past of our region.

Utah: A People's History offers one point of view—not that of a committee. The reader accordingly deserves an explanation of that point of view. A varied procession of peoples have played their part—Paleo-Indians, Desert Archaic, Fremont, Anasazi, Shoshonean (including Utes, Southern Paiutes, Gosiutes, and Shoshone), Navajo, Spaniards, Northern Europeans, Italians, Yugoslavs, Greeks, Blacks, Jews, Polynesians, Southeast Asians, and many more. Important among them in recent times are the Mormons, whose faith began in controversy and has remained there. They became an enduring part of Utah's history in 1847. There is much else about our state's past that is exciting and instructive, but we cannot escape the importance of the Mormon presence and influence here. To ignore it or treat it gingerly in a general history is to assure that we will misunderstand Utah's past. I have accordingly tried to recognize that presence while writing a history that balances reasonably the historical roles of the many peoples who have come here.

Having defined his field, a historian

seeks to explore all the evidence, assess its reliability, reconcile differences among the witnesses, and then arrive at interpretations that derive from and explain the preponderance of the best evidence. Even going carefully through this process, there are often ambiguities that remain. The facts do not speak for themselves and the historian must speak for them—offering interpretations that in his or her judgment best account for them. There, in that matter of "judgment," is the rub. For no author can escape at that point the frame of reference etched by her or his most fundamental beliefs about the nature of man and the wellsprings of human action. He or she must be constantly aware of the limitations of their frame of reference and seek through great exertion to compensate honestly for them.

Moreover, one who would truly understand the past must not be content merely to praise it. Lamentably, history has been altered at least as often by human weakness as by greatness. Some believe that a truly "objective" history would note only the positive and uplifting aspects of human experience. Others insist the badge of "objectivity" can be won only by taking a consistently dim view of the aims and accomplishments of our predecessors. The fact is that the peoples who lived in Utah were not consistently angels or devils. They succeeded wonderfully at times but often failed to accomplish their aims and to honor in practice their avowed principles. They were, in short, human beings, capable of great and glorious deeds and subject to human frailty. To ignore human weaknesses—errors in judgment or faults in character—that have had a discernible impact on the past, is to prettify the record of human endeavor beyond usefulness. A good history must explore the warts where they changed the course of events.

Yet in my judgment the number of wholly malevolent men and women is very few. Far more common are human beings who have competing agendas (often both justifiable from their own perspective), and who are uninformed or careless in understanding others' views. The bitter smoke that arose from the battles of Mormons and Gentiles in nineteenth-century Utah came not so much from good men and women fighting bad as from good men and women misunderstanding one another. Starting from this premise, I have sought not to judge the past, but to understand it. There will no doubt be those who feel I have seen too many faults, just as there will be those who will feel that I have been overgenerous. To such I can only answer that I have tried to be honest and fair to all, to exercise doggedly the skills and concepts that were part of my professional training as a historian, and to compensate through extra effort for those limitations my personal history might place upon my frame of reference.

Any author of a general survey incurs a good many debts. Much very good work on Utah history has been done. Generations of amateur and professional historians have pored over the terrain of Utah's past, exploring virtually every rock and crevice. I have tried to study the vast body of their writing and incorporate that which is helpful into my own. I am indebted to all of them.

I have also had long talks with many currently engaged in studying Utah's past—a varied set whose ideas over the years have helped shape my own so imperceptibly that I cannot always tell where their insights leave off and mine begin. Among them are colleagues with whom I worked in the LDS Historical Department, Ron Esplin, Richard L. Jensen, Bruce Blumell, Gene A. Sessions, Gordon Irving, William G. Hartley, Dean C. Jessee, Glen M. Leonard, Maureen Beecher, Jill Mulvay Derr, Paul L. Anderson, James B. Allen, and Davis Bitton. Others, including Jan Shipps, Klaus Hansen, Larry Foster, Mario De Pillis, Lowell "Ben" Bennion, Brigham D. Madsen, David Madsen, David E. Miller, Richard Poll, Thomas G. Alexander, S. George Ellsworth, Charles S. Peterson, Melvin T. Smith, and Charles Hatch, have added through their excellent study to my vision and to our common stock of understanding about Utah's past. Among the many librarians and archivists who have been unfailingly helpful are Jeffery O. Johnson and Val D. Wilson of the Utah State Archives; Jay Haymond, Linda Thatcher, and Susan Whetstone of the Utah State Historical Society; Ronald Reed, and Robert O. Davis of the LDS Museum of Church History and Art; and Ronald G. Watt, W. Randall Dixon, and William Slaughter of the LDS Church Archives. Many of my students at the University of Utah have, through participation in class discussions and the researching and writing of papers, theses, and dissertations, helped to refine my perspectives and push back the frontiers of knowledge in ways profitable to all of us.

A few historians have served rather more explicitly as models. Leonard J. Arrington has been a friend and colleague for many years, but perhaps more importantly his *Great Basin Kingdom* (only the tip of a cornucopia of scholarship) served to awaken my interest in Utah history and offered insights and challenges enough to stimulate several lifetimes of study (as indeed it has already done among younger historians). It was the only work on Utah history in the select library for graduate history students at Harvard when I studied there, and justly so. Helen Zeese Papanikolas has gently but firmly opened to our understanding the powerful history of the new pioneers to Utah, an accomplishment of immense importance to the state's history. I met Juanita Brooks only a few times, yet always was inspired by her indomitable will, her passion for integrity, her unswerving commitment to truth. Dale L. Morgan, whom I never met, wrote with surpassing style and dogged attention to detail on many aspects of Utah's past, especially the fur trade era. These, to my mind, are the giants whose work has set a standard for subsequent generations. We and subse-

quent Utahns will remain greatly in their debt.

A good many have read all or portions of the manuscript and offered helpful suggestions including Fred R. Gowans, Robert A. Goldberg, Eugene E. Campbell, Gregory C. Thompson, Boone Colegrove, and most of those mentioned above. Betty Sedgley, Margaret Mower, and Heidi Leithead were chief among several who helped to type the manuscript. David Catron, current director of the University of Utah Press, Peggy Lee, and Rodger Reynolds provided constant encouragement, excellent and careful editing, and superb design. Leonard J. Arrington and Gregory C. Thompson read the manuscript for the Press and offered many valuable suggestions, which greatly improved the final product. Among them was Dr. Thompson's proposal to change the working title, which was the same as the TV series, offering one less likely to be confused with Helen Papanikolas' *Peoples of Utah* but perhaps more likely to be confused with Charles S. Peterson's *Utah: A Bicentennial History*. In any case my central aim I hope is clear — of wanting to produce a history of Utah for the people of Utah.

Finally, to my wife, Cheryll, and our children, Tim, Caroline, and Tad, I owe a special thanks. They have been unfailingly patient as I have taken hours and weeks from our common time to advance this book and the television series it emulates. Cheryll has discussed with me every interpretation, been with me over every line of the manuscript, and has always offered wise and thoughtful advice. More importantly, as my best friend and confidante she has patiently helped to see me through not a few sharp vicissitudes of life. Without her I doubt this book could have been written. And behind all this are my parents, Frank Peter May, who died in 1971, Howard F. Rockhill, and Wanda Lowe May Rockhill. Their love and support began long ago and have never diminished.

Utah: A People's History

Salt Crested Rocks at Black Rock, 1899. J. T. Harwood. *Courtesy Utah Arts Council, Alice Art Collection. Transparency provided by LDS Museum of Church History and Art.*

One

Man and Desert

They came to the desert and salt water lakes,
The ground it was teemin' with varmits and snakes,
Beset by wild Indians, Comanche and Sioux,
'Tis a glorious tale how they ever got through!

The verse is from perhaps the best known of all the forty-niner ballads—"Sweet Betsy from Pike." The song sprang up during the gold rush and here seems clearly to speak of Utah country. Of course there was not a place called Utah before late 1850. There were Utah *people*, or the Ute Indians as they came to be known, who inhabited eastern parts of the present state—also Southern Paiute, Gosiute, Navajo, and Shoshone (no Comanche or Sioux). And before them there were the Fremont and Anasazi. Their predecessors were the Desert Archaic; and theirs the Paleo-Indians (the "old" Indians). They were here as early 11,000 B.C.

The folk song is on target, however, as folk songs often are, in etching sharply the image of "desert and salt water lakes." Though there were no lines drawn on a map circumscribing a place called Utah, the land was here long before the people. It is the constant in Utah history, a backdrop across which the people over millennia have come and gone. This is, as the forty-niners were painfully aware, a peculiar land whose unique and distinctive features are deserts and a vast salt-water lake. And, given its austere character, the land has, more than many, required accommodation of its tenants. Thus, the story of Utah is a story of a land and its peoples. But the fixed and enduring part of the mix has been the land.

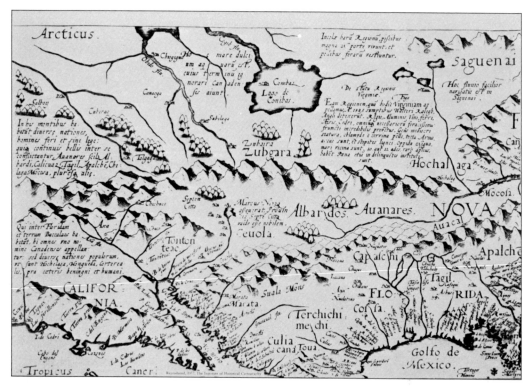

The Land

Utah country was first charted and described by Europeans who approached from the south. In 1540 a scouting party of twelve men under García López de Cárdenas explored northwest from Francisco Coronado's main camp at the Zuni pueblos to investigate reports of a major river in the area. They were suffering from thirst by the time they reached the Colorado and tried in vain to descend through the canyon to the stream itself. Frustrated, they picked their painful way back through the northern Arizona deserts to the main camp, bearing, no doubt, ill tidings of the character of the land they had crossed. They didn't enter present Utah, but they had learned enough to know that the region was forbidding and best avoided. That impression was perpetuated by subsequent Spaniards.

Deserts, impassable canyons, and rumors of a great lake characterized the land the Spaniards came to call Teguayo. A 1593

1593 Map of Utah country prepared by Cornelius de Judais, Antwerp. A large interior lake, Conibus, is shown draining to a northern sea. *Courtesy Yale University Library. Reprinted from Carl I. Wheat,* Mapping the Transmississippi West, 1540–1861, *with permission of Francis M. Wheat.*

map shows a large inland lake called Conibus, connected by an isthmus to a northern sea. A century later another map had abandoned the northern sea but still had a lake, drained by a river to a western ocean. In 1822 maps were produced that did not distinguish between the Great Salt Lake and Utah Lake and kept a mythical river to the Pacific still firmly in place. The deserts and the lake thus dominated the half-imagined view Europeans had of Utah land for two centuries. It was the same view gold-seekers of the late 1840s perpetuated in "Sweet Betsy from Pike."

The Great Salt Lake, a "vast inland sea," is perhaps the most distinctive of all Utah's natural features. Though locals relegate it to a position on their list of Utah's won-

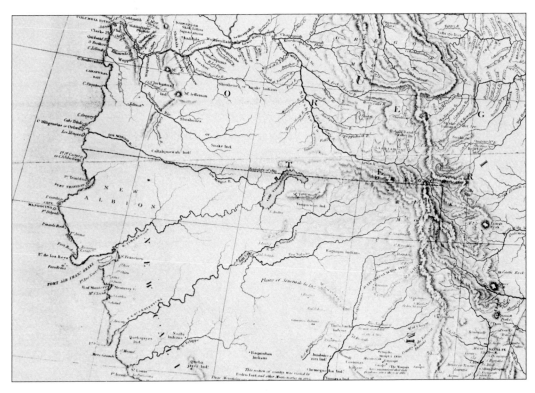

∧ 1822 map by Henry S. Tanner. The Great Salt Lake and Utah Lake are combined. Two rivers flow from the lake to the Pacific Ocean. Sevier Lake is drained by the River Buenaventura. *Courtesy the Bancroft Library, Carl I. Wheat Map Collection. Reprinted from Carl I. Wheat,* Mapping the Transmississippi West, 1540–1861, *with permission of Francis M. Wheat.*

< 1705 John Harris map of the American West. An enormous inland lake drains to a western sea. California is represented as an island. *Printed in Hubert Howe Bancroft's* History of Utah *(1889).*

as the Bonneville Basin. Filling the bottom of a shallow natural dish, the lake is more broad than deep. Its briny waters reach down only about thirty-five to forty-five feet at the deepest points. And a small rise in surface level sends it sprawling outward, flooding recreation sites, bird refuges, saltworks, superhighways, and whatever else might be in the way. On the average the lake spreads seventy square miles for every foot it rises. And as it grows it feeds itself, spawning heavy snowfalls and rains on its eastern shores that return pre-

ders approximating its elevation in the landscape about it, the lake has a way of making its presence known. Its surface fluctuates around 4,200 feet above sea level, occupying the lowest part of a great, shallow, natural basin, known to geographers

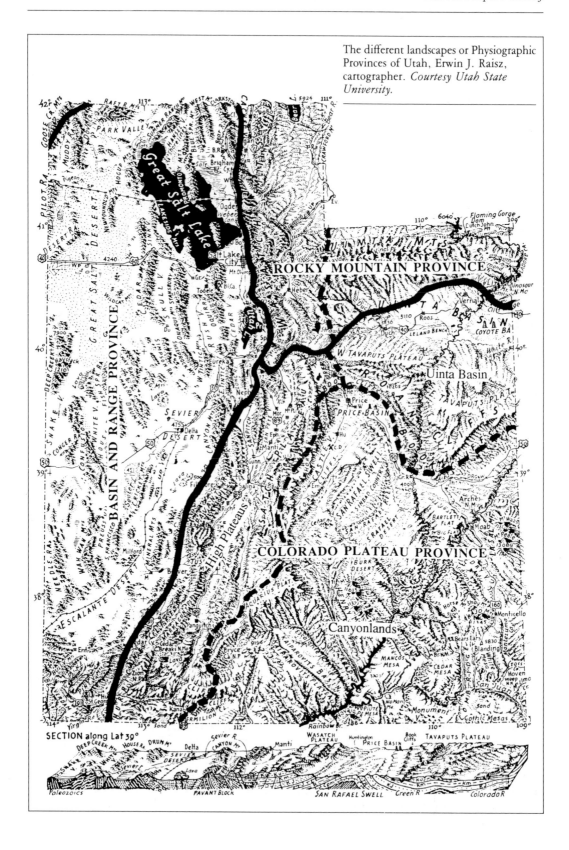

The different landscapes or Physiographic Provinces of Utah, Erwin J. Raisz, cartographer. *Courtesy Utah State University.*

Basin and Range country west of Delta. The normally dry playas on the basin floor appear to be bodies of water from a distance. *Dean L. May photograph.*

cipitation to its waters, reminding even modern man that his tenure here is in some measure subject to nature's will.

The Bonneville Basin reaches from the crest of the Wasatch Mountains westward to Wendover and from Malad, Idaho, southward to Cedar City. It is part of a much greater inland drainage area extending south and west to Death Valley and to Reno, called by John C. Frémont in 1845 the Great Basin. Both are a part of a physiographic region geographers call the Basin and Range Province which stretches from east to west between the Wasatch Mountains and and the Sierra Nevada. It begins in the north, near Klamath Falls, Oregon, and encompasses, as it doglegs southwestward from that point, tracts extending all the way to the big bend of the Rio Grande River below El Paso.

Geographers invented the term "physiographic province" to help them classify and describe landforms that are recognizably similar. There are three extending into Utah; the Middle Rocky Mountain Region of the Rocky Mountain Province; the Colorado Plateau Province; and the Basin and Range Province. You can tell Basin and Range areas, as you might expect, by their numerous nearly flat *basin* valleys, separated by north-and-south-running *ranges* of mountains. A cross-sectional map of the land running westward from the Wasatch Mountains clearly shows the generally flat valley basins separated by short mountain ranges. The Oquirrh, Stansbury, and Cedar chains parallel one another almost perfectly in a series extending altogether only sixty miles west of Salt Lake City.

Though Deseret Peak in the Stansbury Mountains rises to 6,800 feet above the valleys (11,031 feet above sea level), the mountains generally do not project far above the basins. The valley floors are nearly flat, having been filled over eons of time with sediments washing from the mountains. Some, such as Skull Valley, have intermittent lakes, the dry beds of which are called playas, at the lowest point.

The Basin and Range Province is the product of a geological process called block faulting. Around sixty-five million years ago pressures began to break the earth's crust into a series of adjoining blocks, pushing them up on the western edges and causing them to slope towards the east. Volcanic activity had already peppered the crust with intrusions of molten materials, but the faulting contributed to even greater outflows of volcanic matter that filled in the cracks and seams and then hardened. Adjoining uplifted blocks formed rugged V-shaped valleys, which over hundreds of thousands of years received sediments washing from raw mountain faces. Heavy gravels and sands were deposited near the mountain edges. Finer soils settled on the valley bottoms, flattening the basins to the form seen today. The ranges of the Basin and Range province thus became islands projecting from a sea of sediments that form the basin floors.

It is a curious fact that much of the shaping of the region, now known for its aridity, was accomplished by the action of water on rock and soil. Though the whole area was subject to a series of inundations going far back into geological time and forming the sedimentary layers and fossil beds seen all over Utah, the most recent and best documented was that which formed Lake Bonneville, named after Benjamin L. E. Bonneville, an army captain who had in Washington Irving a brilliant press agent. His explorations were made famous through Irving's *Adventures of Capt. Bonneville, U.S.A. in the Rocky Mountains,* published in 1837.

During the Pleistocene period, a time of heavy glaciation, immense lakes dotted the Basin and Range Province. The largest of these filled the basin named after Captain Bonneville. At its highest level the lake was 348 miles long, 145 miles wide, and

covered 19,750 square miles, a little less than present-day Lake Michigan. For thousands of years the lake waters rose until at Red Rock Pass in the extreme northern end of Cache Valley they spilled over the northern rim of the Bonneville Basin into Marsh Creek, a tributary of the Portneuf River, and flowed thence to the Snake, the Columbia, and the Pacific.

The lake stood at its highest level for an extended period, its waves carving a shoreline along the mountain slopes at 5,150 feet above sea level. That shoreline is still clearly visible today on many mountain slopes, marking what is now called the Bonneville level of the ancient lake. As soon as the waters spilled over the rim of the basin, however, they began to cut away the softer soils at Red Rock Pass, rapidly lowering the lake level until they encountered hard rock 300 feet below the Bonneville level. Again the lake was contained and stabilized within its own basin, now forming a lower shoreline, clearly visible at Point-of-the-Mountain, between the Salt Lake and Utah valleys. This shoreline is known as the Provo level. Other stages in the lake's capricious career have left an elaborate series of terraces that can be seen almost everywhere along Utah's mountains and foothills.

Important to later inhabitants of Utah was the deposition by canyon streams entering the lake of millions of tons of sediments to form large deltas. These deltas are not quite level. They slope gently in three directions and are usually crossed by a mountain stream. Thus they were frequently chosen as prime settlement sites by the earliest whites to come here. Numerous Utah towns were built on such sites, including Salt Lake City, Provo, and Nephi.

The waters of Lake Bonneville continued over millennia to evaporate, the body shrinking eventually to the present confines of the Great Salt Lake — about 2,400 square miles. Salts were concentrated as the waters evaporated until the present waters have become a rich soup of minerals — a source of chlorine, magnesium, potassium sulfate, sodium sulfate, and, of course, table salt. Boiling a quart of water from its saltiest solution would yield about a half cup of salt.

The Basin and Range Province is very literally a land of deserts and salt-water lakes. Vegetation is sparse and hardy, able to endure the semiarid seven to twelve inches of rainfall each year. The aromatic artemesia, or sagebrush, is but one of several native plants that fill vast areas of the basins. Native bunchgrasses were also common in the early 1900s, though they have subsequently been grazed nearly out of existence, and cheat grass, a less useful European import, has taken their place. Before settlement bunchgrass was rich and high in the better watered areas, making excellent forage. Cottonwood and willow trees lined the streams and rivers.

The ranges of the Basin and Range Province rarely have trees larger than pinyon pine and mountain juniper (or cedar as the white settlers called it). At the higher elevations some yellow pine and Douglas fir can be found. Though lush in the spring and along waterways, the Basin and Range parts of Utah are inhospitable to plants and animals generally and man in particular. In Rhode Island I have tramped through the countryside and come across the fence rows and foundation stones of seventeenth-century farmhouses, almost invisible under a heavy growth of trees and shrubs. Rhode Island is a land that wants to be forest. In Basin and Range Utah, men nurse the landscape into reluctant verdure, but without constant attention the trees and shrubs wilt and die. Utah is a land that wants to be a desert.

In the early 1800s Americans commonly thought of the whole sweep of land between the Missouri River and the Rocky Mountains as the Great American Desert. Zebulon Pike, who gave his name to the mountain peak near Denver, published journals of his explorations to the Rio Grande Valley in 1810, comparing the tree-

The "Great American Desert." *Printed in* The Times Survey Atlas of the World *(London, 1922)*.

less plains he crossed to the deserts of Africa. Another explorer, Henry Brackinridge, confirmed Pike's account, adding that if settlers were to be successful in the West "a different mode of life, and habits altogether new, would have to be developed." As late as 1849 historian Francis Parkman offered the public a description of a western plain "unbroken as far as the eye could reach. Sometimes it glared in the sun, an expanse of hot, bare sand; sometimes it was veiled by long coarse grass. Huge skulls and whitening bones of buffalo were scattered everywhere."

This American Sahara shrank, however, as successive waves of explorers and settlers filled the empty spaces, proving them to be habitable and fertile. Even in this century cartographers still found substance for the myth, however, in the salt flats west of the Great Salt Lake. A London *Times* atlas of the 1920s clearly shows the remains of the Great American Desert, lying west of the Great Salt Lake and east of Wendover. The myth of the American Sahara

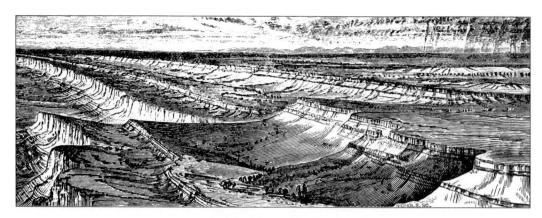

The Grand Staircase of Utah. Successive strata tilt up as the land drops to the Colorado River near Kanab forming a massive staircase of variegated cliffs. This classic H. H. Nichols etching was made for John Wesley Powell's *Exploration of the Colorado River of the West and its Tributaries* (1875). *Courtesy Special Collections, University of Utah Library, Salt Lake City, Utah.*

found its final refuge in Utah's Basin and Range region.

The Basin and Range Province covers only part of Utah, though the other geographical provinces of the state are also forbidding in their own way. More than half of the state's land area is within the Colorado Plateau, a brilliantly variegated landscape carved and shaped into fantastic and unforgettable features. Only California has more national parks than Utah and all five of our national parks are within the Colorado Plateau. Each is unique in its own way. The towering, massive, blocks of granite and sandstone of Zion resonate with all the power and rhythm of a Mahler symphony. Bryce Canyon, on the other hand, is pure Rossini, all whimsy and delight. Arches National Park evokes the symmetry and balance of a Mozart concerto. The grand landscapes of the Colorado Plateau seem to bare the substructure of time and nature herself, thrusting human tenure into a perspective that dwarfs our endeavor and batters our pride. They are a good place to visit.

Most of the Colorado Plateau is within Utah and Arizona, though it extends some distance into Colorado and New Mexico as well. It is called a plateau (French for tray) not because it is flat but because the underlying strata lie generally flat. The casual observer traveling south on I-15 would hardly notice the ending of the Wasatch range at Mount Nebo, above Nephi, or the changing character of the mountains south of that point. Indeed, early explorers, including John C. Frémont, labeled the entire cordillera stretching from the Cache Valley to the Grand Canyon as the Wasatch.

Yet the differences are clearly evident to one looking for them. Faulting in plateau country thrusts large, nearly level chunks of the earth's surface upward, giving the mountains a more rounded and less jagged appearance than the Wasatch, or often leaving summits as flat mesas. Erosion by wind and water has more play in such strata, as sandstone sedimentary layers of different color and texture are worn away at different rates in unpredictable directions.

Though rainfall varies according to elevation, the Colorado Plateau is if anything more arid than the Basin and Range Province. An average annual rainfall of six or seven inches is not uncommon. Violent summer storms and flash floods sweep powerfully between narrow red canyons, engorging the desert washes and projecting red, frothing waters into a network of streams and rivers—the San Juan, the Escalante, the Dirty Devil, and the Green.

Their flow colors the Colorado (the "red" river) and eventually spills into the Gulf of California.

A large chain of mountains extending southward from Nephi into Arizona is called the High Plateaus, a distinct region within the Colorado Plateau Province. Numerous peaks rise to 10,000 and 11,000 feet in elevation, Delano Peak reaching 12,173 feet. The strata in the High Plateau tilt upward as they reach the Colorado, their exposed edges forming spectacular colored cliffs—the Pink, White, and Vermilion Cliffs, known collectively as the Grand Staircase of Utah.

Other Colorado Plateau mountains, such as the Henry and La Sal mountains, were formed by volcanic action, the pressure of molten rock literally pushing the sedimentary layers upward until a mountain was formed, the igneous flow finally breaking through to the upper surface as a volcanic "stock" or spilling out the sides in formations called laccoliths. Some of the peaks of the Henry Mountains are very high, Mount Ellen reaching to 11,615 feet.

The Henry Mountains lie within another section of the Colorado Plateau, called the Canyonlands. Within this area layers of the earth's crust have been bent upward into a series of swells or upwarps, such as the Uncompahgre Upwarp and the San Rafael Swell, the undulating surface sometimes broken by jagged ridges called hogbacks or reefs that run for miles.

Between the Canyonlands and the Uinta Mountains lies a broad basin, the Uinta Basin, also part of the Colorado Plateau. Though in structure a true basin, it is drained by the Green River, which cuts a deep canyon through the Roan Plateau as it coils its way southward. The broken surface of the Colorado Plateau together with the scanty rainfall make the region perhaps even less attractive for human settlement than the Basin and Range Province. Vegetation is sparse. Creosote and mesquite bushes are common at the lower elevations. Where there is sufficient soil or gravel,

sagebrush and hardy grasses will grow. Scrub oak occurs at higher elevations and mountainous areas support juniper, mountain ash, and some yellow pine and Douglas fir.

Though the Colorado Plateau was home to the best known of Utah's early peoples, the Anasazi, it has remained since that time sparsely populated. Settled life has been maintained only in a few oases along the edges of streams and springs. Substantial towns such as Vernal, Moab, and Monticello have been built up, but the region still has a density of only about four persons per square mile. Extensive mineral deposits, including coal, oil shale, and uranium, have led to intermittent periods of rapid growth and stagnation, a condition certain to prolong the intense battle between environmentalists and developers over uses of the region's resources.

Given the arid, desolate character of the Colorado Plateau and the Basin and Range Provinces, Utah would hardly seem a fit place for human habitation. Yet, surprisingly, nearly two million people do live here. But the population centers follow a distinctive pattern. As early as 1855 an Englishman, William Chandless, looked westward across the Salt Lake Valley, saw attractive lands there, and wondered why there were no towns. Had he looked beyond the valley floor to the Oquirrhs he would have quickly found his explanation.

Like most ranges in Utah's arid regions, the Oquirrhs do not have a single stream flowing continuously into the valley. Settlements were on the east side of the valley because there the mountains are of an an entirely different character. At the eastern edge of the Bonneville Basin the great ranges of the Wasatch and Uinta reach abruptly skyward, throwing up a granite wall that the prevailing westerly winds must scale as they cross the continent. The Wasatch and Uinta mountains are called by geographers the Middle Rocky Mountain Region, which is itself part of the Rocky Mountain Province. This is the third

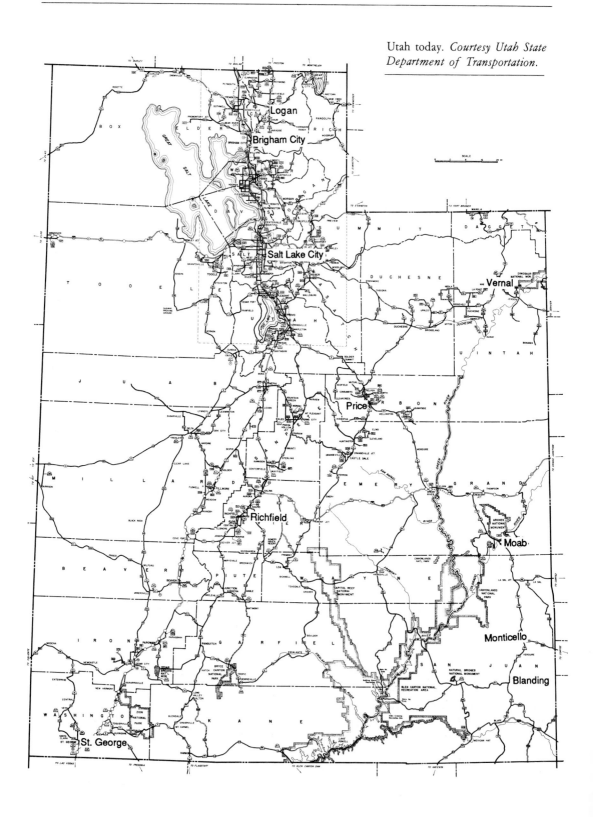

and smallest of the geographical provinces reaching into Utah, but without it 85 percent of Utah's population would have to seek homes elsewhere. The Wasatch Mountains run in a north-south line from Soda Springs to Nephi. They were formed by sharp faulting along the western edge which twisted sedimentary strata almost vertical in places and which accounts for the precipitous 7,000-foot rise from the valley floor all along the Wasatch Front.

The eastern side of the Wasatch is much more gradual and very different in character from the abrupt western edge, providing numerous small, well-watered mountain valleys that, despite a short growing season, make ideal settlement sites. However, on the west, the sudden ascent from valley floor to peaks of 11,000 and 12,000 thousand feet above the sea gives the Wasatch Mountains their scenic beauty, their superlative recreational value, and, most important, their ability to capture water from the upper air, store it as snow, and release it gradually during the summer into small mountain streams that feed the valleys below.

The Wasatch meet the Uintas near Coalville, the Wasatch continuing north and the Uinta Mountains running 150 miles eastward to the Colorado border. The Uinta Mountains are unusual, though not unique, among North American mountains in running east and west. They were formed more by a bending than a rending of the earth's crust and were scored heavily by glaciation. Thus, while higher than the Wasatch, they are characteristically more gentle and rounded in form. Twelve-thousand-foot peaks are common and King's Peak, Utah's highest, rises to 14,498 feet. Three of Utah's most vital rivers, the Bear, the Weber, and the Provo, originate near one another in the high Uintas, then head in different directions, all eventually cutting their way through the Wasatch to mingle in the waters of the Great Salt Lake.

Like most western mountains, the Wasatch and Uintas are rich in vegetation—aspen, fir, spruce, and pine all appearing at higher elevations. Igneous intrusions have left rich deposits of silver, lead, and gold, as well as the gray granite used in building the Salt Lake Temple and the State Capitol Building. The mountains are essential to settled life in Utah, providing vital resources that the Basin and Range and the Colorado Plateau regions lack.

"Sweet Betsy from Pike" curiously does not mention the mountains in its listing of the perils of western overland travel. Utah's mountains were a formidable obstacle to early California-bound emigrants. Most chose to avoid the place altogether, traveling northward from western Wyoming to Fort Hall in Idaho and thence southward up the Raft River and Cassia Creek and past City of Rocks to the Humboldt. Those who did travel over Utah found the mountains very rough going, indeed. The Donner-Reed party of 1846 suffered their most significant delays hacking a road through the thick brush from the Weber River south to Big Mountain Pass and into the Salt Lake Valley. They, like others crossing Utah in 1846, then turned their back to the mountains and headed doggedly into the salt desert, single-minded in their determination to reach the lush land of California ahead of winter snow.

Their perception of Utah's landscape is a fascinating example of how fully our goals influence what we really see and value in our environment. Utah was remembered in the folklore of two decades of westering immigrants as a land of desert and salt-water lakes. For them, and for much of the world to this day the Great Salt Lake is the visible symbol of Utah—a remote, austere, inland sea. Because their hopes were fixed on California and their attention captured by the unusual, the early travelers gave the mountains of Utah hardly a backward glance.

The first whites to settle here saw the scene quite differently. They built their earliest settlements in the Basin and Range areas, where the land was flat enough to farm but always nestled against the western edge of the Wasatch. They did this because the mountains were the source of water, timber, and minerals—all vital to successful settlement by modern man in so hostile a land. The mountains became for them symbols of security and plenty. Where those traveling through saw desert and salt lakes the settlers saw mountains. Dozens of their songs carry the same themes as this one of Joel Hills Johnson, still a favorite among the descendants of Utah's early pioneers:

> O ye mountains high, where the clear blue sky
> Arches over the vales of the free,
> Where the pure breezes blow and clear streamlets flow,
> How I've longed to your bosom to flee!
> O Zion! dear Zion! land of the free,
> Now my own mountain home, unto thee I have come,
> All my fond hopes are centered in thee.

Rarely do they mention the desert and salt-water lakes.

The People

These contrasting nineteenth-century views of Utah are from men and women of European descent. They were only the last of many sojourners in this land, and thus far their stay has been the shortest. While modern Utahns find sustenance for our way of life chiefly in the mountains and the lands that skirt them, our predecessors drew more upon resources offered by marshy areas, including those around the Great Salt Lake and its borderlands. They found food and shelter in places modern man would never think to look.

Utah's earliest peoples, regrettably for us, didn't read or write. Nor did they come in contact with anyone who could. All we know of them is what we can infer from artifacts they left behind—a worn sandal,

a food cache, a stone house, a silkweed net, even human droppings. Anthropologists have ingeniously pieced together from such artifacts a sketch of Utah's prehistory, but enormous gaps remain. We have only vague notions of how many people lived here at various periods in prehistoric times. Some have thought Utah was home only for itinerant bands of early peoples. Recent research suggests there may have been large groups living settled lives along the shores of the Great Salt Lake and other waterways for enormously long periods of time. Some evidence suggests there was considerable continuity between successive occupations, but other evidence indicates long periods of near total depopulation. Many mysteries remain, and what we think we know is subject to radical revision as more evidence is unearthed.

Present scientific evidence suggests that the ancestors of the first Utahns came from Siberia. Their crossing into Alaska did not require any skills in shipbuilding or navigation. They simply walked on dry land. Apparently, around 20,000 years ago the formation of ice packs in the north reduced the water level of the seas enough to expose a broad plain called Beringia, of the which the Bering Strait is a remnant.

There was no prehistoric Columbus who one day chanced upon the route and returned home to start a mass exodus. More likely these peoples gradually expanded their habitat over generations until some found themselves in America. The setting of their migrations must have been spectacular. Great Alaskan mountains surrounded them, the slopes as well as peaks heavily glaciated. They were able to live there, despite the numbing cold, because a network of river valleys provided in summer seasons comparative warmth and sufficient game to sustain life. This network led them gradually east and south on a course that would take their descendants, many generations hence, directly into the American Northwest. There, no longer locked up by formidable mountains, they spread out in all directions, some making their way eventually to Utah.

Perhaps 12,000 years ago a band of these prehistoric migrants trudged over a rise and looked out upon a Utah valley. Unfortunately, we have no record of their thoughts on that occasion, but a brief look at the record of a later group of travelers to the area provides an instructive contrast.

In September 1776 a small party of Spanish explorers led by Father Francisco Atanasio Domínguez crossed into Utah Valley, entering from the east by way of Spanish Fork Canyon. Father Vélez de Escalante wrote in his diary what attracted their attention as they looked out across the valley.

> It is surrounded by the Sierra's heights from which four medium-sized rivers that water it emerge flowing through it until they enter the lake that it has in the middle. . . . [The valley floor] is flat, and with the exception of the marshes along the lake's edges, of very good farmland quality for all kinds of crops. . . . In some sections it produces flax and hemp in such abundance that it seems as though it has been planted purposely. . . . Over and above these finest of advantages, it has plenty of firewood and timber in the adjacent sierra which surrounds it—many sheltered spots, water, and pasturages, for raising cattle and sheep and horses.

Since human perceptions are so strongly shaped by what we are looking for, the first Utahns, or Paleo-Indians as they are called, no doubt saw an almost wholly different Utah from that seen by those of European ancestry who came in 1776. First, they saw in the basins swamps and marshes—a habitat teeming with birds and animals and choked with cattails. Second, they saw signs of game. When the first settlers looked out over a Utah landscape they probably headed precisely for the area the Spaniards found most undesirable—

"the marshes along the lake's edges." Plenty of timber was nothing to the migrants of 12,000 years ago. People who do not live in wooden houses and have only stone axes for felling trees have little interest in forests. Pasture is of no use to those who do not have domesticated animals. What did they care if the land was level enough to plow or if there were streams close enough for irrigation? They knew nothing of farming. To them the evidences of abundance and opportunity lay in the marshes that the Spaniards seemed to disdain. There they saw small animals such as rabbits and ducks and big game—bison, mammoths, and giant sloths.

It must have been a great achievement to bag one of these prehistoric creatures—called megafauna by the anthropologists. The first Utahns hunted them with thrusting spears tipped by beautifully crafted, fluted points. These people also may have made kills by driving the animals into bogs or over cliffs and then finishing them off with spears as historic tribes are known to have done. It seems unlikely, however, that such heroic feats were everyday affairs. By the time the earliest Paleo-Indians came to Utah it is probable that their staple food came from the marshes. Over centuries the megafauna disappeared altogether.

A very different people, known as the Desert Archaic, were in place by 6000 B.C. Among the archeological sites that have revealed much about these people are caves around the edges of the Great Salt Lake. Danger Cave near Wendover housed people intermittently as early as 8000 B.C. Hogup Cave on the western edge of the Great Salt Lake was occupied, off and on, from 6000 B.C. until shortly before Columbus discovered America—a span of 7,500 years. Fortunately, these folks were not very tidy. They dropped table scraps, broken baskets, and worn sandals onto the dirt floor and left them there. Layers of artifacts thus deposited tell much about ancient man in Utah.

Their principal weapon was a device called an atlatl that gives leverage and thrust in throwing a spear, much as a sling does in throwing a rock. With it they killed the small animals and antelope that frequented their habitat, using the flesh for meat and the sinews, hides, and bones for fashioning cloaks and tools. We know that they wove nets of plant fibers and twisted rabbit hide, probably stretching them in a broad semicircle on sticks and driving animals into them. They fashioned duck decoys that lured fresh fowl into the marshes where they could be more readily bagged. Yet recent studies suggest that the lowly cattail, together with salt tolerant plants such as pickleweed, burrowweed, and sedge, provided the basic diet for many of the Archaic peoples. Red meat was for them something of a luxury. Life was not all hunting and gathering, however. Decorated gaming sticks and charming split-twig animals that have been found suggest that they enjoyed gambling pastimes (the first gambling on the desert was not at Wendover) and perhaps participated in rituals to bring good luck to the hunt.

Closely tied to the Great Salt Lake and other waterways, the fortunes of the Archaic peoples were determined by changes in climate and water levels. Dr. David B. Madsen, Utah state archeologist, has concluded that from 6500 B.C. to 3500 B.C. dwellers around the Great Salt Lake lived a fairly settled life. Their considerable population expanded as receding waters exposed more lake edge resources. Eventually, however, the waters dropped so low that groundwater feeding the marshes dried up. This forced the people to draw on upland resources, such as Indian rice grass, mountain sheep, deer, and rabbit, but only in seasonal migration, as they probably retained the vast lake edge as a home base. About 1500 B.C. the fickle lake waters began to rise again. They eventually reached levels not previously known to human settlers, covering some of the lakeside habitats. The waters were then too high for marsh and lake edge subsistence. The population declined drastically. After 6,000 years, the Archaic peoples very possibly disappeared altogether. They left empty lands to a later people whose presence we do not discern until a thousand years had passed.

Around A.D. 500 the dramatically different culture of the Fremont peoples began to spread over much of Utah. Their lives were in some ways very similar to those of the Archaic people—enough so that they could conceivably have been descendants who, through contact with others, picked up enough new habits and tools to make them appear to be an entirely different race. Certainly they, like the Archaic people, continued to live mostly in those narrow strips of Utah where water meets land. But, whatever their habitat or ancestry, their new technologies were enough to make them an entirely different people.

For example, one can shoot a projectile many times farther, with greater velocity and better accuracy, using a bow than the atlatl of the Archaic peoples. Because they had the bow and arrow, the Fremont people were able to bag game more consistently than their predecessors. But this is only the beginning. Caves may have been convenient as homes, in that they required a minimum capital investment—one quick check to make sure the previous occupants have moved on and you're ready to move in. Caves, however, tend to be drafty and clammy at times, and awkwardly situated. Somewhere, the Fremont peoples learned to build shelters. Their shelters were partially underground, with poles and dirt forming a roof. Smoke and people emerged from the house through holes in the ceiling. They were much more cozy in scale than, say, Hogup Cave. More important, such shelters could be built wherever food and water were available.

In addition to pit houses, the Fremont built rectangular granaries above ground, made entirely of adobe or unmortared stone. Often several homes and granaries

Roof beams and latticework in ceiling of 700-year-old Fremont granary near Richfield. *Dean L. May photograph.*

were built close together to make villages. Granaries? But where did they learn to farm? We do not know that for sure, either, but sometime around the beginning of the Christian era they picked up the art of growing maize, or what we call corn, and probably beans and squash. They grew a particular variety of dented corn that was especially drought resistant, required only a short growing season, and seems to have originated in the Great Basin. Though they did not farm extensively, it is evident they did supplement their diet with home-grown vegetables. Equally important, the Fremont people made pottery. A simple, gray coiled product, it was adapted to many uses such as boiling food—uses unknown to the Archaic people whose only vessels were woven baskets and animal skins.

The distinctive pictograph style of the Fremont people often shows heroic-sized human figures with broad, triangular shoulders and heavy, elaborate necklaces. This same style is echoed in clay figurines found at a number of Fremont sites, sometimes together with foodstuffs. The figurines are very carefully made of unfired clay and painted in shades of ochre, tan, and green. We don't know what the figurines or pictographs meant to those who made them. Some think that because they are associated with game and crops, they were magical charms invoking successful hunts and harvests.

Fremont decorative arts can also be seen in jewelry and in pottery. Designs were pressed into wet clay and, in later periods, also painted on the pots. Perfectly round clay balls have been found that apparently were used for games of some kind, and incised bone gaming devices like those used by the Archaic cultures were probably used like our modern dominoes or dice.

The Fremont peoples probably lived in family groupings or clans. Their range of commerce and contact with other groups was much greater than one might suppose. It is generally believed that agriculture and pottery making originated in the Southwest and that these, as well as other aspects of Fremont culture, came from there. Some scholars, however, have noted obvious borrowings from interior Indians, such as paddle-and-anvil vessels that look similar to artifacts from the Great Plains. Some even speculate that the Fremont peoples originally came from the Plains.

Whatever their origins, it is clear that Utah's Fremont people were not as isolated and provincial as is often assumed. They freely borrowed and adapted from others. Indeed, their culture can be seen as an amalgam of influences surrounding them both in space and time. In their own distinctive way they drew in all directions survival skills others had developed to cope with their harsh Basin and Range and Colorado Plateau environments.

Their panoply of skills was not enough, however, to sustain them through the incursion of Shoshonean peoples of historic times. The Shoshoneans entered the area about A.D. 1200 or 1300. As they arrived, the Fremont, for reasons not altogether clear, were passing from the scene, leaving their haunting images on canyon walls and their artifacts in village sites the length and breadth of Utah.

The best known of the prehistoric Indians of Utah were those who lined the canyons of the San Juan River region with their adobe and masonry cliff dwellings. We call these people the Anasazi, from a Navajo word meaning "the ancient ones." The Anasazi lived at the same time as the Fremont. Yet, their villages, often precariously perched along canyon walls and masterfully conceived and erected, are a far cry from the subterranean pit-house villages of the Fremont. Anasazi pottery, its design bursting with confident energy, represents an achievement far different from the common gray Fremont pot. While the Fremont had patches of corn, beans, and squash here and there, the Anasazi became heavily dependent upon agriculture, building impressive systems of dams and canals to water their fields—even when those fields were terraced in canyon walls or situated on high mesas.

Since Anasazi development can be traced from about the time of Christ, 500 years before the Fremont appeared, one would think that the Fremont probably were simply an Archaic people who copied, in a clumsy way, some of the culture of their neighbors to the south. The evidence suggests otherwise. The Utah Anasazi lived only in the southeastern part of the state. The earliest signs of Fremont culture appear, however, in the north. The Fremont artifacts of later periods are found progressively southward—the opposite of what we would expect if the Fremont were country cousins, feeding on crumbs from the Anasazi cultural table.

More likely, the two groups had a common ancestor somewhere in the Southwest. Their migrations, over hundreds of years, could have taken them on different geographic and cultural paths. Because the cultural development of the Anasazi has been

carefully studied, we know much more about them than we do about the Fremont. At least six developmental stages have been identified and dated. These stages cover their entire 1,300-year growth from a basketmaking people—barely distinguishable from the Desert Archaic tribes—to their peak as accomplished farmers and masons. The basketmaking period extends from sometime before A.D. 1 to about A.D. 750. After A.D. 750 the Anasazi developed rapidly in pottery-making, agriculture, and house building.

Their astonishing achievement in house building had modest beginnings. The first pueblos were made of adobe and pole, adobe and stone, or simply cut stone. They were grouped in L-shapes, semicircles, and rectangles. Often a pit house would be in the center of such a village. A common structural feature was the "jacal wall"—made by setting a row of posts or logs upright in the ground close to one another and filling the spaces with adobe. Such complexes became more elaborate over time until about A.D. 1150. Then began the great Pueblo period when they built large villages—often nestled under protective sandstone cliffs. These pueblos contained hundreds of rooms. Many of the walls were of fine masonry, the interiors sometimes plastered with adobe and decorated with red, yellow, and black designs.

The Anasazi's great investment in such structures was practical only if they were able to stay in one place over long periods. Their development of agriculture made this possible. They raised not only corn, beans, and squash, but also cotton—spinning, dyeing, and weaving the fibers into decorative patterns. In addition, they domesticated turkeys, adding dependable supplies of meat to their regular vegetable diet, and denying the people of present-day Moroni the right to claim that they brought turkey culture to Utah.

Religious ritual became elaborately developed among the Anasazi. The pit house evolved into the kiva—a round under-

Handprints of Anasazi masons, Westwater Village. *Dean L. May photograph.*

ground room entered by a ladder through the roof and used for religious and fraternal ceremonies. To their achievements in decorative arts, they added turquoise necklaces, leather robes, and flint knives. Their pottery took a variety of forms and was skillfully decorated in contrasting black and white geometrical patterns.

In 1300, at the height of their powers, the Anasazi disappeared. More than a thousand years of cultural development went with them. The Anasazi apparently just packed up and left. They headed south into Arizona and New Mexico, leaving their massive pueblos to the ravages of time, weather, and vandals. We still do not know why they left. Tree rings show a severe drought struck in 1276 and lasted most of the rest of the century, so, perhaps they were simply starved out. Others have wondered if migrations of historic Navajo and Apache from the north might have decimated the essentially peaceful Anasazi. We may never know the full answer, but it is clear that they, with the Fremont, disap-

peared from Utah about the year 1300, never to return.

Though they have long since left, the legacy of the first Utahns, which began in the marshes, is rich and powerful. Their story reminds us that Utah has always been, to some extent, a crossroads. Over the last 10,000 years, several tides of people have swept across the face of this land, settling down for short or long periods and then moving on. Although the various Archaic people had little technology, they had a homing instinct for that vital zone where water met desert land. There they enjoyed a long and, from all appearances, contented tenure.

The Fremont, a true crossroads people, borrowed freely from predecessors and neighbors. Leaving the marshes, they spread out over the whole state and built an eclectic and vigorous civilization. Of all the early groups, they are identified most uniquely with our state. The Anasazi were brilliant outsiders whose Utah settlements were provincial and peripheral to their main residential centers.

All of these ancient peoples seem to have been gentle — there is little evidence of warfare, their arts reflecting domestic and religious life. Understanding these peoples is useful in helping us understand ourselves. If they could look at the salt marshes we avoid and see here a great opportunity for settled life, we are made to pause and ask, what else do the limits of our culture keep us from seeing? Where are our blinders? History helps us push back the blinders and broaden our field of vision.

Finally, their story is useful in giving us a sense of perspective of our own place in the totality of human experience in the Great Basin. Whole civilizations have come here, settled down for thousands of years, and then disappeared from human ken. We know them only from what little they left behind.

They discarded or misplaced enough for us to know that these were alert, sentient, creative people. No doubt if we could somehow transport ourselves to their time, we would discover that not one of them expected to see the day when their race had ceased to exist. Not one would have imagined that their trinkets, tools, houses, their very bones, would provide the stuff of romantic legend and folklore for a later people. It is hard for people to imagine that one day they might be the ancient ones.

Thus, Utah history is very much the story of human interaction with a difficult and challenging landscape. In this saga modern man thus far has played only a bit part, our predecessors counting their tenure here in millennia; we in decades. And certainly our continuance here, as was theirs, will be largely determined by the kinds of accommodations we ultimately make with the land.

For Further Reading:

Histories

The Land. The broader geographical context of which Utah is a part is described in Wallace W. Atwood's *The Physiographic Provinces of North America* (1941). A beautifully designed and very informative reference book on Utah is the *Atlas of Utah*, published in 1981 by Brigham Young University Press and Weber State College. It is the kind of book one can curl up with for hours. More than a hundred graphically illustrated, pithy essays on landforms, climate, vegetation, peoples, economics, and other topics cover virtually every aspect of Utah's past that can be better understood with maps, charts, and graphs. Brigham Young University professor Robert L. Layton's "Utah: The Physical Setting," in *Utah's History*, edited by Richard D. Poll, Thomas G. Alexander, Eugene E. Campbell, and David E. Miller (1978), is readable and informative. Lehi F. Hintze's *Geological History of Utah* (1973) is widely cited, but the average reader may find it somewhat technical.

The People. A brief and readily available introduction to the earliest human history of the region is former University of Utah professor Jesse D. Jennings's "Early Man in Utah" in the January 1960 *Utah Historical Quarterly*.

S. Lyman Tyler, former director of the University of Utah's American West Center, provides an excellent overview of what is known of the first Utahns in "The Earliest Peoples," a chapter in *Utah's History*. Utah state archeologist David B. Madsen's work, including (with C. Melvin Aikens) "Prehistory of the Eastern Area," in *Handbook of American Indians*, vol. 11, *Great Basin* (1986), has substantially revised that of earlier researchers, suggesting a larger and more stable population in some areas of the Great Basin than had previously been thought. See also Madsen's "Get it Where the Getting's Good," in *Man and Environment in the Great Basin*, Society for American Archeology, *Papers*, No.2, ed. David B. Madsen and James F. O'Connell (1982).

Eyewitness Accounts

The Land. In subsequent chapters I will direct the reader to some of the most readily available accounts by those who participated in and thus helped to make Utah's past. These might be diaries, letters, reminiscences or other documents created by people of Utah. In many cases (sad to say) they are more instructive and interesting than the works of historians who draw from them. Of course there were no eyewitnesses who described the great geological changes that shaped Utah's landscape or could write of the prehistoric animals or peoples of our region. We can nonetheless have a type of firsthand encounter by studying what they left behind. We can still see the consequences of geological change in such monuments as Zion National Park, the Grand Canyon, or the many benches formed by Lake Bonneville; we can piece together the fossil remains of prehistoric animals; and we can study the tools, crafts, and ruined villages of prehistoric man.

The Brigham Young University Geology Department makes available at low cost a *Geological Highway Map of Utah* that is useful in helping to find and identify important geological features in the state. One of the largest quarries of prehistoric animal fossils in the world is at Dinosaur National Monument in Vernal. There visitors can watch excavation in progress while gaining a clear and comprehensible understanding of both the geological and biological processes that led to the formation of this remarkable deposit. The Utah Museum of Natural History at the University of Utah also has an excellent display of dinosaur fossils as does the Prehistoric Museum at the College of Eastern Utah in Price.

Early explorers and geographers left descriptions of Utah country that have much of the character of a firsthand account. Several reprintings of John C. Frémont's published reports are available, but the most useful is Donald Jackson and Mary Lee Spence, *The Expeditions of John Charles Frémont* (1970–73). The memoir of Charles Pruess, *Exploring with Frémont* (1958) provides a valuable view by one of Frémont's closest associates. Other classic works are John Wesley Powell's *Report on the Exploration of the Colorado River of the West* (1875, reprinted 1961) and *Report on the Lands of the Arid Regions of the United States with a More Detailed Account of the Land of Utah* (1878). Also important are Grove Karl Gilbert's *Geology of the Henry Mountains* (1890) and *Lake Bonneville* (1890); and Clarence E. Dutton's *Geology of the High Plateau of Utah* (1880). Many of these studies are available in reprint editions or on microfilm in larger libraries. A fascinating view of changes in the way European settlers saw this country is in a collection of maps printed by Carl I. Wheat as *Mapping the Trans-Mississippi West, 1540–1861* (1957–63). It can be found in most major libraries, and its maps communicate with much of the immediacy and charm of an eyewitness narrative.

The People. The Utah Museum of Natural History at the University of Utah and the Prehistoric Museum at the College of Eastern Utah in Price display artifacts and dioramas that help communicate directly to us something of the lives of ancient man in Utah. More specialized are the Edge of the Cedars State Park in Blanding, on the site of an ongoing excavation of an Anasazi village, and the Fremont Indian State Park, on Interstate 70 in Clear Creek Canyon between Cove Fort and Joseph. The rock art of prehistoric man can be seen in most parts of Utah. *Petroglyphs and Pictographs of Utah* by Kenneth B. Castleton is an excellent guide to those wishing to visit sites in their area. A thirty-minute videotape, "Doodling on the Rocks," dealing mainly with Utah rock art, can be viewed in the audiovisual area of the University of Utah's Marriott Library. Some village remains can be visited, such as Hovenweep National Monument, a magnificent remnant of the Anasazi, in southeastern Utah. Whenever visiting such sites, however, one must remember that the rock art, artifacts, and ruins are priceless, irreplaceable documents, helping us better to understand human experience in the Great Basin. It is against the law and shamefully irresponsible to alter or remove such artifacts.

Rendezvous. This watercolor, by Alfred Jacob Miller, is from sketches he made at the 1837 rendezvous on the Green River between New Fork and Horse Creek. Jim Bridger can be seen among the Indians in the left foreground sporting a suit of armor just given to him by a Scottish adventurer, William Drummond Stewart. *Courtesy Walters Art Gallery, Baltimore, Maryland.*

Two

An Opening to Europe

In a day when we can jet from New York to London in four hours and land men on the moon there are many alive who remember the first automobile to come to Utah. Learning to live with a dizzying pace of change is one of the great challenges to men of our time. There were also dramatic changes in the lives of early Utahns, as subsistence animals disappeared, capricious lake waters opened and then flooded habitats, droughts parched the land or new peoples pushed their way in. Nonetheless, the surviving evidence makes it clear that the lives of early Utahns were far more stable than our own. Traditional clothing, tools, foodstuffs, and housing often did not change for hundreds of years. The Paleo-Indians were here for perhaps 4,000 years; the Desert Archaic for 2,500. The Fremont and Anasazi knew this land for no more than 1,300 years, from A.D. 1 (A.D. 500 for the Fremont) until A.D. 1300 and then left it to a new people, the Shoshoneans.

The Shoshoneans came, as near as we can tell, from the southwest. They proceeded to settle in and practice a hunting and gathering life-style somewhat between that of the Fremont and the Archaic peoples. Like the Fremont, they were an upland people. They gathered roots and seeds, including the pinyon nut, a tasty delicacy that can be gathered on mountain foothills in the fall and stored and

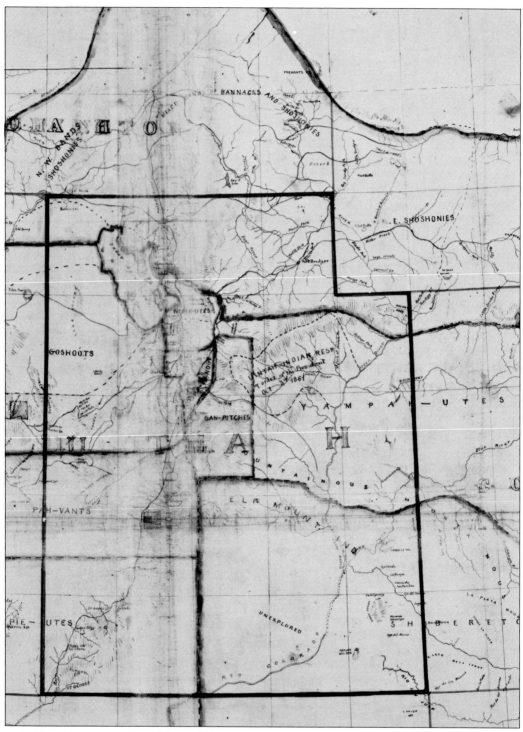

This map, showing the homelands of Utah's Indians, was prepared for the Utah Superintendency of the U.S. Bureau of Indian Affairs in 1860. The Gosiutes were based in the northwest quadrant of the territory, Southern Paiutes the southwest, Navajos the southeast, and Utes the central and eastern portions. The Shoshoni were in the north. *Courtesy Cartographic Records, National Archives (RG75, Map 372).*

ground to provide winter food. They also caught fish and small animals for food, and raised some vegetables—corn, squash, and beans. They had the bow and arrow and made good baskets and some pottery. They sometimes lived in pit houses like the Fremont, though they also used brush shelters called wickiups and lakeside caves during some phases of their annual migrations. They lived in small family bands, with little or no tribal organization, and seem initially to have had very little conflict between groups.

Four main Shoshonean peoples inhabited Utah country—the Shoshone in the north and northeast, the Gosiutes in the northwest, the Utes in the central and eastern parts of the region, and the Southern Paiutes in the southwest. They had been in place but a short time—around three hundred years—when the approach of another people, entirely alien to the Great Basin, brought significant change to their lives. These armored, mounted intruders were Spanish Europeans, moving northward from their already established bases in Mexico.

The Spaniards

The Spanish conquests in the Americas had been pursued with remarkable speed and efficiency. Barely thirty years after Columbus's landing, the West Indies had been taken, parts of Central America occupied, and the Aztec capital of Tenochtitlán or Mexico City conquered. Hopes based on reports of great cities and abundant gold to the north were quashed by Coronado, whose expedition in 1540 found the reportedly gilded Seven Cities of Cíbola to be dusty Indian pueblos.

A scouting party under Cárdenas made its way to the Grand Canyon but, thoroughly intimidated by the landscape, retreated to the base camp at the Zuñi pueblos. The expedition did not reach Utah and ventured no further in that direction. Coronado's pessimistic report slowed the

The European Conquest as seen by Indians. An Aztec drawing of the Spanish attack on Tenochtitlán (Mexico City). *From Paso y Troncoso's rendering of the drawing as printed in* Historia de las Cosas de Nueva España *by Fray Bernardino de Sahagún (Madrid, 1905–7).*

Spaniard advance into North America but did not stop it. Through the rest of the 1500s silver strikes in central Mexico led a steady stream of miners, adventurers, and priests gradually northward. Finally, in 1598 a colonizing party was sent to establish the province of New Mexico, and in 1610 the capital city of Santa Fe was founded, just three years after the first permanent English settlement of Jamestown, in Virginia. Santa Fe was to remain for the next two centuries a remote, precarious frontier outpost.

As the 1700s drew to a close, international rivalries elevated this provincial capital to a position of some importance in Spanish imperial politics. Exploration of the west coast of North America had begun with Juan Rodríguez Cabrillo's voyage up the coast as far as Oregon in 1542. Sixty-one years later Sebastián Vizcaíno followed essentially the same route. For the next 135 years, however, no follow-up was made, and the California coast, remote and difficult to supply and maintain, was left unsettled by Europeans. It took the Russians to get Spain really interested in Upper California. Beginning in 1725, the Russians pushed into the American arctic and gradually expanded down the coast toward California. To make matters worse, England, Spain's archenemy, seemed to be showing interest in the Pacific coast.

This all took place at a time when the European states were involved in a series of wars, the stakes being control and possession of overseas colonial lands. Any unsettled territory in America was up for grabs, and it finally became clear to the Spaniards that if they expected to keep Upper California they had better settle there. And they did. San Diego was established in 1769 and Monterey the next year. These outposts, far beyond the frontiers of Spanish settlement, were weak and vulnerable. During their infancy they needed regular contact with other Spanish settlements and a steady source of supplies, so imperial attention turned once again to northern outposts in New Mexico. In the 1770s overland expeditions were sent to the California coast from New Mexican and other inland settlements, helping to secure the coastal missions. However, all crossed perilous deserts through hostile Indian territory. A less hazardous route, perhaps more to the north, would be useful.

Thus Santa Fe, for a brief moment, came into her own. Exploring parties had already ventured into the surrounding terrain and begun to dispel its obscurity. One, under Juan María Antonio Rivera, had in 1765 entered into present-day Utah, exploring as far north as Moab. Little, however, was known of the inland areas to the north. In 1776 Franciscan Father Francisco Atanasio Domínguez was appointed to head a party commissioned to explore the interior and hopefully discover a more feasible overland route from Santa Fe to the northern coastal outpost of Monterey. He chose as his co-leader a young priest still in his twenties, Francisco Vélez de Escalante, who kept a detailed record of their journey. Though

the Rivera expedition and other Spaniard traders and adventurers traveling without license may have ventured northward into present-day Utah, this expediton, because of the journal and because of a map by another of the travelers, Don Bernardo Miera y Pacheco, was the first to open Utah to European eyes.

This errand into the wilderness had both political and religious aims. In fact, the fathers made little differentiation between the two, for as they saw it, the cause of God was the cause of Spain. The little company of twelve men, with pack animals and riding horses set out from Palace of the Governors in Santa Fe on July 29, 1776, the same time that the English colonists, 2,000 miles to the east, were in the process of declaring their independence from England.

The explorers traveled in familiar country for the first three weeks. Spaniards had, after all, been in the area for almost 170 years. Early in their journey, on August 17, they came across fresh Indian tracks, "quite recent tracks of Yutas," as Vélez put it. Already, they begin their descriptions of the Utes—the most powerful and widespread of Utah's historic Indian peoples. They were to see much of the Utes during their journey.

The Utes

By 1776 the Utes were dramatically different from their great-grandfathers who had lived in Utah when the Spaniards first settled Santa Fe. One of the important changes contact with the Spaniards had brought was adoption and use of the horse. Of all the groups Domínguez and Vélez were to encounter on their journey, the Utes—and especially those they now encountered in western Colorado—had adapted most successsfully to the equine culture. The range of their normal habitat was greatly increased. Mounted Utes could travel easily forty miles a day, whereas before they could walk only fifteen or twenty

Ute Indians near Fort Bridger, 1857. Photographer unknown. *Courtesy Smithsonian Institution (Photo No. 55,078).*

and bring very little gear with them. Shortly after contact with the Spaniards, some Utes began to range widely in search of buffalo, frequenting most of eastern Utah, western Colorado, and parts of northern New Mexico. Their contact with Plains Indians led to the adoption of leather clothing, beaded decoration, feathers, ceremonial dress, and the use of the tepee, that most beautiful and functional dwelling of the plains.

The horse also affected social organization, for the increased range of the Utes made it desirable to organize into groups larger than the small clan or family, with chieftains presiding over the affairs of the group. This organization was not rigid or greatly formalized when the Domínguez party set out, and there remained considerable uncertainty as to how widely the authority of any particular chief was recognized; but a distinct change had occurred from the days of small wandering family bands. The Spaniards recognized two main groups of Utes, the eastern, mainly Colorado- and New Mexico-based Utes, and the western or Utah Utes. But there were, as the journal makes clear, many local bands within these broader groups.

A warrior on horseback can have a terrifying effect on unmounted people, speed and height lending a formidable advantage. Exploiting their access to horses, some bands of Utes became warlike, raiding neighboring tribes to plunder goods and even kidnap individuals to sell as slaves in the Spanish settlements. Other Utes lived quite sedentary lives, fishing from mountain lakes, raising corn and other vegetables, and making pottery. Generally, however, the Utes were widely known, feared, and respected. It is not surprising that they were the first Indians encountered by the Domínguez party.

When the explorers first spotted Ute tracks on August 17, they decided to try to find the Indians, assuming the Utes had already seen them and might think they were up to no good. Besides, as Escalante put it, "One of them might be able to guide us or furnish us with some hints for continuing our journey with less difficulty

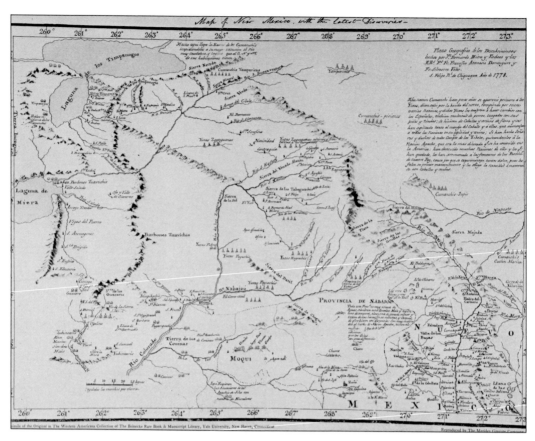

A Spanish view of Utah drawn by Bernardo Miera y Pacheco in 1778. The Great Salt Lake and Utah Lake are joined by an isthmus and drained by a river to the west. The River Buenaventura is a fanciful composite of portions of the Green and the Sevier and flows into Sevier Lake, which in this rendering seems to have no outlet. *Courtesy of Yale Collection of Western Americana, Beinecke Rare Book and Manuscript Library.*

or hardship." They did not find a Ute until six days later, however, and when they did, near the Gunnison River, he wanted to trade with the whites, offering his services as guide in exchange for a knife and some glass beads.

Traveling up the north fork of the Gunnison they were led to the villages of the Sabuaganas Utes, where they found two Laguna or Timpanogotzis Utes far from their home near Utah Lake. The priests were delighted to enlist their services as guides. One they named Silvestre; the

other, a boy of eleven, they dubbed Joaquín. Not entirely confident of the good faith of their guides and suffering some internal dissension as well, the party continued in a meandering northerly course, finally entering present-day Utah near Jensen. There they were fortunate to succeed in a buffalo kill which they celebrated with a day of rest and recuperation. They crossed the Green River and then made their way up the Duchesne, Sevier, and Strawberry river drainages. Crossing over the crest of the Wasatch into the Diamond Creek drainage, they descended it and the Spanish Fork River. As they approached Utah Valley their Indian guide, Silvestre, was so anxious to get home that he "vanished in the forest at every step, and we knew not where to follow him because, what with the great density of the forest, there neither was a foot path nor could his track be discerned in many places. He was

Utah Valley from Dominguez Hill. *Dean L. May photograph.*

ordered to go slow and always within our sight."

On September 23 the Domínguez party climbed up a ridge at the mouth of Spanish Fork Canyon and, as they put it, "caught sight of the lake and the spreading valley of Nuestra Señora de la Merced of the Timpagonotzis. . . . We also saw that they were sending up smoke signals on every side, one after another, thus spreading the news of our coming." This was for them the high point of their journey, an occasion made auspicious by their arrival on the feast day honoring Mary as liberator of captives, or Our Lady of Mercy, which gave them their name for the valley. As they recorded it, "This coincidence seemed like a happy omen of the good disposition of these captives, whose liberty we desired and besought of the Redeemer of the world through His immaculate Mother's intercession."

Thanks to the good report of their guides Silvestre and Joaquín, their Christian teachings were warmly received, some of the natives urgently requesting baptism. The fathers decided not to baptize them, however, until a permanent Christian settlement could be made in the valley. They described the people in some detail:

> We found them all very simple, docile, gentle and affectionate. . . . [They] live on the lake's abundant fish. . . . Besides this, they gather the seeds of wild plants in the bottoms and make a gruel from them, which they supplement with the game of jackrabbits, coney, and fowl, of which there is a great abundance here. They also have bison handy not too far away to the north-northwest, but fear of the Comanches prevents them from hunting them. . . . Their dwellings are some sheds or little wattle huts of osier [willow], out of which they have interestingly crafted baskets and other utensils for ordinary use. They are very poor as regards dress. The most becoming one they wear is a deerskin jacket and long leggings of the same. For cold seasons they wear blankets made of jackrabbits and coney rabbit furs. . . . They possess good features, and most of them are fully bearded.

The land pleased them as much as the people. They described each stream and river crossing the valley: Spanish Fork, Hobble Creek, the Provo River, and the American Fork River. They were impressed by the abundance of flat, tillable land, producing "flax and hemp in such abundance that it seems as though it had been planted purposely." They noted that the climate was warm and that there was plenty of firewood and timber in the mountains, in addition to "many sheltered spots, waters, and pasturages, for raising cattle and sheep and horses."

After a brief sojourn it came time for them to take leave of the Ute villages. Young Joaquín and a new guide, called Jose Maria, agreed to accompany them. "The hour arrived," the fathers wrote, "and all bade us farewell most tenderly, especially Silvestre, who hugged us tightly, practically in tears. And they began charging us once more not to delay our return too long, saying that they expected us back within a year." On September 27 the Spaniards crossed into Juab Valley and continued southward, meeting little bands of friendly Utes until they reached the Sevier River.

While in Utah Valley the padres learned of another body of water connected to Utah Lake on the north, the waters of which "are harmful and extremely salty, for the Timpanois assured us that anyone who wet some part of his body with them immediately felt a lot of itching in the part moistened." The lateness of the season prevented them from checking out the story for themselves, though thousands of subsequent tourists to the Great Salt Lake would be happy to confirm the rumor.

The Gosiutes

Had the fathers ventured north to test the waters they would have come across another of Utah's historic native tribes, the Gosiutes, a branch of the Western Shoshone. The Utes described them as a "numerous and secluded nation . . . [which] lives on wild plants, drinks from various springs or outlets of good water encircling the lake, and they have their small dwellings made of grass and sods." The description was accurate as far as it went.

The Gosiutes were, of all Utah's tribes, the least touched by Spanish influence. They lived in small family groups, much like the first Shoshoneans to come to the region. They followed seasonal migrations in search of pine nuts, rabbits, berries and roots, and even crickets, which they dried, ground into a meal, and then baked into cakes. Subsequent white visitors called them "Diggers" and thought of them as the most impoverished and pitiful of Indian tribes. In fact, the Gosiutes were most ingenious in extracting food and supplies from their very sparse Basin and Range environment. They had a rich oral tradition of storytelling, including charming tales of the clever coyote who repeatedly outsmarts the other animals. Their blankets were crude but serviceable. They were skilled with the bow and arrow and in making various trapping and netting devices with which to bag rabbits. They were, in addition, peaceful and almost devoid of the skills of warfare, which may have been a reason for their being relegated to this most inhospitable of environments.

Something of their social values can perhaps be inferred by an 1859 account of a meeting with an old man and his crippled son by army surveyor Captain J. H. Simpson:

> At 7 P.M. the good old Indian, crippled as he is, came in and we discovered by his words and gestures that though he was very much fatigued, yet he had a good heart toward us. He made signs to show that his helplessness was such as to make it necessary for him to be lifted bodily from his horse. He was taken off and carried to near the cook fire, and I had a supper prepared for him. All hands feel grateful to him for his extraordinary kindness to us. He had permitted his son, who was his only support and protector, to go away with the guide-party for several days, and now he had done us the signal service, crippled as he was, to

conduct our mules to water and thus possibly save them from perishing and us from failing in this portion of our route. Of course we all felt grateful and testified it by some presents to him and his son. . . . At his request I have permitted him to sleep in camp, the only strange Indian to whom this privilege has been granted on the trip.

Missing the opportunity to bring Christianity to these docile desert dwellers, the fathers hurried southward, hoping to keep ahead of winter's cold. Just after crossing the Sevier they encountered twenty of still another tribe of Indians, "as docile and agreeable as those before." These were "more fully bearded than the Lagunas, . . . [and] in their features . . . more resemble the Spaniards than they do all the other Indians known in America up to now."

The Southern Paiutes

Though there is some debate on the question, these may well have been Southern Paiutes, a Shoshonean-speaking tribe who in life-style were much like the Gosiutes, though linguistically more like the Utes. Their habitats on the Virgin and Santa Clara rivers, the Kaibab Plateau, and in the Moapa and Las Vegas valleys of Nevada were warmer than those of the Gosiutes but even more arid. They led a more sedentary life than the Gosiutes, planting corn and gourds, and later melons and other crops, watering them from nearby streams. They were highly skilled basketmakers, using intricate techniques to fashion vessels of all sizes and shapes, including even protective hats for the women. They too had the bow and arrow and used flint knives and clubs for hunting but were, like the Gosiutes, a peaceful and gentle people. Later, during the Mexican period, they suffered considerably from raids by slave hunters.

The Domínguez party somehow communicated some elements of Christianity to the Indians they encountered on the Sevier and found them as receptive as the

"The arrow maker and his daughter." Southern Paiutes photographed by John K. Hillers of the John Wesley Powell expedition, October 4–5, 1872, on the Kaibab Plateau. *Courtesy Utah State Historical Society.*

Utes. After only a few hours of teaching, the Spaniards prepared to take their leave, "when all—following their chief, who started first—burst out crying copious tears, so that even when we were quite a distance away we kept hearing the tender laments of these unfortunate little sheep of Christ, lost along the way simply for not having the Light. They touched our hearts so much that some of our companions could not hold back the tears."

So the party took its way southward past present-day Scipio and Milford and into the desert, which has since been named for Escalante. In early October their provisions began to run low. On October 5 their Ute guide deserted them, and to make matters worse it snowed heavily. This caused the leaders to reassess their plans. They concluded that the missionary success of their journey had been sufficient. There was no need to undertake the risk of striking out, short of supplies, an unknown distance to the west, in search of Monterey. They decided to continue south, cross the Colorado, and return to Santa Fe by way of the Hopi and Zuni pueblos.

The decision was unpopular with one faction of the party who hoped for the glory of discovering a new route to Upper California. All agreed to put the matter in the hands of God by casting lots. This took place between present-day Milford and Cedar City on October 11. They placed two slips of paper into a hat, one with the name "Monterey" on it and the other "Cosnina" (Havasupai villages en route to Zuni and Santa Fe). No doubt the padres were greatly relieved that the slip drawn indicated a return to Sante Fe. The company continued southeastward, encountering bands of Southern Paiutes along the Virgin River and elsewhere. They hurried past present-day Hurricane into Arizona but were stopped by the impossible canyon of the Colorado at Lee's Ferry. Working their way up the Paria River back into Utah, they finally found a crossing. The steps they carved in the sandstone to aid their descent to the river were still visible when the waters of Glen Canyon buried them, together with the crossing place, now under 550 feet of water. The site is known as Padre Bay. The crossing was completed on November 7, 1776, about five in the afternoon, the party "praising God our Lord and firing off some muskets in demonstration of the great joy we all felt in having overcome so great a problem."

From there the Franciscans and their party traveled to the Hopi village of Oraibi, now in familiar country, and to Escalante's home mission of Zuni. There they refreshed themselves for nearly three weeks before continuing on to Santa Fe. They arrived the day after New Year's, January 2, 1777, after a journey of almost 2,000 miles. The eleven-year-old Laguna Ute boy,

Joaquín, was still with them and was presented to the governor along with the journal kept by Escalante and artifacts given them by the Indians of Utah Lake.

The fathers failed in their political mission—to open a land route to Monterey. They felt, however, that the trip was amply justified "in having discovered such a great deal of country and people so well disposed to be easily gathered into the Lord's vineyard and to the realms of his majesty." They urgently recommended that the inland Spanish frontier be extended to Utah Valley, hoping to build a mission there and follow up on their promise to bring Christianity to the Laguna Utes.

The failure of their political mission apparently impressed crown officials more than the promise of their spiritual one. With the empire in a general state of decline, Spanish officials were in no mood for expansion. The Lagunas waited in vain for the fathers to deliver on their promise to return before the year was out. It was not the last promise whites would fail to keep, but perhaps the best intentioned.

Though several manuscript copies of the diary were made and circulated among government officials, there is no evidence that it was known to subsequent white settlers in Utah. It was first published in Mexico City in 1854. The German scholar Alexander von Humboldt examined the journal and included parts of its descriptive material and a map of the Utah Lake area in an 1811 publication on New Spain. The Miera map, drawn two years after the padre's return, provides considerable detail and is the first cartographic rendering of large segments of Utah by one who had actually been here. It mistakenly shows a river flowing westward out of the Great Salt Lake and connects the Green and Sevier rivers, suggesting that this composite Buenaventura also flows west from the Sevier to the Pacific. The mistaken notion that major rivers might flow westward from central Utah to the coast would take many years to die.

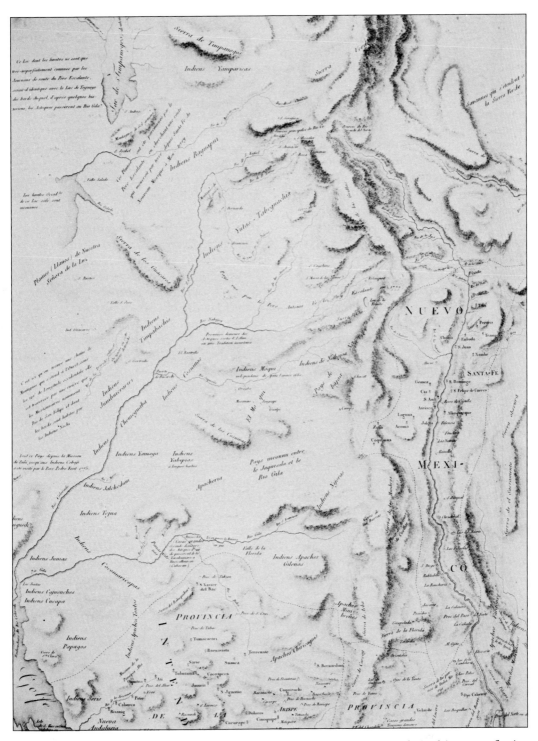

Alexander von Humboldt's map of 1811. Following Miera, Lake Timpanogas is drained by a west-flowing river of the same name. The Buenaventura runs from northeastern Utah to Sevier Lake. *Courtesy the Bancroft Library, Carl I. Wheat Map Collection. Reprinted from Carl I. Wheat,* Mapping the Transmississippi West, 1540–1861, *with permission of Francis M. Wheat.*

The Domínguez party was not the first group from New Mexico to enter present-day Utah, nor were they the last. Under Mexican rule after independence from Spain was gained in 1821, subsequent trappers and traders crisscrossed the area, blazing trails that were used into the nineteenth century. One set of trails, now called the Spanish Trail, led northwestward from Sante Fe into Utah. It crossed the Colorado River at Moab and the Green at Green River. From Castle Dale it curved southwestward through Salina to Parowan, Newcastle, Mountain Meadows, and down the Santa Clara River. It left Utah at Castle Cliff Wash, before heading across the deserts of Nevada and California towards Los Angeles. The 1,200-mile trail from Santa Fe to Los Angeles had become a reality by the 1830s and remained an important thoroughfare through the '40s— but far too late for the purposes that led the Domínguez party into the wilderness.

The Franciscans, through their careful maps and journal, first documented the names, tribal locations, and cultural achievments of Utah's Indians. But ultimately, it may be that the dozens of later, unknown dealers in blankets, horses, and slaves had a far greater impact on the Indian people of Utah than did the better-known Domínguez-Escalante expedition. It was not the one-time heroic event, but the persistent trucking and bartering of Mexican frontiersmen that brought the horse, taught men to prey upon one another, and in countless other ways transformed the Shoshoneans, greatly altering the life-styles of Shoshone, Ute, Gosiute, and Southern Paiute alike.

The Anglo-Europeans

The probing of people of European descent into Utah did not take place from the southwest alone. Indeed, just fifty years after the epic journey of Domínguez and his party, Mexicans were traveling regularly through Utah country from Santa Fe and

Taos, English trappers were descending from the northwest to exploit its resources, and Yankees from North America were intruding from the northeast. All converged here during one of the most colorful and important eras of early Utah history—that of the fur trade.

The earliest Spanish colonies had been sustained by rich harvests of gold and silver. And, as Domínguez and Escalante found, any new territories not promising quick returns were likely to be passed by. Not one of the early English colonies paid its stockholders a significant return. Most were financial disasters. Hundreds of settlers died of famine and disease before permanent bases could be established. The Spanish and English experiences made it clear that the opening of new territory required a product of great value that could be readily gathered and exported. Otherwise, the chances for success were not good.

The beaver was the unlikely bonanza that first opened Utah to European and American eyes. In the 1820s a good beaver pelt could bring $10 in the St. Louis market, the equivalent of perhaps $120 today. The beaver pelt was not used as a fur piece, at least not in the same way a mink or raccoon is today. Rather, the soft underhair was clipped and then pounded to form a felt, used in the making of hats of the finest quality—popular among the well-to-do in all of Europe as well as America. The demand for beaver hats became an enormous stimulus to the exploration and eventual settlement of the Mountain West.

The fur trade had helped sustain the Pilgrims in the 1620s. It flourished in the Far West two centuries later. In 1821 the newly independent Republic of Mexico began to liberalize government control of licenses to trade in their territory (which included all of present-day Utah), releasing a flood of entrepreneurial activity as Mexican trappers began to work the streams of the Southwest. At the same time American and British fur companies were building posts along the watersheds of major

Peter Skene Ogden, leader of the 1825 Hudson's Bay Company expedition to northern Utah. From a daguerreotype taken at Brady's Gallery, New York City. *Courtesy Oregon Historical Society (Negative # OrHi 707).*

rivers — especially the Missouri. Whites and Indians trapped beaver and traded them at these posts for cash, beads, arms, ammunition, and other manufactured goods. Heavy bales of the furs were then easily shipped downriver to St. Louis. But outbreaks of hostility among tribes along the river led some fur companies in the 1820s to look towards the Rockies. Countless mountain streams teeming with a beaver sleeker and heavier of coat than the river varieties promised the opening of a new era in the fur trade. The new hunting grounds were far from major rivers and included parts of the Great Basin.

Some of the earliest trappers to work in the mountains came to Utah country even though more accessible parts of the West were still rich in beaver. This was partly because of British-American rivalry over the Pacific Northwest. In 1818 America and Britain had agreed to a joint occupation of the whole Northwest, with final sovereignty to be determined by later negotiations. As a result, officers of the British Hudson's Bay Company decided to keep the Americans out by eliminating their rea-

son for being there. If the beaver were trapped out, there would be no valuable commodity to attract American settlement and the land would be left to the British.

Acting on this policy, the Hudson's Bay Company in December 1824 sent out a huge expedition from its Flathead, Montana, post. The entourage consisted of 131 persons with 268 horses and 352 traps. Their leader was Peter Skene Ogden, a man of strong opinions and firm resolve. His intent was to trap out all the best streams clear down into Utah country, leaving nothing for the Yankees.

At the same time, however, an American expedition from a St. Louis-based company owned by General William Ashley and Major Andrew Henry was working in the same area. Their main purpose, in true Yankee fashion, was to increase their beaver catch and maximize company profits. Organization of the Ashley-Henry trappers had begun two years earlier in 1822. In that year and again in 1823 the two businessmen placed advertisements in Missouri newspapers:

> The subscriber wishes to engage ONE HUNDRED MEN, to ascend the Missouri River to its source, there to be employed for one, two or three years. — For particulars, enquire of Major Andrew Henry, near the Lead Mines, in the County of Washington, (who will ascend with, and command the party) or to the subscriber at St. Louis. Wm H. Ashley.

Many who responded to ads such as this were to become famous mountain men. Most were young farm boys who saw a chance for adventure and the down payment for a farm at the end of their term. Some worked on salary, their expenses paid and profits claimed by the company. Others were free agents, paying their own expenses and keeping all the profits.

James Clyman was a surveyor who had come to St. Louis in February 1823 to pick up some back pay. There he heard of the Ashley offer, which by then promised a salary of $200 a year and specified that they would be hunting and trapping in the Rocky Mountains. Clyman immediately signed on to help recruit workers. Ashley gave Clyman instructions as to where to find recruits that found an echo in countless western films and in the cantina scene of the first *Star Wars* film of 1977.

> He said he wished then that I would assist him ingageing men for his Rockey mountain epedition and he wished me to call at his house in the evening which I accordingly did getting instruction as to whare I would most probably find men willing to engage which [I] found in grog Shops and other sinks of degredation he rented a house & furnished it with provisions Bread from to Bakers — pork plenty, which the men had to cook for themselves.

As they embarked up the Missouri on their mission he wrote, "On the 8th [10th] of March 1824 [1823] all things ready we shoved off from the shore fired a swivel which was answered by a Shout from the shore which we returned with a will and porceed up stream under sail. A discription of our crew I cannt give, but Falstafs Battallion was genteel in comparison." After an adventuresome ascent upriver the Ashley-Henry trappers left the river and headed west along a route well to the south of established trading posts on the upper Missouri. They were in the Wyoming Rockies by the time Peter Skene Ogden's army of trappers was finalizing plans to move south from Montana — both to meet in northern Utah. It was to be a momentous season.

In the early spring (1824) a small party of the Ashley group began working on the Sweetwater River. From the Sweetwater the Rocky Mountains loom large and forbidding — an intimidating obstacle to those hoping to cross the Continental Divide into the Pacific watershed. But the Ashley-Henry trappers were not easily intimidated. They continued toward the mountains, where there was said to be an opening to the western slope of the Rockies. What they found was not a narrow gorge cutting through the mountain peaks but a gentle ascent through a plain so level that one can hardly tell it is a pass at all.

It was so gentle, in fact, that even wagon traffic could cross the backbone of the continent without great difficulty — a discovery of paramount importance to the westward migration that was to follow. Americans working for John Jacob Astor's Pacific Fur Company had crossed the pass heading east in 1811, but their discovery was not made known to others and was of no consequence. The Ashley-Henry men were immediately aware of the significance of their discovery of South Pass. One of their principal figures, Thomas Fitzpatrick, led a party of three bearing news of the pass and the region's promising beaver streams back to the Missouri, where he reported to General Ashley. Those who remained split into two groups.

Jedediah Smith led the first, a small party that made its way to the Hudson's Bay Company's Flathead Post in Montana. John H. Weber led the second group of perhaps twenty-five to fifty down into Cache Valley where they wintered on the Cub River. Sometime that winter the men began to wonder where the larger Bear River flowed after it left Cache Valley. One of their company, Jim Bridger, was appointed to follow the river downstream and find out where it went. The men followed the Bear River through the narrows connecting Cache Valley to the lower Bear River Valley. Bridger explored the river to the lake and tasted the water. He assumed it was an arm of the Pacific. Thus, Jim Bridger and his small party, in the winter of 1824–25, were probably the first white men to see the Great Salt Lake.

There is one challenger to Bridger's claim to have discovered the Great Salt Lake — Etienne Provost, a trapper of French background, working that same winter up into Utah from New Mexico. Provost was one of the earliest of the many trappers who entered Utah from the southwest, especially

Taos and Santa Fe. It is possible that he saw the Great Salt Lake from the south at about the same time Bridger saw it from the north. In either case, before the summer of 1825 the mountain men had discovered the Great Salt Lake Valley as well as the route across South Pass that would make the valley accessible by wagon. This was not to be the end of their adventures that season.

While Bridger and Provost were discovering the Great Salt Lake, the American party under Jedediah Smith had been giving the British a bad time. As Peter Skene Ogden's brigade moved that spring from their Flathead post towards the Snake River country, they were dogged every step of the way by that "sly cunning Yankee," as they called Smith. Smith and his small party trapped with and sometimes ahead of the Hudson's Bay group. As the Americans approached Utah, they headed south to meet with John Weber's group of Ashley-Henry men. Ogden was disgusted to find that Americans had already trapped nearly every stream along the Wasatch Front. Moving south over the mountains into Ogden Valley and then into the Weber River Valley, Ogden found signs of the American presence everywhere.

But that was just the beginning of his troubles. His men had learned that American companies paid more for furs and charged less for supplies than the British. Some deserted, taking their furs to the American party. On May 22, 1825, at "Deserters' Point" near Mountain Green, Utah, Ogden encountered twenty-five Americans and fourteen deserters. The Americans, stirred by a trapper named Johnson Gardner, challenged the British to a fight. They claimed the British were trespassers on American soil. Actually, they were all on Mexican soil. The United States, but not Britain, had relinquished its claim to Spain back in 1819. Three years later the Mexican revolution had made it part of the new republic. Faced with near mutiny among his own men, Ogden backed down

and discreetly withdrew, leaving the Wasatch drainages to the Americans. Later, in 1828–29, he would lead a company from Montana to discover the Humboldt River—that vital highway across the western deserts—and return by way of the northern Great Salt Lake country.

Thomas Fitzpatrick's group had, in the meantime, informed William Ashley of the fine beaver streams they had found and the discovery of South Pass. It was perhaps Fitzpatrick's news that gave Ashley the germ of an idea that, starting in the summer of 1825, would greatly change the character of fur marketing in the West. Ashley had already realized that it would be inefficient to bring the trappers to St. Louis at the end of each season. That year he decided instead to take supplies to them in the mountains and haul out their furs with pack trains. From 1825 until 1840 trading fairs were held each year at agreed-upon sites in the Mountain West. They called them rendezvous. The rendezvous were raucous affairs—part Mardi Gras and part trading fair—where fur trappers of several nationalities, Indians of several tribes, and traders and suppliers got together for an uninhibited week of revelry and barter.

Perhaps the most famous and respected of all the American trappers to work in Utah was Jedediah S. Smith. Smith was in his early twenties when he first enlisted in the service of Ashley and Henry. He headed the party that discovered South Pass in 1824. He also led the group that became such a thorn in the side of the powerful Peter Skene Ogden and Hudson's Bay Company the next year. Smith attended both the 1825 rendezvous on Henry's Fork of the Green River and the second rendezvous, held probably at the southern end of the Cache Valley—near Hyrum. At this rendezvous, Jim Clyman reported that he and his party had sailed around the Great Salt Lake in skin boats that spring and had been disappointed to find no promising beaver streams or outlets from the lake.

As the rendezvous broke up, Smith headed out in search of virgin trapping grounds. From that point on he became more of an explorer than a trapper. His search for beaver streams and for a navigable river to the Pacific took him past the Great Salt Lake well down into the Mexican-dominated areas of central and southern Utah along a route approximating that of today's Highway 89 past Richfield and west through Clear Creek Canyon. Heading south and west until he struck the Virgin, he followed it to the Colorado. The party then crossed the deserts to the Mojave River, eventually making their way to the San Gabriel Mission near Los Angeles. There they were greeted with hostility and suspicion by Mexican authorities and ordered to leave by the same route they had come. Evading the order they moved northward into the San Joaquin Valley, trapping as they went. Leaving his crew at the Stanislaus River, Smith and two of his men then returned across the Sierra Nevada and the basins and ranges of Nevada. In the spring of 1827, after suffering terribly in the Nevada deserts, they finally came upon the familiar waters of the Great Salt Lake. Of that event, Smith wrote:

> The Salt Lake a joyful sight was spread before us. Is it possible said the companions of my sufferings, that we are so near the end of our troubles? For myself I durst scarcely believe that it was really the Big Salt Lake that I saw. It was indeed a most cheering view. . . . Those who may chance to read this at a distance from the scene may perhaps be surprised that the sight of this lake surrounded by a wilderness of more than 2000 miles diameter excited in me those feelings known to the traveler who after long and perilous journeying comes again in view of his home. But it was so for me for I had traveled so much in the vicinity of the Salt Lake that it had become my home in the wilderness.

Smith and his companions hurried on to the rendezvous site, on the shores of Bear Lake, near present-day Laketown.

There they were greeted with joy by the other mountain men, who had assumed they had died in the deserts or had been killed by Indians.

Shortly after the rendezvous, Smith left again for California, following the same route as the previous year. The journey was plagued with mishap and calamity. Indians attacked them on the Mojave River. Several of his party were killed, and Smith barely escaped with his life. When he reached California, Smith decided to travel up into Oregon before heading back east. Near the Umpqua River the party was attacked again. Only Smith and three others escaped to spend the winter at a Hudson's Bay Company post. They then headed east to the Flathead Indian country in Montana where they trapped through 1829 and '30, attending the rendezvous both years. In October 1830 Smith arrived in St. Louis where he planned to retire from trapping and prepare his journals and maps for publication. He couldn't resist, however, joining Thomas Fitzpatrick in a trading expedition to Santa Fe. In May of 1831, while scouting alone for water along the Cimarron River bed in western Kansas, he was attacked by Comanches and killed. He was just thirty-two.

By that time the northern Utah country had been pretty well trapped out. Shrewd businessmen to the end, Smith and his partners had sold their fur interests at the 1830 rendezvous to the Rocky Mountain Fur Company—a partnership that included such notables as Jim Bridger, Thomas Fitzpatrick, and Milton G. Sublette. They and other trappers, such as Osborne Russell, and Thomas L. (Pegleg) Smith, continued to trap the area into the 1830s.

Enough activity continued to encourage the occasional establishment of temporary trading posts. Little is known of these early posts. Most were in the Uinta Basin and served trappers working out of Santa Fe who dominated that part of Utah. "Kit" Carson established a trading post at the junction of the Green and White rivers as

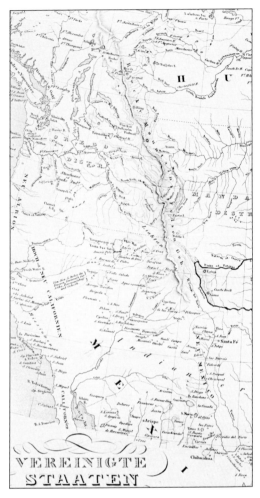

Utah after the Trappers. Jacob Steiler Map of 1834, among the first to show the Great Salt Lake and Sevier Lake as interior basins. *Courtesy the Bancroft Library, Carl I. Wheat Map Collection. Reprinted from Carl I. Wheat,* Mapping the Transmississippi West, 1540–1861, *with permission of Francis Wheat.*

early as 1833—probably the first of the Utah posts. Another, Fort Davy Crockett, was founded in 1837 at Brown's Hole on the north bank of the Green River near the Utah-Colorado boundary. The fort was named in Crockett's honor by its founders, Philip Thompson and William Craig. That same year, another fort was founded by Antoine Robidoux, a trapper working out of New Mexico. He left a message carved on a rock near present-day Harley Dome,

Utah, announcing his plans to build a trading post further north: "Antoine Robidoux passé ici le 13. Novembre, 1837, pour établir maison traitte á la Rv. Vert ou Winte." (Antoine Robidoux passed here November 13, 1837, to establish a house of trade at the Green or Uinta River.) The post was apparently finally located at the Whiterocks Fork of the Uinta, and continued operations until 1844, when it was destroyed by rival traders. The loss was not greatly felt, as the fashion in men's hats had turned to silk and the fur trade was clearly in decline.

Mexican traders continued to travel through central and southern Utah until mid-century—well after the Mormons came—packing blankets to the coast to change for cattle and horses or buying captured Indians to be sold as slaves in New Mexico. A few of the Anglo traders, such as Jim Bridger, couldn't get this country out of their blood. They lingered into the '40s establishing trading posts like Fort Bridger in southwestern Wyoming and Fort Buenaventura on the Weber River. But these posts were to serve the coming overland immigrant traffic more than the fur or Indian trade. Their presence assured that the influence of the mountain men—especially in place names and travel—would remain until permanent settlement of the region.

The mountain men had been the first to literally put Utah on the map. The cartographer Henry S. Tanner in 1822, for example, dimly referred to the Great Salt Lake and Utah Lake, but with no clear differentiation. He showed a river flowing westward to the Pacific out of the Great Salt Lake and other details are confused and misleading. By the 1830s more accurate maps of the region were being printed, thanks in great measure to the mountain men. Even as far away as Germany maps began to portray the area as an inland-drainage basin. Jim Bridger had, after all, discovered the Great Salt Lake in the winter of 1824. Etienne Provost learned that same year of its relationship to Utah Lake and trapped the country between the Utah Valley and the Uinta Basin. The next year Jim Clyman, Moses Harris, and others paddled around the Great Salt Lake in skin boats and found it had no outlet. Jedediah Smith broke new ground all the way to Los Angeles, finding no river to the Pacific. Peter Skene Ogden could offer some hope to westbound travelers, however, with his discovery of the meager Humboldt heading off towards its alkaline sinks south of Lovelock. And perhaps most important, South Pass was charted and its existence made known in the East. The trappers' first-hand knowledge of the terrain would gradually make its way to mapmakers whose works encouraged thousands of Americans to cross the continent with their wagons and families as they came to the West to start a new life. The American victory in the rivalry for influence in the West was clear by 1840, encouraged by the pathfinding the mountain men had accomplished. Americans would shortly flock to Oregon and California—their trails taking them near and sometimes across the Wasatch oasis.

The mountain men were hard-nosed businessmen who, nevertheless, had a touch of the romantic. They opened the West to America, and Utah to future immigrants. More than this, their bravado set a style that has captured the imagination of thousands of Americans. From Maine to California modern-day mountain men meet yearly in traditional dress to shoot black powder rifles, barter knives and fur hats, and imagine themselves to be free, independent, courageous trappers of another age.

In the boldness of their ventures there are some similarities between the mountain men and the astronauts of our time. But the analogy fails at some points. The Apollo lunar landing crews were perhaps more the Lewis and Clarks than the Jedediah Smiths of the space age. They explored but did not harvest. Yet who can say what harvests await the business acumen and derring-do of some modern Jim Bridger or Thomas Fitzpatrick? Surely, should Tranquility Base become the Cache Valley of a new breed of space explorers—out for quick gain and adventure—both that landscape and our own would be greatly transformed by the encounter. In the meantime, the lunar landscape has been imprinted in our consciousness by the men who went there, named the mountains and the valleys, and then left—the evidence of their passage now cluttering some Brown's Hole or Ogden Valley that previously had not known the tread of man.

For Further Reading:

Histories

Indians. A useful general history of American Indians is Wilcomb E. Washburn's *The Indian in America* (1975). Several short studies of present-day Indian tribes of Utah are in the book edited by Helen Z. Papanikolas, *The Peoples of Utah.* The spring 1971 issue of the *Utah Historical Quarterly,* edited by C. Gregory Crampton, has several articles on Utah Indian tribes. Excellent brief overviews are in S. Lyman Tyler's "The Earliest Peoples," and "The Indians in Utah Territory," both chapters of *Utah's History* (1978) edited by Richard D. Poll, Thomas G. Alexander, Eugene E. Campbell, and David E. Miller. On the Gosiutes see *Newe: A Western Shoshone History,* published by the Inter-Tribal Council of Nevada (1976). Ruth Murray Underhill has written *The Navajo* (1971). Also useful is *Dinéjí Nákéé Nááhané: A Utah Navajo History* by Clyde Benally and others, published in 1982 for use in San Juan County schools. The Inter-Tribal Council of Nevada printed in 1976 *Nuwuvi: A Southern Paiute History.* A videotape on Southern Paiute history is available through the library of Southern Utah State College. A useful history by James Jefferson, Robert W. Delaney, and Gregory C. Thompson is *The Southern Utes: A Tribal History* (1971). Also see Wilson Rockwell's *Utes: A Forgotten People* (1956).

The Spaniards. Herbert E. Bolton was the great historian of the areas of North America colonized by Spain. His *Spanish Borderlands* (1921) provides a general background of events leading to the Domínguez-Escalante expedition. A later publication, *Pageant in the Wilderness* (1951) is in part a history of the expedition, together with a translation of the Escalante journal.

Mountain Men. A classic general study of the fur trade is Frederick J. Merk's *Fur Trade and Empire* (1931). See also Edwin E. Rich's *The Fur Trade and the Northwest to 1857* (1967). Dale L. Morgan offers a carefully detailed and as yet unsurpassed study of Utah's fur trade in *Jedediah Smith and the Opening of the West* (1953). David E. Miller's chapter on "The Fur Trade and the Mountain Men," in *Utah's History* (1978) is succinct and useful. Bernard DeVoto's *Across the Wide Missouri* (1964) is lively and readable and illustrated with the marvelous contemporary paintings of Alfred Jacob Miller, George Catlin, and Charles Bodmer. Many biographies of particular mountain men and specific aspects of the fur trade have been printed and are available in local libraries. Of special relevance to Utah history are J. Cecil Alter, *James Bridger, Trapper, Frontiersman, Scout and Guide: A Historical Narrative* (1925); Archie Binns, *Peter Skene Ogden: Fur Trader* (1967); LeRoy R. Hafen, *Broken Hand, The Life of Thomas Fitzpatrick: Mountain Man, Guide, and Indian Agent* (1973), and "Etienne Provost, Mountain Man and Utah Pioneer," *Utah Historical Quarterly* 36 (1968); and Charles Kelly, "Antoine Robidoux," *Utah Historical Quarterly* 6 (1933). Carl P. Russell's *Firearms, Traps, and Tools of the Mountain Men* (1967) makes interesting reading for those wishing to recapture the nuts and bolts of the fur trade.

Eyewitness Accounts

Indians. A chilling account of the conquest of Mexico City was reported by Aztecs to a Spanish Franciscan, Sahagún, in 1555. It is readily available and provides an Indian perspective on their encounter with the Europeans in North America, though of course not in the Utah region. See Bernardino de Sahagún, *The War of Conquest: How It Was Waged Here in Mexico: The Aztecs' Own Story.* Rendered into modern English by Arthur J. O. Anderson and Charles E. Dibble (1978). Regrettably, few narratives by Utah's early historic Indians (who did not have written language) are available in libraries. *Son of Old Man Hat: A Navajo Biography,* is the only one I have found from

Indians whose people had a major influence on Utah history. Collections of legends can tell much of a people, however, and several have been printed, among which are William R. Palmer's set of Southern Paiute legends, *Why the North Star Stands Still and Other Indian Legends* (1957), and *Stories of Our Ancestors: A Collection of Northern Ute Indian Tales,* printed by the Uintah-Ouray Ute Tribe in 1974. The indispensable early white perspective is the Domínguez-Escalante journal itself, with translations printed in Bolton's *Pageant in the Wilderness* and Fra Angelico Chavez, trans., Ted J. Warner, ed., *The Domínguez-Escalante Journal* (1976).

Spaniards. In Herbert Bolton, ed., *Spanish Exploration in the Southwest, 1542–1706,* is printed a variety of firsthand accounts and documents that provide a general background for the Domínguez-Escalante expedition. Their journal is fascinating reading, with translations available as noted above in Bolton's *Pageant in the Wilderness* and Chavez and Warner's *The Domínguez-Escalante Journal* (1976).

Mountain Men. Several eyewitness accounts of mountain men have been published. William Kittson's "Journal, Ogden's 1824–5 Snake Country Expedition" in the *Utah Historical Quarterly* 22 (1954) provides a fascinating view of that momentous season in the mountains. David E. and David H. Miller have edited with Glyndwr Williams *Peter Skene Ogden's Snake Country Journals, 1827–28 and 1828–29,* a set of lively and informative journals. Colorful and often highly exaggerated is *The Life and Adventures of James P. Beckwourth,* ed. Delmont R. Oswald (1972). Jedediah Smith's often eloquent journals covering an important portion of his sojourn in the West are in George R. Brooks, ed., *The Southwest Expedition of Jedediah S. Smith: His Personal Account of the Journey to California, 1826–27* (1977). James Clyman's journals have been edited and printed in Charles L. Camp, ed., *James Clyman, Frontiersman: The Adventures of a Trapper and Covered-Wagon Emigrant as Told in His Own Reminiscences and Diaries* (1960), and Linda M. Hasselstrom, ed., *Journal of a Mountain Man: James Clyman* (1984). A unique and most valuable pictorial record is in Marvin C. Ross, *The West of Alfred Jacob Miller* (1966). Osborne Russell's *Journal of a Trapper,* ed. Aubrey L. Haines (1955), is less colorful than some, but gives very useful insights into the everyday life of a working trapper.

Pioneers camped at Chimney Rock, August 3, 1861. George M. Ottinger. Painted from a wagon while on the overland trail. *Courtesy LDS Museum of Church History and Art.*

Three

White Settlement

Before the 1840s American settlers had barely touched the lands that lay beyond the Missouri River. Yet, thanks in large measure to the mountain men, reports of rich lands in Oregon and California awakened a restive spirit among midwestern farmers. Though the deserts and mountains between the Missouri and the coast were of no interest, the very names of Oregon and California began to take upon them a magical quality. By mid-decade the trickle of American emigrants to the Far West had become a flood. The eastern press was surprised and bemused by the phenomenon, many editors arguing that the prospect of a farm in Oregon or California could not possibly justify the costs and dangers of the journey. One writer maintained that Siberia was at least as inviting as Oregon and no more difficult to reach by wagon. The journey itself, he insisted, would cost more than would be needed to buy "an Illinois farm of the finest land in the world." But there was no stopping that great human tide. Watching the dusty roads to the West swell with the flocks, herds, and wagons of midwestern farmers the editor of a New York journal reluctantly concluded that "we might as well undertake to stay the sun and the moon in their course over the peaks of the Rocky Mountains, as emigration to the west by the hardy nomadic population of our country." Certainly, as opportunities on the coast faded, a part of that flow would have been attracted to Utah country. But the first Americans in Oregon and California had barely cleared their lands when another migration of Americans chose to pull up some thousand miles short of the coastal settlements. These were the Mormons. Their decision to settle here in 1847 changed the history of this region. The story of white settlement in Utah begins, curiously enough, in the beautiful, well-watered lake country of upstate New York when it was itself just past frontier times.

Mormon Beginnings

While the mountain men were reaping Utah's first harvest of valuable beaver pelts, a farm boy half a continent away in New York State was embarking on a search for another kind of treasure that would in time, unlikely though it might have seemed, transform the direction of Utah's history. Joseph Smith formally organized his following into a religious body in 1830, the same year another famous Smith—Jedediah—left the Rockies for the last time. Sixteen stormy years later, the Salt Lake Valley, which Jedediah had called his home in the wilderness, would again become a home in the wilderness—this time for several thousand of Joseph Smith's followers.

The family of Joseph Smith, Sr., in which the Mormon movement had its beginnings and found its first leaders, was prior to 1820 hardly distinguishable from hundreds of other Yankee farm families of the early 1800s. They, with others, suffered a series of economic reverses in the early years of the century and in 1816 joined a considerable migration of New Englanders to western New York. There, in an economy booming with the advent of the Erie Canal, which was to open a vast hinterland surrounding the Great Lakes to Atlantic traffic, the Smiths worked at odd jobs until they scraped together the means

to make a down payment on a hundred-acre farm close to the town of Palmyra.

The Smith's were pious and close to a strain of folk religion mixed with magic common among rural people of the time. They did not associate with organized religions, however, until the late 1810s and early '20s when waves of revivalistic enthusiasm began to sweep through towns in their vicinity. The mother, two sons, and a daughter joined the Presbyterians, though the patriarch of the family remained aloof. The junior Joseph, then in his fifteenth year, leaned towards the Methodists but, according to his 1838 account, found himself hopelessly confused by the conflicting claims and doctrines of the various revivalists.

Deeply disturbed by the centrifugal forces tearing at his own family, at organized religion, and at the broader American society, he sought a resolution by praying in a grove near his father's farm. There he had a religious experience that transformed his own and his family's lives, and eventually those of thousands of his followers.

The direction of that transformation seems clear. Smith, above all, was attempting to resist, even to reverse the trend towards individualism and disorder he saw all about him in the exuberant young America of his time. More than that, he was attempting to counter the most powerful trends of modern times by building an enclave of order and unity in a world he saw as increasingly chaotic and fragmented.

Given the dimensions of the task he set for himself, it is hardly surprising that he encountered opposition and persecution at every turn. The maxims of everyday life in America were becoming permeated with such notions as "it's a free country ain't it?" and "every man for himself and the devil take the hindmost." People who held to such sentiments would resist Smith's movement with all the power at their command. And, as often happens, that very resistance would prove to Smith's followers the rightness of their position, increasing the solidarity of those Saints—as they called themselves—who stayed with Smith and insulating them from other Americans. In this way they became to a considerable degree the unified and orderly society Smith had hoped for. The historical experience of the Mormons reinforced Smith's teachings, moving this people, even after the founding prophet was dead, in directions counter to those of the nation.

One of these teachings was that Smith had been called by God to be a prophet to mankind in the last days. Through his agency the Book of Mormon was published in 1830. The book tied the New World to the Old as a setting for God's revelation to man. Its "coming forth" reinforced Smith's assertion of unique prophetic powers. While others might receive counsel and revelation from God in managing their own affairs, there was only one prophet who had been given authority by God to convey His will to all men. Smith's revelations were often written down and became accepted by the faithful as the express will of God to His people. This concept of continuing, current, and immediate revelation introduced a valuable element of flexibility to doctrine and cloaked church policies in the language and authority of holy writ. It would have been clear to the discerning viewer by December 1830, when Smith announced a revelation telling the New York congregations to pull up stakes and move to Ohio, that the prophet's followers were remarkably responsive to the counsel and commands he gave them.

Shortly after moving to Ohio, Smith designated Jackson County, Missouri, on the western frontier of America, as the central gathering place for Mormons. Some began that summer to move to Missouri, and for the next seven years there were really two main centers of Mormon activity in the United States, the Kirtland, Ohio area,

and a succession of Missouri sites. Different experiences in each center reinforced the doctrinal teachings of Smith.

A most important doctrinal innovation leading to a strong sense of community was enunciated with great clarity in Kirtland—that of "the gathering." Converts were early put on notice that theirs was no camp meeting conversion from which they could return, albeit more piously, to their ordinary walk of life. In Boston, New York, and Philadelphia, as in farm villages of New England and the middle states, recent converts were asked to sell their possessions and "gather" with the Saints, preferably to Missouri, but Kirtland would do as well. Implicit in their doctrine was the idea that the non-Mormon world was subject to corruptions and influences from which the faithful must flee, clearly adding a physical separation to the widening doctrinal rift between the world of the Saints and that of other Christians. Particularly important in this process were the beginnings of a cooperative economic system called Consecration and Stewardship, practiced mainly in Missouri, and the commitment of the people to an enormous public project—the building of the Kirtland Temple.

Consecration and Stewardship was first described in revelations received in February 1831, very shortly after Smith's arrival in Kirtland. The system required all church members to "consecrate" or give all their earthly possessions to the church, whereupon they received in return from the church a "stewardship" or grant of real property and the materials to make a living in their chosen profession. They were then given entrepreneurial freedom to "improve" their stewardship and enjoy the benefit of their creativity and energies "according to circumstances . . . wants and needs." Any surplus beyond these needs was to be again consecrated to the church storehouse at the end of each year. Through these consecrations the social welfare of the Saints would

The Kirtland Temple, symbol of community.
George Edward Anderson photograph. *Courtesy
LDS Church Archives.*

be funded, and new stewardships would
be provided to impoverished converts and
to youth coming of age. The consecrations
would also be used to finance the administrative and missionary activities of the
church. The marketplace still allocated essential goods and services, but the consecrated surplus provided a capital fund that
could be used by the church hierarchy to
shape and plan for the balanced economic
growth of the whole community. The program was a revision of the extreme individualism apparent in America at the time.
It led towards a more communal economics, though leaving some elements of individualism, particularly individual opportunity and responsibility, still clearly in place.

Though practiced in Missouri between
1831 and 1833, Consecration and Stewardship occasioned some friction in the community. It was later discontinued under

Joseph Smith's direction, in favor of the
"lesser law" of tithing. The experience of
attempting to live it, together with the continuing promise that it would be reinstituted when the Mormons were sufficiently
selfless, helped break down distinctions between secular and religious lives, asking
members to sacrifice substantially and systematically to community needs and goals.

Equally important in building a sense
of community among the early Saints was
the construction of the Kirtland Temple.
In the extremity of poverty, Joseph Smith
announced in December 1832 that his followers were to build a major edifice to be
used as both a school and a meetinghouse
and in which God would further reveal his
will to them. The building was constructed
at great financial sacrifice. Women worked
long hours spinning wool to provide clothing for the workers; when it was time to
plaster the sandstone walls many gave their
china and glassware to be ground into the
plaster so the walls would glisten in the
sun. Dedication services were held in March

1836, many testifying that they heard heavenly choirs and experienced other heavenly manifestations at the dedication services and thereafter. The building became a visible symbol of community, representing sacrifice of individual for common needs. It remains one of Ohio's finest early nineteenth-century church buildings.

The sense of community it symbolized was heightened when Joseph Smith began to teach that the Mormons were in fact a latter-day Israel, thus beginning a profoundly important identification with the ancient biblical covenant people of God. "Ye are the children of Israel, and the seed of Abraham," Mormons were told in an 1834 revelation. They began in Kirtland to see themselves as a covenant people with a special relationship to God and under sacred obligation to undertake special responsibilities and obligations. In all these ways Mormons became identified as not just adherents to a new denomination but citizens of a community that exacted a level of commitment and loyalty uncommon among religious bodies of the time.

Events in Missouri reinforced these and added still other dimensions to the Mormon character. The Missouri migrations had begun in the summer of 1831, shortly after Smith had designated Jackson County as the American Zion. A temple site was dedicated and settlements were made under the direction of the first Mormon bishop, Edward Partridge. Things went well in 1831 and 1832, but as Mormons began to pour into the area, older settlers, mainly from Kentucky and Tennessee, began to fear the growing influence of the New England Yankees. The Mormons published a newspaper and opened stores and shops. It seemed they would before long gain political control of the area. Worse, they were freesoilers, had converted some free blacks, and had announced that they hoped to convert the Indians.

In July 1833 the prior settlers, greatly disturbed by all these developments, organized open resistance. They destroyed the Mormon press, the store, and the blacksmith shop, and tarred and feathered prominent church leaders. Opposition became so intense that in November the Mormons were forced out of the county, crossing the Missouri northward into Clay County where they were provided with food and temporary shelter by local residents. Upon hearing of the expulsion, Joseph Smith led a party of two hundred from Kirtland to help reinstate the Saints, but the expedition, called Zion's Camp, failed in its main aim. It did, however, provide valuable experience in group migration that the Mormon leaders would later draw upon.

Eventually, a gentlemen's agreement was made by which a new county, Caldwell County, would be created primarily for Mormon occupancy in sparsely settled lands northeast of Clay County. There the Saints began building once more and by 1838 had established several towns, including Far West, a thriving little community of four to five thousand. A temple site was dedicated there, and cornerstones for the structure laid—the only identifiable remnant of the town still visible today. In the meantime, a Kirtland, Ohio, bank sponsored by Joseph Smith without state authorization had failed. Local citizens were stunned to find their investments frozen and understandably placed the blame on Smith. Threats against his life soon began to surface. By early 1838 the situation had become so grave that the prophet fled Ohio, joining the Missouri Mormons at Far West.

By the time Smith arrived in Missouri the Mormon presence was already causing anxiety among residents of neighboring counties. As other Ohio Mormons arrived, conditions worsened, and in October open violence broke out. Several confrontations led the governor to issue an order that the Mormons leave the state or be exterminated. Subsequent skirmishes led to several deaths, including the massacre of seventeen Mormons huddled for protection in a blacksmith shop at Haun's Mill. Smith was jailed in Liberty, Missouri, and the

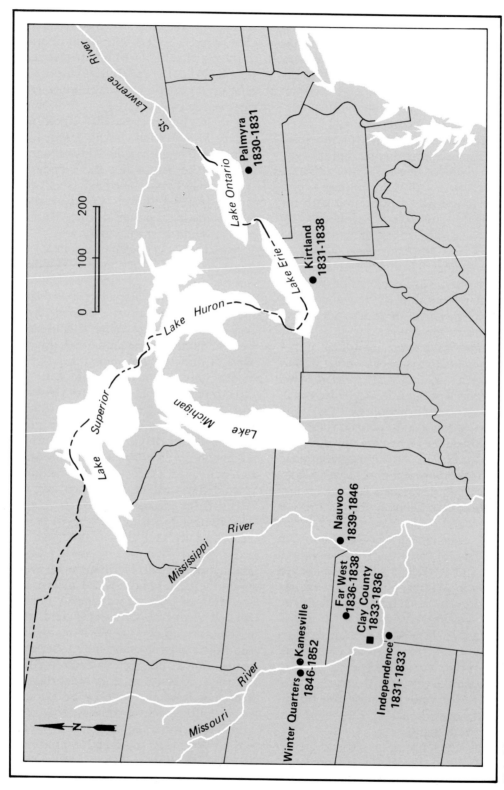

Main Mormon centers through 1846. *Drafted by Gene Ockinga.*

Saints, again in the dead of winter, made their way eastward across the Mississippi to Quincy, Illinois. There they were welcomed with compassion and cared for by the residents of the town.

The Missouri experience had shaped the Mormons in significant ways. It had made the theme of unjust persecution an indelible part of their consciousness. From that time on the retelling of stories of mob violence, of threats of extermination, and of flight became a ritual that helped define Mormon attitudes towards others and reinforce their sense of separateness. In addition, the Missouri experience gave the Mormons, however painfully, repeated experience in migration and organizing new settlements.

Their last settlement site in the Midwest was on a broad bend of the Mississippi River, north of the refugee camps at Quincy. Purchases of lands began in April 1839, shortly after Smith escaped imprisonment in Missouri and rejoined his scattered flock. Under liberal charter from the Illinois legislature, the city—called Nauvoo—grew rapidly. An embryonic university was founded, and a disciplined town militia, the Nauvoo Legion, organized.

Doctrinal developments in Nauvoo were dramatic, adding a strong Old Testament flavor to the religion and injecting elements that seemed almost calculated to provoke non-Mormons and try the faith of Smith's most loyal followers. Especially inflammatory was the initiation of plural marriage—the taking of more than one wife. Though the revelation announcing plural marriage was not written until July 1843, it had secretly been communicated and the practice introduced sometime prior to that. In June 1844 a group of apostates set up a newspaper openly critical of Smith's leadership and exposed the practice of plural marriage. Smith, as mayor, called a town council meeting, which ordered the press destroyed. This disregard of the long-held American principle of freedom of the press brought an immediate response from non-

Mormons. Smith was jailed in nearby Carthage and on June 27 an armed mob broke into the jail, shot him and his brother, and then fled. After some uncertainty, leadership of the church fell upon Brigham Young, president of the Twelve Apostles.

The death of the prophet only temporarily appeased those who feared and distrusted the Mormons. In September 1845 anti-Mormons began burning Mormon homes in outlying settlements. Church leaders responded with an announcement that they had been planning an orderly, gradual evacuation for some time and would begin to leave Illinois in the spring. Mob pressures increased, however, and on February 4, wagons began to pull out of the city to ferries waiting to take them across the Mississippi. By coincidence, that same day, another group of 238 Mormons from the East Coast, led by Samuel Brannan, embarked by sea in the ship *Brooklyn* from New York, bound for California. Mormon congregations from Mississippi were also organizing companies to head west and join the Saints. And later that summer, after the main migration made it halfway across Iowa, a government recruiter enlisted a battalion of their young men to march as federal troops to San Diego as part of U.S. military operations in the Mexican War.

Thus, by the winter of 1846, there were Mormons camped along the Missouri, Mormons heading north from Mississippi in wagons, Battalion Mormons moving southwest and northwest from Santa Fe and Brannan's flock in northern California—all planning to rendezvous the next summer in one of the valleys of the Rocky Mountains. It was to be an exodus of major proportions and one that would transform Jedediah Smith's old home in the wilderness almost beyond recognition.

As this crowd of refugees fanned out across the American West they and their adversaries would have agreed on at least one thing. They had become by this time quite clearly a peculiar people, quite unlike the Americans who had driven them beyond the borders of the United States. Their prophet's teachings and their historical experience in New York, Ohio, Missouri, and Illinois had reinforced one another, striking a distinctive stamp firmly upon them.

They had developed an unusually strong sense of community. They had come to believe that cooperation was better than competition; that mutual concern and watchfulness were superior to rugged individualism; that people ought to live close together spatially as well as socially, in towns rather than on individual farmsteads. Moreover, they believed their community enjoyed a special relationship to God and owed him special obligations. They increasingly saw themselves as separate and distinct from the world. Their sense of community became, in fact, very nearly a sense of nationality—a separate Mormon nation.

The Mormons had also developed an unusual respect for authority—at least the authority exercised by their own leaders. In an age of increasing anti-authoritarianism this voluntary acceptance of their leaders' authority was highly unusual—vexing to their critics, but powerful in its effect upon their cooperative accomplishments. The strong sense of community and almost instinctive willingness to respond to trusted authority made the Mormons a remarkably orderly and unified people. Dissent was frowned upon; lone genius was not honored. They prized choirs over soloists, the dance over sculpture, theater over novels. The finest accomplishments of mankind in their eyes, were those of the community—not of individuals.

And what did all this mean to Utah? It's interesting that in 1846 several immigrant trains came through Utah, some finding the place attractive, but none of them stayed. Utah was too remote, too far from sources of supply in famine, too distant from civilization for men to settle down in. It was far beyond the frontier of settled lands. New settlement in remote lands had always taken a great toll of lives and energies and in the end as often succeeded as much by luck as by pluck. But surely there was never a people better equipped than the Mormons to settle a remote and distant land. Not only had they had the practical experience of building new settlements several times within a few years, but they in addition had developed a distinctive subculture that made them ideal pioneers. Their sense of community, respect for authority, and commitment to unity and order within their society, now, as they moved far beyond the frontier, would greatly favor their enterprise.

Crossings West

The Mormons were not the first Americans to push beyond the Missouri to the Far West. Their migration was a minor early surge in a flood of settlers bound mainly for the lush coastal lands of Oregon and California. Yet only a small eddy of that great stream passed through present-day Utah. The mountains and salt deserts of the region were formidable obstacles, causing immigrants to avoid Utah, even when it meant going several hundred miles out of the way. Those passing through the Wasatch Front before 1847 did so out of ignorance or because of high-pressure tactics from the promoter of an untried shortcut to California. Most were sorry they had come and glad to be on their way at the first opportunity. To the 300,000 people who came by wagon to the West between 1840 and 1860, Utah was best known as a place to be avoided.

Most overland travelers in the early 1840s took leave of the states from the same place, whether heading to Oregon, California, or New Mexico. This was the little town of Independence, Missouri, the same town which for a brief time a full decade earlier, had been the Mormon Zion. There, people with western fever outfitted themselves and began to coalesce into immigrant trains. After leaving Independence, those bound for Oregon and California

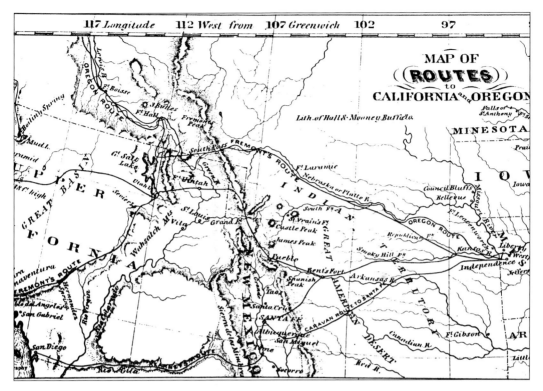

Wagon roads West. From Steele's *Western Guide Book* (1849). The Mormon Trail followed the Oregon route, though it left from Council Bluffs and ran north of the Platte River until Fort Laramie. The Mormon Battalion followed the "Caravan Route to Santa Fe" and then "Kearney's Route" to San Diego. *Courtesy the Bancroft Library, Carl I. Wheat Map Collection. Reprinted with permission of Francis M. Wheat.*

crossed the verdant northeast corner of Kansas and moved up into Nebraska where they struck the Platte, now traveling toward the sunset, along the south banks of the river. This was their grand highway to the West, well watered, grassy, and nearly level. It crossed all of present Nebraska past important landmarks such as Chimney Rock and Fort Laramie. Its northern fork continued a third of the way across Wyoming.

Finally, the North Platte turned south and immigrants were obliged to cross it, striking west up the Sweetwater River. Some stopped to carve their names on Independence Rock or marvelled at the sight of the Sweetwater seething between the nar-

row cliffs of Devil's Gate. By this time the Wind River Mountains were in sight, and they approached with trepidation the Rockies. South Pass, to their great relief, turned out not to be an awesome mountain gorge but a series of brush-covered hills. When they reached Pacific Springs and saw the waters coursing westward they knew they had indeed crossed the backbone of the continent.

The trail now was mainly downhill to the Little Sandy, then the Big Sandy River, and thence to the Green. Some headed due west from there; others dropped southward to Fort Bridger, founded by Jim Bridger in 1843 to serve overland traffic. After Fort Bridger they went northwest to the Bear River, stopping at the famous bubbling waters of Soda Springs, and then hurrying on to Fort Hall. From there the Oregon-bound headed northwest, continuing across Idaho to eastern Oregon. If bound for California, they veered off to the southwest till they found the Humboldt River. The Humboldt took them almost to the Truckee, though with a bad desert crossing between them. From the Truckee they climbed one of the passes over the Sierra and down into California. The community of overland immigrants called their journey "seeing the elephant," a phrase that aptly captured the awesomeness of the experience. As one 1852 overlander put it,

> To enjoy such a trip . . . a man must be able to endure heat like a toad, and labor like a jackass . . . he must cease to think, except as to where he may find grass and water and a good camping place. It is a hardship without glory, to be sick without a home, to die and be buried like a dog.

There were instances of overland immigrant travel in the 1830s, but, not counting the mountain men who wandered ceaselessly over all of Utah, their numbers were very few. Mass travel along these dusty highways didn't begin until the 1840s and the total in any given year was little more than 100 until 1843. In that year, 900 people traveled, to use their phrase, "the plains across."

One of the earliest overland companies passed through northern Utah in 1841, picking a trail through lands so forbidding that no one ever again would use their exact route. Their adventure began in the spring of 1841 when Missourian John Bidwell gathered together in Independence sixty-nine men, women, and children willing to stake their meager fortunes on an enormous journey into the unknown. "We knew only that California lay to the west," Bidwell later wrote.

John Bartleson was chosen as captain, so the group is often called the Bartleson-Bidwell company. Fortunately for them, Thomas Fitzpatrick and a party of other mountain men joined the train and served as guides until they reached Soda Springs. From there the trappers and about half the immigrants headed northward to Fort Hall. The rest, thirty-four in number, including the wife and teenage daughter of one immigrant named Benjamin Kelsey,

moved southwest in what seemed the shortest line towards California. After wandering around the marshes near Corinne, they struck westward over Promontory Summit, the route surveyors would choose for the transcontinental railroad almost three decades later. From there they skirted around the desolate western edge of the Great Salt Lake Desert, their wagons miring so badly in the salt flats that two were abandoned before they reached fresh water flowing from springs at the base of Pilot Peak. Heading west, they wandered past Silver Zone Pass west of Wendover to Johnson's Springs. They'd been hoping all this time to find a major river flowing west so they could refashion their wagons into rafts and float to the Pacific. Disappointed in this hope, they loaded what they could onto their animals, gave the rest to a no doubt bewildered Indian, and then headed northwest until they struck the meager Humboldt. They were to endure further privations crossing the Sierra but, finally, at the end of October stumbled into California's San Joaquin Valley.

The Bartleson-Bidwell Company had brought the first white woman and child through the Utah region. No whites before them had driven wagons across the Great Salt Lake desert or refreshed themselves at the Pilot Peak Springs. But most important, they were the first sizeable immigrant party to make their way across the continent from the states to the Far West. Theirs was, by any measure, an epic journey.

Fremont's Explorations

Even though California immigration would grow to reach 1,500 in 1846, no immigrant trains came through Utah for five more years. Another group did, however, though with an entirely different purpose in mind. This was the exploring party of the great pathmarker, as he has been called, John C. Frémont, on his second western expedition. It began in May 1843

Sunset on Gunnison Island, 1882. Alfred Lambourne. An example in painting of the romanticism of Frémont's writing. *Courtesy LDS Museum of Church History and Art.*

in St. Louis with the purpose of exploring possible wagon routes to Oregon. But at Soda Springs Frémont's curiosity about the Great Salt Lake country got the better of him. "The region possessed a strange and extraordinary interest," he wrote. "We were upon the waters of the famous lake which forms a salient point among the remarkable geographic features of the country, and around which the vague and superstitious accounts of trappers had thrown a delightful obscurity."

He and a party set out south and shortly found themselves bogged down in what became later the Bear River Migratory Bird Refuge. Disappointed in their efforts to approach the lake from the north, they moved eastward onto higher lands along the edge of the Wasatch Front. From the top of Little Mountain, west of the Weber River, they finally gained a panoramic view of the lake. Their journal reads:

> To travelers so long shut among the mountain ranges a sudden view over the expanse of silent waters had in it something sublime. Several large islands raised their rocky heads out of the waves; but whether or not they were timbered, was still left to our imag-

ination, as the distance was too great to determine if the dark hues upon them were woodland or naked rock. Then, a storm burst down with sudden fury upon the lake, and entirely hid the islands from our view.

Frémont's romantic description of the lake is a perfect literary rendering of the romantic landscape paintings of his contemporaries Thomas Moran, Albert Bierstadt, and Alfred Lambourne.

Eager to explore further, Frémont and his company inflated a primitive boat—much like an eight-man rubber raft of today. On the morning of September 9, 1843, they set out from near the mouth of the Weber to explore the lake. Unfortunately, their raft began to leak. Pumping furiously to keep afloat, they reached the closest island about noon and climbed to its summit. From the peak they surveyed the lake and prepared the first reasonably accurate map of its shape and the placement of its various islands. Finding "neither water nor trees of any kind," they named it Disappointment Island. A later explorer, Captain Howard Stansbury, renamed it Frémont Island, in honor of his predecessor's visit. While the survey was taking place, Frémont's mountain man guide, Kit Carson, carved a cross onto an unusual outcropping of rock near the summit. Though the diminutive petroglyph

Carved Cross on Fremont Island. *Dean L. May photograph.*

Pilot Peak from edge of Cedar Mountains. *Dean L. May photograph.*

clearly visible near the summit of Frémont Island would not seem to qualify as the "large cross" Carson described, many are convinced that it is, in fact, the work of the Frémont party.

Before leaving the area, Frémont boiled down a sample of water from the lake. He found that five gallons would yield "fourteen pints of very fine-grained and very white salt"—the first attempt to analyze the briny waters. He also took readings that allowed him to set the lake's elevation very accurately at 4,200 feet above sea level. After this brief exploration the party made its way back to Soda Springs and on to Vancouver. The following May they crossed back through Utah Valley on their way to St. Louis.

Frémont lost no time in arranging his notes and preparing an account of his explorations. The volume, published in Washington, D.C., in 1845, was widely circulated, especially among those who had an interest in western settlement. Brigham Young and other Mormon leaders had copies of the journal and studied it carefully before leaving Nauvoo. They could hardly have failed to notice Frémont's explanatory note accompanying his maps.

The Great Basin: diameter: 11 degrees of latitude, 10 degrees of longitude: elevation above the sea between 4 and 5 thousand feet: surrounded by lofty mountains: contents almost unknown, but believed to be filled with rivers and lakes which have no communication with the sea, deserts and oases which have never been explored, and savage tribes, which no traveler has seen or described.

Congress determined these mysteries should be resolved and funded another trip for Frémont which he undertook immediately. His party entered Utah in the fall of 1845 by way of eastern Colorado. They spent a month exploring Utah Valley and the Great Salt Lake area, visiting and naming Antelope Island. Frémont then settled down to the most important of his goals—the scouting of a route to California from the Salt Lake Valley.

Their biggest problem had also plagued the Bartleson-Bidwell company in 1841: What was the best route from the lake to the Humboldt? Frémont and his party moved out to the southwestern edge of the Great Salt Lake and then fixed their sights on a mountaintop a considerable, but unknown, distance across the desert to the northwest. Traveling all that night they arrived the next afternoon at the base of the mountain. Frémont proceeded to name it Pilot Peak. Having thus made a trail across the Great Salt Lake Desert, the party moved on west to explore large parts of Nevada. They finally arrived at Sutter's Fort in California in early December.

Hastings's "Longtripp"

It happened that Lansford W. Hastings, one of the most avid of California boosters, was at the Sutter's Fort that winter as well. He and Frémont had long conversations that were to be of great consequence to several parties traveling westward the next year. By the time of his meeting with Frémont, Hastings had already published *An Emigrant's Guide to Oregon and California*. In it, Hastings, who had moved to California from Oregon, portrayed his newfound home as a veritable paradise. But he did more than just extol the advantages of California. He offered immigrants advice on how to make their way there. And in his enthusiasm, he suggested that they could greatly shorten the trip by heading directly southwest from Fort Bridger across the Salt Lake Valley rather than digressing northward along the main immigrant route to Fort Hall.

Hastings wrote: "The most direct path would be to leave the Oregon route, about two hundred miles east of Fort Hall; thence bearing west-south west, to the Salt Lake; and [in an incredible understatement] thence continuing down to the bay of San Francisco." He published the recommendation in 1845 without ever having been over the route himself. Hastings's conversations with Frémont confirmed the former's belief that wagon traffic over the trail was possible. He rode east that spring in a personal effort to divert the flow of traffic from the main immigrant road down across the new proposed cutoff. Tracking Frémont's trail across the salt desert, he followed his mountain man guides, James

Excavated wagon tracks from the Donner era crossing the desert of mud. The track runs horizontally across the photograph. The narrow dark shadow is cast by the bottom lip of the tire impression. Archeological work by the Utah State Historical Society under the direction of David B. Madsen. *Dean L. May photograph.*

Clyman and James Hudspeth, up Parley's Canyon, to Mountain Dell, then north over Big Mountain Pass to Echo Canyon and on out to Fort Bridger.

From there, he sent a letter east recommending the route to incoming trains and then settled down to wait for their arrival. In July, as immigrant companies approached, Hastings promised personally to guide them over the cutoff, no doubt assuring them that Frémont had traversed it the previous season with no problems. The magic name of John C. Frémont, together with the promise of personal guidance from the author of the best-selling guidebook of the season, was enough to convince a number of parties. Over the next few weeks at least four companies of immigrants pulled away from the main stream of traffic and headed southwest toward Echo Canyon. They were soon to find that Hastings promised much more than the terrain could deliver. He had not yet worked out the best route from Fort Bridger to Echo Canyon, and he began with the assumption that after leaving Echo Canyon, the Weber River Canyon would provide the easiest crossing into the valleys.

Prominent in the first group were a newspaperman, Edwin Bryant, and a traveling companion, William Russell. Altogether, the Bryant-Russell party consisted of only nine men on horseback. Even without wagons they found the recommended route harrowing, especially in the lower Weber Canyon where, as they put it, they were "frequently passing under, and some times scaling immense overhanging masses and projections of rock." They nonetheless made their way successfully out of the canyon near present-day Ogden, then down across the south end of the Great Salt Lake to the springs in Skull Valley. By August 3 they were at the north end of the Cedar Mountains looking across what Hastings had said was a forty-mile desert to Pilot Peak. According to their account, Hudspeth said, "Now boys, put spurs to your mules and ride like Hell!" They did that, and though they found the crossing closer to eighty miles, made it to Pilot Peak and on to California.

The next group, led by George W. Harlan and Samuel C. Young, was larger and risked taking some forty wagons down the Hastings Cutoff, following roughly the same route as the Bryant-Russell party. They lost at least one team and wagon at Devil's Gate in Weber Canyon but emerged otherwise intact into the valley below. They had a terrible time crossing the salt flats, losing both livestock and wagons to "the desert of mud."

Another party of but four men, led by Heinrich Lienhard, was hard on the heels of the Harlan-Young group. The Swiss immigrant's journal provides fascinating details of the trip and descriptions of the terrain. By the time the Lienhard party set out, Hastings had determined the most direct route from Fort Bridger to Echo Canyon, which gave them some advantage over the earlier companies, but the guide didn't

catch them in time to warn them away from the dangerous Weber Canyon. After finally reaching the Humboldt on September 8, Lienhard wrote wryly in his journal that the route they had followed "might much better be called Hastings' Longtripp" rather than Hastings Cutoff.

The last group to follow the ill-advised route that summer was led by George and Jacob Donner and James Reed. Following the now well-marked route into Echo Canyon, they emerged near Henefer to find a note prominently stuck in a stick along the trail. It was from Hastings. He advised them against the wagon-smashing Weber Canyon road, suggesting they stay there until he and Clyman could show them the route they had traveled earlier that year. James Reed and two companions went ahead, finding Hastings near the northern edge of the Oquirrhs. He hurried back with them far enough to give them a general description of the route he now recommended. Reed and his companions then returned to the main party, now camped four days at Henefer. From there they turned up Main Canyon. They spent twelve days cutting a road along Dixie Hollow and up part of East Canyon Creek until they reached Little Emigration Canyon and a pass to the west over Big Mountain. They labored up over Little Mountain and down into Emigration Canyon. Even then their troubles didn't end. They found the mouth of the canyon blocked with seemingly impassable boulders. Rather than clear them out, they spent a full day double-teaming their wagons to lift them up and over the steep Donner Hill, today itself clogged by staring condominiums. Finally, on August 23, they rolled across the Salt Lake Valley and camped near the Jordan. From Henefer to the Jordan, their trip had taken eighteen days—a delay that would prove far more costly than any of them could ever dream.

The desert of mud extracted its usual toll of livestock and wagons. After a string of misfortunes, they reached Truckee

Lake—now Donner Lake—in late October, about the time the Bartleson-Bidwell company had reached that point in 1841. There, for the Donners, disaster struck. Early snows trapped them beside the lake, and before help came forty-four of the original eighty-nine persons in the group had died. Theirs is a tragic story of both courage and human frailty pitted against overwhelming natural obstacles.

The migration of 1846 thus ended on a tragic note. Hastings Cutoff had been trying for all and disastrous for the Donners. Later, when the Salt Lake Valley was settled, the cutoff became practical for travelers to both northern and southern California. Even then, however, the Fort Hall route remained the established and popular way to the coast, for the sufferings of the pioneers of '46 would be long remembered by subsequent travelers.

The 1846 immigration of 2,700 to the West Coast doubled the next year, then dropped to but 1,700 in 1848. The gold rush filled the overland trails with 25,500 in 1849 and 50,000 in 1850, but the biggest year on record was 1852 when 60,000 hardy immigrants "saw the elephant" in their crossing to California and Oregon. The Utah immigration was but a tiny fraction of the great mass movement.

One aspect of the 1846 immigration is most intriguing. Several dozens of immigrants took eighty or more wagons across the Salt Lake Valley that summer. Why did it not occur to one of them to stop and settle down? The Domínguez party had described the parts of the region they saw in glowing terms in 1776; so did a number of mountain men in the 1820s. John C. Frémont, after his 1843 visit, had recommended the area for raising cattle and grain in a book that many of the immigrants of that season carried in their wagons.

Why not settle down and leave the harrowing salt flats and the Sierra passage to someone else? Heinrich Lienhard, an 1846 immigrant, was rhapsodic in his descriptions of the Salt Lake Valley.

The land extends from the mountains down to the lake in a splendid inclined plane, broken only by the fresh water running down from the ever-flowing springs above. The soil is rich, deep black sand composition doubtless capable of producing good crops. The clear, sky-blue surface of the lake, the warm sunny air, the nearby high mountains, with the beautiful country at their foot, through which we on a fine road were passing, made on my spirits an extraordinarily charming impression. The whole day long I felt like singing and whistling.

Yet Lienhard and company sang and whistled their way right out into the boggy salt flats and on to California. Why did they not stop? There were doubtless many reasons. Their hopes, after all, had long been fixed on California. They could not have stopped, one guesses, without feeling they had not been made of stern enough stuff; that they had been forced by nature to settle for a lesser prize. Indians seemed a constant threat to any small garrison of white men living so far from others of their kind. There were no markets nearby for whatever they could get the arid soil to yield.

But at the bottom of all this they were intimidated by the loneliness of the place. This was a sublime landscape, even cheering after being shut in the mountains for so long; but here the wind blew incessantly across a broad, flat expanse of water in a valley where not one of civilization's comforts could be seen from horizon to horizon. Only here and there along the streams did a comforting vertical line, a clump of cottonwood or willow, break the stretch of plain and water. In the Willamette Valley or somewhere near Sutter's Fort were houses and people—civilization. There one could settle down, but not out here, a thousand miles from the nearest settlement.

Heinrich Lienhard wrote further in his journal that day, "had there been a single family of white men to be found living here, I believe that I would have remained. Oh, how unfortunate that this beautiful country was uninhabited!" Thus, by the end of 1846 the route to the Great Salt Lake had been laid out, the path marked, the road tried the whole way. And those who risked life and limb to accomplish this herculean task left it all to struggle across the desert of mud and on to California. The next move would be up to someone else.

A New Land

While the 1846 immigrants were pioneering the harrowing trails through Utah the Mormons were contemplating their own errand into the wilderness, to commence the following spring. Perhaps 8,000 or 9,000 of them occupied hastily thrown-up log cabins on both sides of the Missouri near Omaha. The settlement on the Nebraska side was called Winter Quarters. That on the Council Bluffs, Iowa, side they later called Kanesville, after Thomas L. Kane. Some had wintered in towns downriver, such as St. Louis or St. Joseph. Many remained in Nauvoo, or in major East Coast cities. Nearly 10,000 were in England, awaiting word as to where the Camp of Israel would settle, so they might join them.

Some five hundred miles west of Winter Quarters, near Pueblo, Colorado, the Mississippi group and the sick detachments of the Mormon Battalion made up a community of nearly 300. Still further west the remainder of the Battalion, 350 strong, served as occupation troops in San Diego and Los Angeles. Other Mormons were in Northern California, primarily the 238 who had sailed round the Horn the previous year. A few others had come to California with earlier overland migrations. Tens of thousands were making preparations to respond to Apostle Orson Pratt's clarion call:

> We do not want one saint to be left in the United States. . . . Let every branch in the East, West, North and South be determined to flee out of Babylon either by land or by sea.

And flee they did. By the spring of '47 they could be found in many parts of the West, preparing to converge that summer somewhere in the vicinity of the Great Salt Lake.

The Mormon migration of 1847 is noteworthy for its relative ease and efficiency. Their worst suffering by far had been while crossing Iowa the previous spring and camping on the Missouri the winter of '46–'47. In 1847 they were by no means moving out into unknown or uncharted lands. Between 1840 and 1846 more than 8,000 persons had traveled over the route the Mormons were to use, at least as far as western Wyoming. And in the year the Mormons traveled, 5,400 others crossed to the West. They met people often along the way. In fact, to avoid meeting others, which might lead to competition for forage and campsites and exposure to contagious disease, they stayed away from the main Oregon Trail on the south side of the Platte where possible, making their own trail on the north side of the river.

All that winter of 1846–47 they worked on detailed plans for the pioneer journey. Among their visitors at Winter Quarters was the famous Jesuit, Father De Smet, who offered advice based on his own travels in the Rocky Mountains. In January Brigham Young announced to his followers a revelation that set out the basic organizational structure of the traveling companies, dividing them into groups of ten, fifty, and one hundred, with a captain presiding over each. The companies were to divide the poor and the families of the Battalion members among them so no one group would bear an undue burden. The revelation offered general instructions concerning appropriate ethical and moral behavior together with words of encouragement, including the promise that they would be led by the God "who led the children of Israel out of the land of Egypt; and my arm is stretched out in the last days, to save my people Israel."

In their typically practical fashion, however, the Mormons did not rely on God's arm alone. Whatever scientific instruments could be found were gathered together—including sextants, barometers, thermometers, telescopes, and such. Maps of the main route to Oregon were prepared for all the pioneer companies, undoubtedly based on the one prepared by John C. Frémont during his 1843 expedition, which had been published in 1845. Seeds, plows, saws, and other equipment essential to new settlement were gathered, together with men skilled in a variety of needed crafts and trades. Lectures were held on the methods of irrigation, should they find the rainfall insufficient for raising crops. They even carried with them a large leather boat equipped with seines and fishing gear.

Early in April, members of the select pioneer company began to gather a short distance west of Winter Quarters. This was a crack team—mainly tried and experienced men—commissioned to mark the trail, choose a settlement site, and begin construction of shelters. The pioneer company consisted of 143 men, 3 women, and 2 children, and included 3 black slaves—Green Flake, Hark Lay, and Oscar Crosby.

On April 16 they began their journey in earnest. Fearing possible Indian encounters, Brigham Young imposed a military organization overlaying the revelatory order of tens, fifties, and hundreds. They had no unpleasant encounters, however, except for occasional pilfering and the loss of a few horses. Brigham Young presided over the expedition, supervising every detail and offering continuous advice and occasional reprimands when evening and Sunday recreation became too rowdy.

Under camp rules issued by Young a bugle sounded at 5:00 A.M. The whole company was to breakfast, harness the teams and be prepared for travel by 7:00. They were to be on the road until 8:30 P.M. and be ready for bed by 9:00. It was a bracing regimen and one that paid off in rapid travel. William Clayton had been charged with the tedious task of estimating distance traveled by counting the revolutions of a wagon wheel and multiplying by the measured circumference of the wheel. After three weeks he enlisted the skills of Orson Pratt and Appleton Harmon, and they built an odometer that automatically ticked off the revolutions of the wheel as they moved up the valley of the Platte. By its measurements fifteen- to twenty-mile days were not uncommon. In thirty-nine travel days (they generally laid over on Sundays), the company arrived at Fort Laramie, averaging fourteen miles a day for the 573-mile leg of their journey. Yet another crew was now designated to prepare and plant markers every ten miles along the way from Fort Laramie to their destination. This first half of their adventure had been easy going. The mountains and deserts of the second half would be a greater challenge.

Young appointed tasks to various crews for the journey. Orson Pratt, the company's scientific observer, made regular readings with his instruments, taking notes on geological formations, plants, and animals. He described Laramie Peak on June 7, "its top whitened with snow, that acts the part of a condenser upon the vapour of the atmosphere which comes within its vicinity, generating clouds which are precipitated in showers upon the surrounding country." He noted while passing a series of bluffs on June 10 that "the rock in the bluffs would make excellent grindstones, being of fine grit sandstone." Young appointed hunters to provide game, reprimanding them on at least one occasion "for being wasteful of flesh . . . killing more than was really needed," a temptation many travelers succumbed to when they encountered an abundance of game along the plains.

After crossing to the south side of the Platte the company paused to shoe animals, repair wagons, and freshen up for the arduous mountain trails ahead. There an advance contingent of the Pueblo Saints caught up to them and informed them that others were following. They learned, in addition, that an enormous Oregon-bound immigration of at least 2,000 wagons was behind them on the trail. From this point they were back on the regular immigrant road, following the Platte to its crossing near the mouth of the Sweetwater.

At the last crossing of Platte, before striking the Sweetwater, they unloaded their leather boat, the "revenue cutter," as they called it, and ferried themselves and other westward-bound immigrants across the swollen waters. Ever pressed for hard cash, they were delighted to learn that Oregon-bound immigrants would pay $1.50 to $2.00 a wagon for the ferry service. Another crew was given the task of building a large raft, capable of carrying a loaded wagon across the river, and ten men under Thomas Grover were left at the ferry to man the operation.

After South Pass, along the Big Sandy and the Little Sandy rivers, the company ran into several parties of travelers, including mountain men Moses Harris, Jim Bridger, and Miles Goodyear. Harris favored the Cache Valley as a settlement site and Bridger, Utah Valley. Both voiced some reservations about the enterprise—Harris thought there wasn't enough timber; Bridger feared the growing season might be too short. But their overall communication to the pioneer company was positive. It may well have been these discussions that convinced Brigham Young that the Mormons would settle in the Salt Lake Valley.

The strongest dissenting voice came from a fellow Saint, Samuel Brannan. Brannan, with but two companions, had made a heroic spring crossing of the Sierra, noting the grim remains of the Donner tragedy as he passed. He then hurried up the Humboldt, north to Fort Hall and east to the Green, where he met Brigham Young's pioneer company in late June. He had already set up a press in California, bringing with him the first sixteen issues of his *California Star*. He also brought the news

that California, then a Mexican possession, had been occupied by the United States and would almost certainly become part of the U.S. His settlement on the San Joaquin River had been established, and the Saints there were making plans to receive the main companies when they arrived. Why not, he argued, come on to California, where the climate is mild, the soil proven fertile, and where thousands of acres of well-watered land can be had for the taking?

It may well be that the fate of the Mormon movement hung in the balance as Young pondered Brannan's enthusiastic advice. California even then was something of a magic word, stirring up images of physical comfort, a bounteous nature, and the good life. At the time, probably no more than 2,500 Americans had settled there. Vast tracts of that rich land could fall under Mormon control if Brigham Young would only give the word.

No one can say what was in the Mormon leader's mind at that moment. Apparently without discussion he rejected Brannan's proposal. The company moved on to Fort Bridger. "The Fort," Orson Pratt wrote with obvious disappointment, "consists of two adjoining log houses, dirt roofs, and a small picket yard of logs set in the ground." From there they left the Oregon Trail, continuing on Hastings Cutoff over a route that Pratt noted "is but dimly seen as only a few wagons passed over it last season."

As they moved down Echo Canyon the company spread out, partly because of outbreaks of an unknown disease they called mountain fever—apparently Colorado tick fever, carried by wood ticks. After emerging from Echo Canyon a scouting party under Orson Pratt considered the Weber Canyon route to the valleys used by most of the 1846 parties. However, a five-mile ride down the canyon convinced Pratt and John Brown that they should return and search for the Donner-Reed tracks. They shortly found them, partially overgrown with grass, and began to improve the road their predecessors of the previous season had blazed. Continuing to work the road as they moved, Pratt's party on July 19 gained glimpses of the Salt Lake Valley from Big Mountain. On July 21 he and Erastus Snow descended Emigration Canyon, climbed Donner Hill, and gazed in awe upon the panorama spread out below them. "Beholding in a moment such an extensive scenery open before us," Pratt wrote, "we could not refrain from a shout of joy which almost involuntarily escaped from our lips the moment this grand and lovely scenery was within our view." After a brief exploration the men returned to their camp.

The next day, July 22, Pratt guided the first wagons to the mouth of Emigration Canyon where they worked four hours clearing a path to avoid the steep hill the Donner party had so laboriously climbed. They then rolled into the Salt Lake Valley and camped in the vicinity of Fifth East and Seventeenth South. The next morning they moved north to about Fourth South and Main, and began plowing. That evening Pratt dedicated the land as a home for the Saints.

Two days later the last wagons pulled out of Emigration Canyon. Brigham Young, recovering from a severe bout with mountain fever, had his driver stop the carriage and gazed upon the scene. He later recalled that as he did so "that darkness which had rested over every place where we had been in the states vanished altogether . . . and I felt assured that our enemies would never accomplish anything more towards our destruction than what they had accomplished." Wilford Woodruff many years later remembered that Young was wrapped in vision for a few moments, then said, "It is enough. This is the right place. Drive on." In his diary entry of that day, however, Young wrote only the following: "I started early this morning and

after crossing Emigration Canyon Creek eighteen times, emerged from the canyon. Encamped with the main body at 2 P.M. About noon, the five acre potato patch was plowed, then the brethren commenced planting their seed potatoes. At five, a light shower accompanied by thunder and a stiff breeze."

Having found a suitable place to settle, this advance party began immediately a communal effort to civilize the region. July 25 was a Sunday, and the day was devoted to sermons and speeches. During the next week crews were appointed to undertake the various immediate tasks. Plowing and planting continued; surveyors, fence builders, and sawyers were organized. A "bowery" was built to provide shelter when public meetings were held. One crew was appointed on July 27 to explore the canyons of the Wasatch Mountains to search for timber. Another was to explore westward to the Oquirrhs. Brigham Young led a party to explore northward. After noting the warm springs at the northern end of the Salt Lake Valley, Young's party decided to climb the foothills so they might gain a better view of the landscape. They headed for a peculiarly rounded nob that stood out clearly from the rest. From its summit they could see the Jordan River from its narrows, near Point-of-the-Mountain, to where it discharged its waters into the Great Salt Lake. They also could see the courses of several other streams that crossed the valley from the east to flow into the Jordan.

Completing their bird's-eye survey, one of the party commented that this would be an ideal place to raise a flag or ensign. Brigham Young agreed, and wrote in his diary that night, "I ascended a hill north of the city site, which I named Ensign Peak." They took no flag on their hike that day and had they raised one it would probably not have been the Stars and Stripes. The fact is that the Mormons were in a resentful mood about their treatment at the hands of government officials in the Midwest and felt no great loyalty to the United States. One of their songs, for example, complained that:

> The blood-stained wicked nation
> From whence the Saints have fled,
> Expressed their approbation
> And wished that they were dead.

However, the widespread wish to be separated from the United States had a more positive and broader dimension. On August 6, two weeks after the pioneer company reached the Salt Lake Valley, Brigham Young ordered that one of the creeks be dammed to form a pool. He then was immersed in a ritual rebaptism, each of the apostles following him, and then most of the rest of the company. It was a solemn, but joyful occasion. "We had as it were entered a new world," Erastus Snow explained, "and wished to renew our covenants and commence a newness of life."

The use of the word "new" three times in that short sentence is profoundly significant. Clearly rebaptism on that occasion represented far more than just a call to repentance. It was, as Snow stated, a recognition that in a new land it may be possible to begin society anew, consciously shaping it so as to root out all that is unjust and undesirable in the old. From the earliest settlement of America the thought of a new world had awakened the reformist impulse in men, arousing in many a desire to build a better society.

This wish to build a better world, untrammeled by customs and traditions of the past made the isolation of the Great Basin, which other passersby had feared, a great attraction to the Mormons. Whereas the doughty Swiss immigrant Lienhard would gladly have stayed in 1846 had there been earlier settlers, the Mormons gladly stayed because there were no earlier settlers. The Salt Lake Valley was as many days from the Missouri as New England had been in the 1600s from London, and it took nearly as long to get to the nearest

California settlements on the West Coast. The Mormons had leaped far beyond the advancing line of settlement to a remote land a thousand miles in any direction from the nearest major population centers. In their present mood they wanted nothing so much as to be left alone. Not even the streams and rivers mingled with those on the outside, which suited the Mormons just fine.

They were soon to find that isolation a mixed blessing. While it was no doubt comforting that there were none here "to hurt or make afraid," as their hymn put it, the corollary of that fact was that there were likewise none to assist or supply in case of need. Previous pioneering in remote frontiers, such as the settlement of Jamestown, had often been attended by terrible privation and loss of life, followed by a long, costly period of dependency on the mother society. This land was unknown and her soils untried. No one knew for sure that a large number could survive here.

There were, however, factors favoring the Mormon enterprise. Visitors from the time of the Domínguez-Escalante expedition had praised the bench and valley lands, often mentioning that they were particularly adapted to grazing and, according to Frémont's assessment, to raising wheat and other grains. Moreover, Miles Goodyear had established the previous August a trading post, or at least a cabin, on the site of present-day Ogden and by the summer of 1847 had corn and other vegetable crops well under way.

The Mormons themselves were for the most part favorably impressed by the new homesite, though their trek across western Wyoming would likely have made the most withered of grasses look lush. Woodruff called it a "vast, rich fertile valley . . . clothed with the heaviest garb of green; . . . abounding with the best fresh water springs, rivulets, creeks, brooks, and rivers of varied sizes." Orson Pratt noticed, however, that "the grass had nearly dried up for want of moisture" and that the drier places were "swarming with very large crickets, about the size of man's thumb." Nonetheless, Pratt and others were pleased with the site, if less enthusiastic than Woodruff.

Time would show that irrigation was vital to successful agriculture in the Great Basin. In this respect the Mormon choice for an initial settlement site was extremely fortunate, as the Salt Lake Valley was crossed from east to west by seven small streams, fed most of the summer by snows melting from the Wasatch Mountains. A small brush diversion dam would in most instances be sufficient to lead a canal the two or three miles needed before lands could be irrigated from the next stream. This was of vital importance, as the Mormons had almost no capital and needed to put land into immediate production. There were few places in the arid West where this could be done as expeditiously as in the Salt Lake Valley.

They were fortunate for another reason as well. Many areas of the Great Basin, including Utah Valley, just south of the Salt Lake Valley, were the regular habitat of Indians. There were Northern Shoshone to the north, Gosiutes and Western Shoshone to the west, Utes to the south, and Paiutes to the southwest. The Great Salt Lake Valley, however, had for some time been open to visits from the various tribes, with none putting forth a clear claim to it.

The Mormons thus were not encroaching on the territorial claims of any particular group. As they began to look beyond the Salt Lake Valley for settlement sites, however, they were intruding upon established territory in almost any direction they moved. Their good fortune was that the full implications of their settlement in the Great Basin did not occur to native leaders until the Mormons were present in sufficient numbers to be able to withstand Indian resistance. There were other whites in the territory as well, including Miles Goodyear at Ogden and the Mexican traders who regarded central and southern Utah as their special preserve. But Goodyear

seemed happy to sell out to the Mormons, and the Mexicans had no established settlements in Utah, minimizing conflicts between the two groups.

The final circumstance favoring their enterprise came from their own group character and the experiences they had been subjected to over the previous sixteen years. Had each gone out to settle his own farm or gone prospecting, or had great numbers been enticed by Sam Brannan's preachments on behalf of California, the Mormon story might have been greatly altered. Instinctively obedient to the men they saw as legitimate authorities commissioned by God to lead this enterprise, they moved in directions urged by their leaders in spite of grumbling and occasional expressions of dissent.

It would have made more sense, from one point of view, to build a home for one's wife and family than to spend time on a community bowery or plow a common field. But to have done so would have been repugnant to Mormon notions of authority, unity, and order. The principles that were to shape Mormon utilization of this land were worlds away from the highly individualistic approach seen in most other western settlements. In meetings on July 25, Brigham Young enunciated the basic philosophy of Mormon settlement in the Great Basin: "No man should buy or sell land. Every man should have his land measured off to him for city and farming purposes, what he could till. He might till it as he pleased, but he should be industrious and take care of it." There would be no private ownership of streams, wood, or timber, and only dead timber could be used as fuel.

Working under these rules, they laid out the city in ten-acre blocks, constructed a fort with adobe walls on three sides, harvested salt from the lake, put a whipsaw into operation, built a boat, hewed out a canyon road, set up a blacksmith shop, established an adobe yard, and began other necessary work. By December 7, John

Taylor reported, they had planted 2,000 acres of fall wheat.

Certainly they had work aplenty to do. Hard on the heels of the pioneer company were the sick detachments of the Mormon Battalion and the Mississippi Saints. Behind them were four more companies of immigrants numbering 1,500 souls. Before winter set in, the first of the discharged Battalion members would arrive from California.

With the initial labors well under way, Brigham Young turned the reins of government over to a High Council of twelve men under Joseph Smith's uncle, John Smith, and returned with a substantial company to Winter Quarters. From there apostolic letters would be sent to the scattered Saints throughout the world proclaiming that a settlement place had been found and that they should come to "the Valley," as it was already being called, at the first opportunity. Latter-day Israel was soon to be gathered to the land they would call Deseret, after the Book of Mormon word for honeybee.

For Further Reading:

Histories

The Mormons: Richard L. Bushman's *Joseph Smith and the Beginnings of Mormonism* (1985) is a sympathetic and compelling account of the cultural and family context within which Mormonism arose. Perhaps the most balanced general history of the Latter-day Saints is James B. Allen and Glen M. Leonard, *The Story of the Latter-day Saints* (1976). Thomas F. O'Dea's *The Mormons* (1957) and Dean L. May's extended essay, "Mormons," in *The Harvard Encyclopedia of American Ethnic Groups* (1980) emphasize distinctive cultural traits of the Mormons. The cooperative character of Mormon society is the principal theme in Leonard J. Arrington, Feramorz Y. Fox, and Dean L. May, *Building the City of God: Community and Cooperation among the Mormons* (1976). The Kirtland period of Mormon history is treated in Milton V. Backman, Jr., *The Heavens Resound: A His-*

tory of the Latter-day Saints in Ohio, 1830–38, (1983) and the Nauvoo period in Robert B. Flanders, *Nauvoo: Kingdom on the Mississippi* (1975). An excellent, highly readable account of the pioneer migration to Utah is Wallace Stegner, *The Gathering of Zion* (1964). Also see relevant chapters of Leonard J. Arrington's *Brigham Young, American Moses* (1985).

Crossings West. William H. Goetzmann's *Exploration and Empire: The Explorer and the Scientist in the Winning of the American West* (1966) is a significant and brilliantly written study that provides the essential context for the events discussed in this chapter. Gloria Griffen Cline's *Exploring the Great Basin* (1963) focuses more directly on the Utah area and is highly readable. The story of overland migration is detailed in John D. Unruh, Jr., *The Plains Across: The Overland Emigrants and the Trans-Mississippi West, 1840–60* (1979). George R. Stewart's *The California Trail: An Epic with Many Heroes* (1962) is a lively book that includes the Utah portions of the trail. A useful one-volume study of the career of John C. Frémont is Allan Nevins, *Frémont, Pathmarker of the West* (1939, rev. 1955). Perhaps a better understanding of Frémont's work can be gained from the two volumes of his writings edited by Donald Jackson and Mary Lee Spence, *The Expeditions of John Charles Frémont* (1970–73), which has much useful explanatory and interpretive material by the editors. *West from Fort Bridger*, edited by J. Roderick Korns as volume 19 of the *Utah Historical Quarterly* (1951) is primarily a printing of edited documents relating to the 1846–50 migrations across Utah, but the introductions and notes provide much useful background material.

Eyewitness Accounts

The Mormons. Happily, a fascinating volume of readings from a variety of eyewitnesses to the early years of Mormonism has been edited by William Mulder and A. Russell Mortensen, *Among the Mormons: Historic Accounts by Contemporary Observers* (1958). It is widely available and will direct the reader to further such readings. An 1847 pioneer, William Clayton, wrote a guide to help subsequent wagon trains on their journey to Utah. It has been edited by Stanley B. Kimball and reprinted under its original title *The Latter-day*

Saints' Immigrant Guide (1983). A number of libraries will have *William Clayton's Journal: A Daily Record of the Journey of the Original Company* (1921). *The Autobiography of Parley P. Pratt* (1874, repr. 1961) is widely available and offers a lively account by an important early Mormon. Other absorbing accounts are in *On the Mormon Frontier: The Diary of Hosea Stout, 1844–1861* (1964, repr. 1982), edited by Juanita Brooks, and *A Mormon Chronicle: The Diaries of John D. Lee*, 2 vols. (1955, repr. 1983), edited by Robert G. Cleland and Juanita Brooks.

Crossings West. Dale L. Morgan has edited a most useful collection of overland diaries, *Overland in 1846: Diaries and Letters of the California-Oregon Trail* (1963). John Bidwell's journal is readily available in *A Journey to California, 1841; The First Emigrant Party to California by Wagon Train: The Journal of John Bidwell* (1964), introduction by Francis P. Farquhar. Several reprintings of Frémont's published reports are available, but the most useful is Donald Jackson and Mary Lee Spence, *The Expeditions of John Charles Frémont* (1970–73). The memoir of Charles Pruess, *Exploring with Frémont* (1958), provides a valuable firsthand view by one of Frémont's closest associates. Lansford W. Hastings's *Emigrants Guide to Oregon and California* and Edwin Bryant's *What I Saw in California* are both available in reprint editions. *West from Fort Bridger*, edited by J. Roderick Korns, noted above, prints excerpts from the journals of James Clyman, Edwin Bryant, Heinrich Lienhard, and James Reed. Much of the same material is in Dale L. Morgan's edited volume *Overland in 1846*, also noted above.

The Salt Lake Theatre in 1862, the year it was dedicated. Painted by
George M. Ottinger. *Courtesy David Glover. Transparency provided
by LDS Museum of Church History and Art.*

Four

A New Land

On July 22, 1847, William Clayton accompanied the first sixty wagons of the pioneer train into the Salt Lake Valley. "At this place" he wrote, "the land is black and looks rich. . . . The grass grows high and thick on the ground and is well mixed with nice green rushes. Feed here for our teams is very plentiful and good and the water is also good." Looking beyond the watered areas close to the creeks, Clayton saw cause for concern but was still determined to be upbeat. "The land looks dry and lacks rain," he added, "but the numerous creeks and springs must necessarily moisten it much."

What we see in a landscape depends much on when we look at it and why. Another 1847 pioneer, Wilford Woodruff, wearied from crossing the Wyoming badlands and hoping this would be the future home of the Mormons, described it as "the land of promise held in reserve by the hand of GOD for a resting place for the saints. . . . We gazed with wonder and admiration upon the vast rich fertile valley . . . abounding with the best fresh water springs rivlets, creeks & Brooks & Rivers of various sizes." Though more reserved, Orson Pratt and William Clayton were nonetheless optimistic. Clayton concluded ambiguously that "for my own part I am happily disappointed in the appearance of the valley of the Salt Lake." Sam Brannan, recently arrived from California's rich San Joaquin Valley, saw the Salt Lake Valley as barren and desolate, a land where icy waters and frequent frosts would prohibit any hope of agricultural success. All were to gain a more balanced view as time passed and as they became familiar with the region extending beyond the Salt Lake Valley; all but Brannan, that is, who left the Salt Lake Valley that year, never to return.

Colonizing the West

The fact is that the pioneer company had landed smack in the middle of what geographers now call the Wasatch Oasis and in a season when, though the green of June had faded, the brown of August did not yet prevail. Thinking back across years of toil, they remembered the landscape as worse than their first diary entries indicate. But given that they by then had gained the perspectives of seasonal change and regional familiarity, they were probably closer to an accurate assessment of the whole region's character the second time than the first. The number of hospitable niches in the Great Basin was definitely limited. Even in 1981 only about 4 percent of Utah's land area was actually cultivated for crops.

Brigham Young soon found that those Utah lands that were well-watered were usually too cold for any but a limited agriculture. And those that were warm were too dry. Only in a few oases where water flowed all summer in streams large enough for irrigation could farming settlements be established. Yet in 1847 there were as many as 9,000 Mormons waiting on the Missouri and many thousands more in England. If homes were to be found for these, not to mention the tens of thousands of new converts Young confidently expected, it was essential that the Mormon net of influence be cast wide. Thus, no sooner had the pioneer company alighted in the Salt Lake Valley than Young dispatched exploring parties to identify and claim further

oases for Mormon occupation. Over the next three years, exploration continued until nearly all habitable sites in the Utah area had been identified.

Perhaps the most important initial influence on the direction these explorations took was the experience of the men of the Mormon Battalion. Early in June 1846 President James K. Polk responded to Mormon pleas for assistance by offering to enlist a volunteer force of several hundred men in Iowa and march them to San Diego as part of military operations in the war with Mexico, which had just broken out. Shortly thereafter, Captain James W. Allen, acting under orders from Colonel Stephen W. Kearney, was in the Mormon camp of Mount Pisgah, Iowa, 130 miles east of Council Bluffs. In an announcement circulated among the Mormon camps Allen explained:

> This year is an opportunity of sending a portion of their young and intelligent men to the ultimate destination of their whole people, and entirely at the expense of the United States, and this advance party can thus pave the ways and look out for land for their brethren to come after them.

Brigham Young was faced with a hard decision. The loss of so many able-bodied men would impose considerable burdens on those remaining with the main group. When non-Mormon friend and advisor Thomas L. Kane assured him that the federal government had no ulterior motive, and Young, desperately in need of hard cash to finance the migration, lent his support to the recruitment. Altogether 549 persons, including some families, set out from Council Bluffs in mid-June. They marched south, down the Missouri River to Fort Leavenworth where they were equipped and readied for the expedition. They then continued past Independence and followed the well-established Cimarron Trail to Santa Fe.

At Santa Fe and later as the Battalion moved south along the Rio Grande most of the women and children and about 150 men suffering from malaria and other infirmities were sent north to Pueblo. The rest continued down the Rio Grande Valley to near the present town of Hatch, New Mexico. They then crossed the desert in a southwesterly direction to where the Arizona and New Mexican boundaries meet at the Mexican border. After penetrating into Mexico a few miles, they turned north to Tucson and from there bore northwest to the Gila River, south of today's Phoenix. Following the Gila River until it flowed into the Colorado, they then struck out across the desert to San Diego, arriving January 29, the first to bring wagons across the Southwest to the coast. They suffered greatly from thirst, hunger, and exposure. But their only dangerous encounter was with a large herd of ill-tempered wild bulls south of Tucson. During all this journey they were noting areas that seemed promising as future settlement sites. In the 1870s and '80s, as the oases near the Wasatch became over-populated, settlements were made at Mesa, St. David, Benson, Thatcher, and other sites along the Gila and San Pedro rivers, all areas the men of the Battalion had found attractive. (See the 1849 Steele Map in chapter three, portion labeled "Kearney's Route.")

Perhaps even more important, Jefferson Hunt, senior Mormon officer of the Battalion, after leading a group from northern California to the Salt Lake Valley in 1847, returned immediately to Los Angeles through southern Utah and Nevada. On his way back to Utah he searched for settlement sites, minerals, and other resources, reporting this information to Brigham Young. His report encouraged Young to send an exploring party southward from the Salt Lake Valley under Parley P. Pratt in the fall of 1849. Their exploration in turn led to the Iron County Mission the next winter. Thus it is fair to say that the Mormon Battalion experience did much to impart a southerly orientation to Mormon

colonization—pointing them toward settlement of Parowan, Las Vegas, San Bernardino, St. George, southern Arizona, and finally, in 1885, northern Mexico.

There were other influences as well. Certainly the drive for self-sufficiency oriented Brigham Young towards the south, where he hoped cotton, sugarcane, madder (a plant producing a red dye), indigo, and other semi-tropical crops could be raised to complement the row crop, grain, and livestock capabilities of the north. And with South Pass and the Sierra passes sealed shut five or six months each year by winter snows, the hope of maintaining a year-round route to Utah led Young to foster a string of southern colonies leading down to San Bernardino.

That southern bias was complemented and in some cases modified by exceptional circumstances leading to the founding of particular colonies. Cedar City was established in 1851, for example, because it appeared that resources there would sustain a badly needed iron-producing effort. Missions to establish outposts in Idaho (Fort Lemhi), Nevada (Las Vegas), and east-central Utah (Elk Mountain) were sent out in 1855 as part of a renewed concern for missionary work among the Indians. Fillmore was settled in 1851 to be the seat of the newly formed territory of Utah. Thus dozens of colonies were founded because of specific needs, without regard to the general direction and pattern of colonization.

Of all the needs compelling Mormons to found new colonies in the West, the most important and persistent was that for farmland. Most of the oases the Mormons settled were so limited in land, water, and timber that the population was already crowding these resources before the children of the founding families began to form families of their own. The only way to provide opportunities for the growing tide of youth and the thousands who continued to emigrate from Europe was to found new colonies. Brigham Young saw

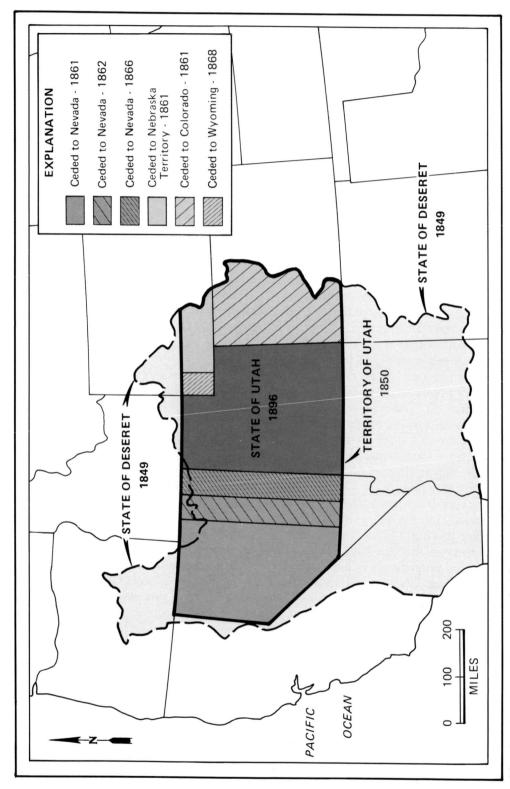

The changing shape of Utah. *Drafted by Gene Ockinga.*

this need from the beginning and set the borders of his empire as broadly as possible.

The first boundaries of the provisional state of Deseret, organized in 1849 without authorization from the United States Congress, covered a vast area, including most of present-day Utah, Nevada, and Arizona, and large parts of Wyoming, Idaho, Oregon, Colorado, New Mexico, and California. The California salient included the Pacific coastline from Los Angeles to the present Mexican border. This ambitious plan was nipped back substantially when Congress, as part of the Compromise of 1850, created Utah Territory. The territory included western Colorado, Utah, and Nevada, with the 42nd parallel as the northern boundary and the 37th as the southern boundary. Nevada Territory, created in 1861, was given large strips from western Utah in 1862 and 1866. Also in 1861, Colorado Territory was created, taking a large segment of eastern Utah. That same year Nebraska Territory, which included present-day Wyoming, was given the northeast corner. This portion was enlarged and given to Wyoming in 1868, leaving Utah with her present boundaries, substantially less than Brigham Young had hoped for in 1849. The allotment of Deseret-claimed lands to surrounding states complicated, but did not stop, the outmigration of Utah Mormons and the founding of new colonies outside of Utah.

The bridgehead in the West had, of course, been secured in the Salt Lake Valley in 1847. That same year the settlement of Bountiful began. The next year settlers moved up into lands recently purchased from Miles Goodyear at the site of present-day Ogden. In 1849 Tooele and Provo were founded and, at the Ute Chief Walker's request, the town of Manti, in the Sanpete Valley. More distant colonies were established in subsequent years — places like Parowan, San Bernardino, and Carson Valley, Nevada — but the great bulk of the population was involved in a more gradual pattern of expansion.

First settled were the most desirable locations along the Wasatch Oasis, on the eastern edge of the mountains. Next, towns were founded in mountain valleys east of the earlier settlements. Gradually the area of settlement was extended until population pressures forced moves to more remote and difficult environments — such towns as Sunset and St. Joseph, settled in 1876 on Arizona's Little Colorado River, or Bluff, settled by the heroic San Juan Mission or "Hole-in-the-Rock" expedition of 1880. Trying to find the most direct route to the southeastern corner of Utah the Hole-in-the-Rock pioneers took their wagons down to the Colorado River through an incredibly steep defile, across a road literally tacked on to a sheer sandstone face, and then painfully labored through miles of the most tortured, difficult terrain on earth — a remarkable example of perseverance in trying to extend the pale of Mormon influence.

When a particular need required movement far beyond the advancing line of settlement, church leaders often resorted to the central planning of a new colony and "calling" or assigning of leaders to launch the enterprise. As soon as the new colony was established, satellite towns grew up spontaneously in the vicinity until all available settlement sites were filled. Not all of these Mormon settlements survived, however. Problems of water supply and control were a major cause of abandonment. The settlers of the charming town of Grafton, for example, lost their small strip of arable land to the flooding Virgin River. Settlers of three colonies on the Muddy River, in the Moapa Valley, west of St. George, gave up their effort in 1870 when a government survey determined that they were in Nevada. Nevada officials promptly assessed back taxes payable in cash only, which settlers could not raise. The Mormons had no choice but to abandon their homes and farms and move back to Utah. The Mexican revolution of 1910 imperiled the lives of Mormon colonists in Chihua-

Brigham Young in 1857. From daguerreotype, photographer unknown. *Courtesy Special Collections, Marriott Library, University of Utah.*

hua and Sonora, forcing a hasty flight in 1912 of most of the colonists there. Geographer Lynn Rosenwall has calculated that in all the West about 69 of 497 Mormon settlements were eventually abandoned, an impressive record when one takes into account the nature of the terrain in which most of the settlement took place.

The acknowledged leader of the whole enterprise was Brigham Young, successor to Joseph Smith as leader of the Mormons. Young was appointed by President Millard Fillmore as the first governor of the territory of Utah, an act that moved the grateful Mormons to name a county and their first capital city after him. They were perhaps the only Americans so to immortalize the otherwise eminently forgettable Fillmore. Young was born a Vermont Yankee in 1801. He later joined a great migration of New Englanders to New York where he settled in the town of Mendon, a few miles from the Joseph Smith home. There he pursued the trade of painter and glazier. He was introduced to Mormonism through

his family, becoming one of Joseph Smith's most able and devoted followers in 1832. Smith chose him in 1835 to be an apostle in the recently founded church. After Smith's death, Young gained the confidence of the greater portion of Latter-day Saints and, by virtue of his authority as senior member of the apostles, assumed leadership of the church. He supervised completion of the temple in Nauvoo, the administering of temple ordinances, and the exodus from Nauvoo. After shepherding the pioneer company to the Great Basin, he returned to Winter Quarters, on the Missouri River just north of present Omaha. There, on December 27, 1847, he was sustained by a conference of church members as president and prophet. Returning the next spring to the Salt Lake Valley, he directed a series of far-ranging economic and political plans for the development of the Great Basin, including the extensive Mormon colonization of the West.

The many letters and sermons Young wrote from his office reveal him to have been a practical, down-to-earth man, homely in speech, and always direct and to the point. He was fond of hyperbole and quick to see the humor in a situation. Complaining of the quality of livestock contributed to the church, he said on one occasion that although

> once in a while you would find a man who had a cow he considered surplus, . . . generally she was of the class that would kick a person's hat off, or eyes out, or the wolves had eaten off her teats. You would once in a while find a man who had a horse that he considered surplus, but at the same time he had the ringbone, was broken-winded, spavined in both legs, had the pole evil at one end of the neck and a fistula at the other and both knees sprung.

To a disaffected Mormon who wrote asking him to take her name off the church records, Young responded,

> Madam: I have this day examined the records of baptisms for the remission of sins in the

Church . . . and not being able to find the name of "Elizabeth Green" recorded therein I was saved the necessity of erasing your name therefrom. You may therefor consider that your sins have not been remitted you and you may consequently enjoy the benefits therefrom.

His use at times of forceful and direct language and his extensive involvement in practical matters of economics and politics caused some to see him as a hard, tyrannical ruler who countenanced no opposition. It is fair to say that he was harsh when he felt the occasion demanded. He was also unwise in some of his pronouncements, possibly causing some of his more zealous followers to feel justified in illegal and perhaps at times violent acts. Yet an overwhelming body of solid evidence makes it clear that the key to Young's effectiveness as director of colonization lay not in intimidation but rather in his style of leadership. The alternative view springs largely from observers, past and present, who have been bewildered by the loyalty of Mormons to their faith and its leaders and have not been imaginative enough to gain an understanding of Mormonism on its own terms.

Brigham Young, despite his taste for many of the finer things in life, was preeminently a man of the people. He oversaw the planning of many of the colonies in great detail, visiting the settlers at the first opportunity and thereafter making annual peregrinations during which he visited most Mormon towns. On these occasions he not only met with local officials but walked about the town calling people by name, inquiring into the health of their children and the condition of their crops. A non-Mormon, Elizabeth Wood Kane, described interviews she saw:

> They talked away to Brigham Young about every conceivable matter, from the fluxing of an ore to the advantages of a Navajo bit, . . . and he really seemed . . . to be at home, and be rightfully deemed infallible on every subject. I think he must make fewer

mistakes than most Popes, from his being in such constant intercourse with his people. I noticed that he never seemed uninterested, but gave unforced attention to the person addressing him, which suggested a mind free from care. I used to fancy that he wasted a great deal of power in this way; but I soon saw that he was accumulating it.

He was not called "President Young" or "The Prophet" so much as "Brother Brigham," an eloquent expression of the confidence and trust his people had in him. He ruled Utah absolutely, but with a hearty handshake, more than an iron fist.

Young was assisted in this work by his counselors in the First Presidency, who included at various times an old neighbor and friend, Heber C. Kimball, George A. Smith, Willard Richards, Jedediah M. Grant, and Daniel H. Wells. The twelve apostles formed a quorum of able and loyal men who counseled the church president, served on missions, and perhaps most important took the lead in establishing and presiding over new settlements. The rotund George A. Smith, after whom St. George was named, led the expedition that settled Parowan. Ezra T. Benson was spiritual leader of the Cache Valley settlements. Lorenzo Snow presided benevolently over Brigham City; his distant cousin Erastus over Utah's Dixie; Orson Hyde over the Sanpete Valley; Charles C. Rich over the Bear Lake settlements; and Franklin D. Richards over Weber County.

Complementing these men was a broader group of advisors known as the Council of Fifty. This body of fifty prominent men was first organized by Joseph Smith in 1844. They were not a clandestine, shadow government of Deseret, secretly controlling the destiny of the region, as some have suggested, but rather a body that affirmed and disseminated decisions made at the top by Brigham Young, his counselors, and the Quorum of Twelve Apostles. It is nonetheless true that they, together with the leaders above them, were vitally important in helping to plan and carry out the extensive colonization of the West by Mormons in the nineteenth century.

Perhaps the real heroes of the enterprise were, however, the ordinary people whose names are unknown to any but their descendants. They left homes and fields, undertaking grueling winter journeys to new settlement sites, plowing, planting, and building, often time and time again. Joseph Grafton Hovey, for example, wrote in his diary on November 6, 1850,

> The President Called out some Hundred to go and make a Settlement in Iron County on the Little Salt Lake. I Joseph being caled to go also not withstanding my harde labours since I have been in the valley. I am willing to forsake all and go build up the Kingdom of God. I have laboured with all my might and god has bless me with helth and strength and my famly. I had my mind made up this winter to rest a litle and enjoy my labours hence there seams to be no stoping place for a man but he must do the will of God.

Hovey's poignant private thoughts are worth volumes on the Mormon settlement process in Utah.

Drawing on the experience in Missouri and Illinois, the Mormons evolved a procedure for town founding that they followed as if by instinct. If this were to be a "called" mission, opening up new territory or planned for a special purpose, such as lead mining, coal mining, or cotton culture, announcements requesting volunteers appeared in the *Deseret News* some months before the projected enterprise. If the volunteer force was insufficient, or lacked essential crafts and trades, "calls" were then issued, sometimes at general conferences, sometimes by local bishops, to participate in the "mission," as the enterprise was called. The colonists were instructed in what to bring and the mission departure date set. They often left in the fall so the company could árrive at the site, build mills, a meetinghouse, and homes, and complete

irrigation works before time for spring planting. The settlers met before their departure to receive pointed sermons emphasizing that their mission was a religious as much as a secular pursuit and that brotherhood and cooperation should characterize their effort. Each colony was initially under the supervision of one man — or delegation of men — who organized the migration, was fully informed on the various skills and crafts represented in the group, had an inventory of seeds, machinery, and tools in the company, organized major projects requiring collective effort, and directed worship services.

A classic example is the Iron County Mission which set out from Salt Lake City on December 7, 1850, under George A. Smith. On January 10, a month after departure, the 167 colonists reached the wholly unsettled site of their future home. On January 15 nominations were made for county officials, with elections following two days later. On January 28 crews began hewing logs for a meetinghouse. That day, George A. Smith wrote to Washington, D.C., asking for a post office for the new town of Parowan.

During the next few months the settlers organized a school, built canals and roads, raised houses, put a gristmill into operation, and scouted a site for an iron works. On the Fourth of July the leader was pleased that the celebration had been "respectably calm and placid: 'All was silent, not a gun fired, nor a drunken man seen in the streets.' " He wrote the lines without apparent awareness that his casual reference to the peaceful streets of Parowan attested eloquently to the remarkable accomplishment of the colonizing mission. When the year began, this had been a solitary stretch of salt grass and sagebrush, disturbed only by occasional wagon trains traveling to or from southern California or wandering groups of Indians. Now there was a village surrounded by fields heavy with ripening wheat and concern that lo-

The last spike. Mallet and spike of Utah iron used at dedication of Utah Central Railroad. *Courtesy LDS Museum of History and Art. Dean L. May photograph.*

cal rowdies might disturb the peaceful streets in their celebration of the national holiday.

By the end of the century more than five hundred communities from Alberta, Canada, to Chihuahua, Mexico, and from Bunkerville, Nevada, to the San Luis Valley of Colorado, would bear the distinctive stamp of Mormon colonization. The brick houses of the old Mormon towns are plain, even severe in design. Green lawns, gardens, and fields fade quickly to sun-baked desert where the line of irrigation ends. Tourists are often amazed by the determination of these villagers to stay and maintain their homes in such a forbidding land. But the Mormon leaders of the nineteenth century had designated this place a refuge and domicile for their people. Recognizing that in most places and at most seasons it was no paradise, the people determined nonetheless to plant their roots deep and stay. For well over a century, shelter, food, and clothing have been worried from this hard land. The launching of an economy sufficient to support even this meager a living was no easy task as we shall see.

A Bootstrap Economy

In 1852 a crew of tough, sweaty iron-workers gathered hopefully around a home-made blast furnace near Cedar City. As a trickle of crimson molten iron began to flow, a general cry went up of "Hosanna, Hosanna, Hosanna, to God and the Lamb." In 1870, when Brigham Young dedicated the railroad connecting Salt Lake City to the transcontinental line at Ogden, he pointedly used not a golden spike but one made of Utah iron, driven with a mallet inscribed with the words "Holiness to the Lord." Every branch of ZCMI—Zion's Cooperative Mercantile Institution—in more than a hundred Mormon towns and villages displayed the same motto, often accompanied by such symbols as hands clasped in brotherhood or the all-seeing eye of God. Now we see such symbols only on the most sacred of Mormon structures—the temples. But in early Utah the distinction between earthly and religious pursuits was not always so clearly drawn. In Brigham Young's view, economic problems were religious problems. And every religious problem had its economic aspects. Why, he felt, make an artificial distinction between the two?

A clear example of how the religious and economic aims of early Utah's leaders were intertwined was the problem of peopling the western Zion. The arduous journey from Nauvoo to the Salt Lake Valley had not been undertaken to improve the economic lot of its participants. It was an almost desperate leap into the wilderness, three months from the nearest settlements. And the Great Basin choice was made, rather than California, to isolate themselves so they could attempt without interference by outsiders to build their model of the ideal society. "We do not intend to have any trade or commerce with the gentile world," Brigham Young told the company almost immediately upon their arrival in the Salt Lake Valley, "for so long as we buy of them we are in a degree dependent upon them. . . . I am determined to cut every thread of this kind and live free and independent, untrammeled by any of their detestable customs and practices."

The thousand miles separating Utah from the frontiers of settled country solved with a vengeance the problem Mormons had always had with old settlers and other neighbors. It created for them, however, a set of new problems, forcing their leaders willy-nilly into the worlds of transportation, banking, manufacturing, and marketing. If Brigham Young was determined to cut every thread binding Mormons to the gentile world, he would have to show

equal determination in teaching Mormons to make threads of their own. And this, as every leader of a developing third-world nation today knows, is a formidable, all-absorbing task.

Brigham Young's first economic problem involved transportation: how to get the eight or nine thousand Mormons on the Missouri across Nebraska and Wyoming to Utah, and more troublesome, how to bring the tens of thousands of British and European Saints to the new Zion. The major instrument for accomplishing this was the Perpetual Emigrating Fund Company. Through donations a fund was created to finance immigration of the poor, who then were to pay the company back after they got on their feet in Utah. Incorporated in 1850, the company first concentrated on bringing the Mormons in settlements on the Missouri to Utah. By 1852 this had been accomplished, and company officials turned their attention to the greater challenge of bringing European converts to Utah.

The PEF (as the company was commonly called) chartered whole vessels on a regular basis, planning their departure, usually from Liverpool, in late winter or early spring so the entire trip could be made in a season. Typical was the journey of 333 Mormons on the *Kennebec*, which left Liverpool on January 10, 1852. The Atlantic crossing for the *Kennebec* passengers was, as one of them noted, "A long, rough voyage." Supplies ran low when the ship became stuck in the silt of the Mississippi off the Louisiana coast. Freed after ten days, the ship made its way to New Orleans where agents were on hand to help the immigrants find passage on river boats to St. Louis. At St. Louis they transferred again for the last part of the 1,200-mile trip upriver to the Mormon settlement of Kanesville, near present Council Bluffs. This was perhaps the most hazardous part of the journey, as severe outbreaks of cholera were common along the river in the early 1850s. Disaster struck when one of the river boats, the *Saluda*, blew up, killing some thirty passengers and scalding and injuring as many more. Finally making it to Kanesville, the company suffered an outbreak of cholera. In one family of nine the father, mother, and three children died, leaving four orphans to undertake the overland journey alone. Henry Ballard, appointed to help the family, recorded part of the tragedy in his journal:

Our troubles was not at an end for . . . Bro George May the father soon took sick with the Cholerhee and Died June 23 and his youngest Daughter also Died on the 27. In the morning with same at the same hour the oldest Daughter Elizabeth took Sick and although she was a strong robust young woman just past 20 years yet about sundown she was reduced to a Skeleton and died and we buried her about 10 Oclock that night with very sorrowful feelings. . . . [July] 4 The mother now Secumed after being Sick nearly all the way but now the effect of the Cholerha and worn out by the long journey and when she was dead it fell my lot to lift her out of the Wagon after She was sewed up in a sheet and that was all the preparation we could furnish and buried her.

The surviving children made their way west in the immigrant company of Eli B. Kelsey, which set out on July 4, arriving in the Salt Lake Valley October 16, 1852. It had been ten months and more than 4,000 miles since the beginning of their fateful journey. After an initial stay in Salt Lake City they, like most of the immigrants, made their way to villages where laborers were needed or land was yet available. Though different in detail, and usually attended by less suffering, the experience was repeated hundreds of times before church-sponsored immigration ceased in 1890. Altogether the Perpetual Emigrating Fund Company helped in transporting between 50,000 and 85,000 persons to Utah during its thirty-seven years of operation.

The Perpetual Emigrating Fund Company provided the financial backing and organizational structure for immigration. But the precise means of travel varied from time to time, as different plans were devised for increasing the speed and efficiency of the journey. One of the most novel was drawn up by church leaders in 1856. It proposed that immigrants walk across the plains, reducing their belongings to the bare minimum that could be pulled in a two-wheeled handcart. Furniture and larger items would be carried in a team and wagon, one for every twenty handcarts.

Though the scheme sounds half-baked at first hearing, there was actually some pretty sound economic reasoning behind it. The cost of wagons and teams on the Missouri was a major part of the overall cost of the journey. The carts promised a reduction in immigration cost from fifteen to nine pounds per head. A thousand British pounds could bring 111 to Utah under the handcart plan, but only 66 with teams and wagons. In addition, the management of wagon trains was difficult and cumbersome in the common situations where both teams and drivers were untrained and inexperienced in overland travel. Any able-bodied person, even if he did not know the hames from a cooper strap, could pull up the handle of a cart and carry several hundred pounds with no great difficulty. Each cart was to carry the provisions and a few personal effects of four or five persons.

The idea seemed so practical and promising that 1,900 persons signed up for handcart immigration in 1856. They were outfitted at Iowa City, Iowa, organized into companies of 100 carts, and spread out along the 1,200-mile trail to Salt Lake City. The first company arrived in September without mishap. Two later companies followed them, the immigrants seemingly more robust and healthy upon arrival than those in team and wagon trains. The final two companies were delayed, however, waiting for their handcarts to be built. They left Iowa City July 15 and 28 under James G. Willie and Edward Martin. Though experienced travelers advised them not to journey beyond Winter Quarters that season, their eagerness to reach the valley overcame their judgment. Both companies were overtaken late October and early November by winter storms near South Pass, Wyoming. John Chislett wrote of the experience:

> I set out on foot alone to do my duty as rearguard to the camp. The ascent of the ridge commenced soon after leaving camp, and I had not gone far up it before I overtook a cart that the folks could not pull through the snow, here about knee-deep. I helped them along, and we soon overtook another. By all hands getting to one cart we could travel; so we moved one of the carts a few rods, and then went back and brought up the other. . . . Thus by travelling over the hill three times—twice forward and once back—I succeeded after hours of toil in bringing my little company to the summit.

The exposure from such painful labors took a heavy toll on those already weakened by a severe rationing of food. Rescue teams sent out from Salt Lake City did not arrive in time to prevent a terrible loss of life. Over 200 of the 1,076 immigrants in the two companies died.

The tragedy dealt the handcart immigration scheme a blow from which it never fully recovered. Over the next four seasons five more handcart companies traveled to Utah, but 1860 was the last year of handcart immigration. Altogether about 3,000 persons carried their possessions in handcarts across the immigrant route during a four-year period when about 5,200 came by wagon. The handcart migration was but a fraction of the whole epic of Mormon travel to the West, but, like the pony express, it stirred hearts and imaginations, looming far larger in the people's memory than the actual accomplishment would seem to merit.

Brigham Young hoped to support handcart migration through the Brigham Young Express and Carrying Company (often called the "YX" company), organized in 1857, which was to provide an extensive

mail, freight, and passenger service from the Missouri to Salt Lake City, including even a pony express. The plan failed, however, when the federal government revoked an important mail contract at the beginning of the Utah War. Another, more enduring solution to the transportation problem began in 1859 with the sending of church wagon trains east each spring to meet the incoming migration at the railhead and return the immigrants to Utah. Driven by men sent as missionaries for the project, the trains operated successfully until the completion of the railroad finally resolved the immigrant transportation problem.

Transporting people was but one of the economic problems caused by the extreme isolation of early Utah. The isolation meant that Utah had to be self-sufficient in the production of foodstuffs and provide a surplus to feed the incoming migration each year. Brigham Young thus urged his followers to fill the vital need for foodstuffs before any other economic need. The *Deseret News* began publication in the summer of 1850, circulating suggestions for improved farming techniques. The Deseret Agricultural and Manufacturing Society was organized in 1856 to experiment with different varieties of crops and livestock, determining which might be suitable to the Great Basin. They sponsored the first fairs in Utah, eventually evolving into the State Fair Commission. Medals, awarded for Utah-grown fruit displayed at a fair in Philadelphia by the Deseret Agricultural and Manufacuring Society in 1873, were the pride of the territory. Thus Utah, not well adapted to agriculture, nonetheless began building its economy on farming. In this it was unlike any of the other Mountain States, all of which began as mining camps.

The production of adequate foodstuffs most years did not, however, make Deseret self-sufficient. A pound of nails might cost ten cents in Atchison, Kansas, in 1850. By the time it reached Utah, freight charges had doubled or tripled its cost. Heavy goods, such as iron; high bulk items, such as bolts of cloth or paper; and fragile products, including window glass, pottery, and china, all were in great demand in early Utah and at premium prices because of the high cost of transportation.

By 1848 the supply of such goods brought by the early settlers was almost exhausted, the people unable to replace worn-out goods themselves and too poor to order new ones shipped across the plains. The problem was temporarily resolved in what seemed to the Mormons a miraculous manner. California-bound gold-seekers began streaming into the valleys in 1849 and 1850, willing to pay hard cash for foodstuffs, supplies, and fresh livestock. They often abandoned wagonloads of scarce merchandise in their eagerness to beat others to the gold fields. This "Harvest of '49," as Leonard Arrington called it, was at best only a stopgap. As the population grew, the demand for eastern goods grew with it, causing a constantly adverse balance of trade and draining hard cash away from Utah.

The solution, as Brigham Young preached on every possible occasion, lay in building up manufacturing. "The Kingdom of God cannot rise independent of the gentile nations," he concluded, "until we produce, manufacture, and make every article of use, convenience or necessity among our own people." And so it is no surprise that during all the nineteenth century the Mormon church did everything possible to encourage the growth of manufacturing in Utah.

For example, the first *Deseret News* was printed June 15, 1850, on imported paper. But the quantity of paper that had to be hauled by wagon across the plains to keep even a weekly newspaper in operation was staggering. Thomas Howard, an English convert with experience in paper manufacturing, was asked to save the day by putting together a paper mill. He had one designed by the fall of 1851, though

his first paper was grey and coarse in texture. He improved the quality when new machinery was ordered in 1853 and again in 1860. However, there remained a constant shortage of rags for raw material. To help solve the problem George Goddard was called on a three-year "rag mission" in 1861 and went from door to door asking for rags to keep the mill in business. As he explained, "For over three years, from Franklin, Idaho in the north, and Sanpete in the south, my labors extended, not only visiting many hundreds of houses during the week days, but preaching rag sermons on Sunday." The mill had become so successful by 1869 that it withstood the competition of eastern firms shipping by rail, continuing operations until 1883.

The year after the paper-making efforts began, church leaders tried to fill two other basic, but very different needs—that for iron, so essential to almost every aspect of modern life, and that for sweets, perhaps less essential but no less in demand. Again, it was British converts with experience in iron manufacturing who were asked to develop this most basic of industries in Utah. Sent to found Cedar City in 1851, where both iron ore and coal were available, they put their all into what turned out to be a discouraging venture. Their small blast furnace turned out a quantity of iron in 1852, which was an occasion for great rejoicing. By 1855, eleven tons or more of iron were produced and the operation seemed well on the road to success. Then a plethora of problems descended—drought, famine, flood, and finally the dislocation caused by the Utah War of 1857–1858. The records show that the population of the town declined drastically in 1858, and the iron making effort was abandoned that October. Not until the capital of giant companies was brought to the region in the twentieth century did Utah produce significant amounts of iron.

The story of sugar manufacuring in pioneer Utah is similar. The search for something to satisfy a healthy sweet tooth had led early Utahns to distilled carrot juice, boiled willow shoots, and eventually to black molasses—a thick, sticky, heavily flavored syrup. An older generation of Utahns ate molasses on everything from pancakes to their frequent bread and milk suppers. Most who tasted it were surely sympathetic to the enormous effort apostle John Taylor put into the attempt to make sugar in Utah. In 1852 Taylor brought to Utah a supply of sugar beet seed from France and all the machinery for a factory. It took forty huge Santa Fe wagons, each capable of carrying up to five tons, and four hundred draft animals to pull the equipment to Utah.

In 1855 a three-story adobe factory was built on Parley's Creek, four miles south of the downtown, to house the enterprise. The neighborhood is still called Sugar House today, after the old factory. But the workers succeeded in producing only an unpalatable molasses and finally gave up the effort. In the 1890s the Mormon church invested again in the industry, this time launching a successful plant at Lehi. Again, it would appear that the early effort had failed mainly for want of capital and expertise sufficient to take it beyond the founding stage.

Other early manufacturing efforts included the making of pottery, furniture, nails, silk, tanned leather, and, perhaps most important, woolen and cotton textiles. A 240-spindle mill was set up near the mouth of Big Cottonwood Canyon in 1863. Later, it was dismantled and shipped to southern Utah where a stone mill was built at Washington, near St. George, to house the enterprise. The mill continued operations until 1910. In 1873 a large woolen mill was opened in Provo, built as part of the cooperative movement of the late 1860s. The Provo Woolen Mills Company, as it was called after 1889, continued to operate until the Great Depression. Several smaller towns, such as Brigham City and Parowan, also had mills in the nine-teenth century, producing almost entirely for the local market.

In all this it is clear that the early Utahns scored a few wins, but some pretty costly losses as well. It is difficult, however, for us to imagine the odds against any kind of success at industrialization in Utah in the 1850s. Imagine what a wealthy New York banker would have thought had one gone to him in 1851 and said, "We don't have many sheep and our population is only 15,000, or so, and it's 1,000 miles by wagon to the nearest outside markets, but our prospects are good. Could we borrow $300,000 to start a textile mill?" He would, no doubt, have had a hard time suppressing a smile. The fact is that in 1850 industrialization, even in the northeastern U.S., was in its early stages.

The Mormon efforts enjoyed the advantages of an automatic tariff, imposed by high transportation costs. In addition, they had a well-trained pool of workers—drawn directly from Great Britain, the most highly industrialized nation in the world. But they were plagued by persistent and nearly insoluble problems of capital formation. How could a people, barely able to buy the wagons and teams needed to transport themselves across the plains, save enough to finance the launching of industrial development? They didn't even have the means to construct dams and canals beyond the rudimentary pioneer ditches, because each fall 2,000 to 3,000 new immigrants arrived, hungry and destitute, and requiring food and care until the next harvest.

The first input of capital into Utah's economy, minimal though it was, came from the federal government in the form of payments to the Mormon Battalion members. Funds from this source went to help the migration effort, but some $1,950 of it was used to purchase the land Miles Goodyear claimed at the site of present-day Ogden. Second, the gold rush, as we noted, brought in goods and some gold at a critical time. Gold dust brought to Utah

Deseret Store and Tithing Office. *Courtesy Special Collections, Marriott Library, University of Utah.*

from California provided a circulating medium in the remote territory. Utah coins were minted by the Mormon church in 1848, until the dies broke, and then again with new, better dies, in late 1849. Various printed currencies were used as well, including even a reissue of the old Kirtland Safety Society notes, still in the possession of church leaders. Also of importance was the brisk trade created by military posts in Utah—Camp Floyd, established in 1858, and Camp Douglas in 1862. They paid cash for supplies furnished them, a portion of which found its way into the church treasury.

Retail stores were established in Utah in 1849, despite Brigham Young's displeasure at such operations. Some of them, such as the Walker Brothers enterprise, evolved into banks. Frederick and Samuel Auerbach began their retail business in the 1860s, and after the railroad and the rising of the mining industry in the 1870s, a number of banks were established. But no doubt the biggest commercial and financial in-

stitution in early Utah was the Tithing Office, located where the Hotel Utah was later built. It was the Mormon institution of tithing, which, more than any other, skimmed off the capital Brigham Young needed to launch the various industrial enterprises undertaken under his auspices. The office was described by an early visitor to Utah as a place where the

> shelves and the deep ware-rooms of the all-devouring theocracy groan and bulge with everything it is conceivable that mankind should sell and buy on this side of the Rocky Mountains. Here are piles of rawhide . . . bins of shelled corn, . . . wheat and rye, oats and barley; casks of salt provisions; wool, homespun, . . . indigo; cocoons and raw silk; butter, cheese, and . . . even the most destructible of vegetable growths,—not only potatoes, turnips, and other root crops, but even green pease and beans.

Though many of these commodities were used for relief of the poor, any surplus that could be marketed was, the proceeds going to a general church fund used for industrial capital as well as for other purposes.

The tithing system greatly facilitated exchange, and in addition involved itself in taxation, public works projects, welfare, warehousing and general distribution, retail and wholesale merchandising, cooperative livestock management, and banking. Probably most important, however, it was an instrument church leaders could use to control economic development, diverting surpluses from one activity and allocating them to others; supporting colonization in one locality, but not another; working ever to increase the general productivity of the commonwealth and, insofar as possible, to fulfill Young's wish that the threads binding the Mormons to the outside world be cut.

As time went on, the taste for imported goods increased in spite of the strong opposition of Brigham Young. "I would rather see every building and fence laid in ashes than to see a trader come in here with his goods," he said in 1858. The consequence of Young's policy was that an increasingly brisk business in trading fell almost entirely into the hands of non-Mormons.

By the mid-1860s it was clear that the impending arrival of the railroad would increase the trade in imported goods. Faced with this fact, Young did an about-face, concluding if the trend was inevitable it should be controlled by Mormons. In 1866 he supported a boycott of non-Mormon stores, and by early 1869 he had pieced together a blueprint for a church-sponsored mercantile system, Zion's Cooperative Mercantile Institution. A mother store in Salt Lake City would serve as the major importer and wholesaler of manufactured goods. Community stores would be founded in every town as local retail outlets. Stock issues for both the wholesale and retail stores were to be in small denominations so all could invest. Eggs, cheese, or any other local commodities

could be used to purchase stock. Stores in the system could be identified by the ZCMI logo, and citizens were urged to patronize only stores carrying the symbol. Regular disregard of such counsel could and did result in a stern interview with the bishop or priesthood quorum leaders, urging support for the system.

Given these advantages the ZCMI system flourished. Over 150 local cooperative stores were organized in all parts of the Mormon commonwealth. Many continued for decades as local general stores — often the only such store in the community. In time, however, the five- and ten-dollar shares drifted into the hands of the more wealthy and able citizens of the communities they served, the stores losing much of their cooperative ownership and often their community-interest managerial aims as well. The co-op store buildings still dot the Utah landscape, mute testimony to the powerful impact of what was surely one of Brigham Young's most successful economic innovations. Today's giant ZCMI department store chain is a much-altered living remnant of the cooperative system begun by the Mormons in 1869.

The founding of ZCMI did not represent in Young's mind, however, a capitulation to the inevitability of Utah's dependence on outside manufacturers. It was Brigham Young's aim that the substantial profits realized by the cooperative stores be reinvested in the founding of local industries. In some towns the store served as a base for expansion into a great variety of community-owned enterprises. Hyrum, Utah; Paris, Idaho, and a number of other towns were noted for the extent of cooperative industry in the town, but the granddaddy of them all was Brigham City.

Under the benevolent eye of Lorenzo Snow, Brigham City's cooperative store, founded before ZCMI, in 1864, grew to foster a truly remarkable array of home industries: a pottery shop, a tin shop, a brush factory, various administrative departments, public works and education departments and even a tramp department to provide jobs for itinerants who came to the town seeking handouts. The Brigham City Tabernacle — a splendid building and the pride of the city — was constructed by the public works department of the town around 1876. The town eventually became 85 percent self-sufficient, goods being distributed through the use of two kinds of scrip, Home Department scrip — or Home D, as it was known, good only for locally produced goods — and Merchandise scrip, good for imported items. So successful were the Brigham City cooperatives that Edward Bellamy reportedly visited the town while he was writing *Looking Backward,* his famous critique of nineteenth-century American capitalism. The cooperative, known as the Brigham City Mercantile and Manufacturing Association, reached the peak of its activities in the late 1870s. Then due to a series of reverses, including the loss by fire of a textile mill and the imposition by hostile federal officials of taxes on the scrip, the association began gradually to divest itself of its various departments until only the store was left. It closed in 1895.

Young's hope of building a society that in economic as in other affairs would be separate from the world was never quite realized. Brigham City was its best urban fulfillment, though many remote towns, such as Pocketville or Grafton, achieved a degree of meager independence they no doubt would happily have done without. Even Brigham Young found it necessary to involve himself with the gentile world, making deals with industrial and transportation firms in order to bring about the level of economic growth needed to supply the basic wants and needs of his people. And, as he had feared, in time locally developed industries were often either taken over by outside interests or succumbed to their relentless competition. But Young's priorities, in building a bootstrap economy, would seem in retrospect to have been the right ones. He began by stressing agriculture as the essential base for the development of the developing common-wealth. At the same time, he urged Utahns, as resources permitted, to commence small manufacturing and mining of industrially useful resources, such as lead, iron, and coal. He rightly sensed that Utah industries meant jobs for Utahns and that the pay of workers remains in local circulation to stimulate the growth of the region. After the railroad came in 1869, precious metal mining became of great importance, transforming the agricultural and small manufacturing base Young had built by adding new industries that remain vital parts of the Utah economy.

The success of these later enterprises, however, would have been greatly inhibited had there not already been a ready supply of foodstuffs and labor to support them. Mining development in all the surrounding states was heavily dependent in the 1880s and '90s on the truck gardening capabilities of the bootstrap economy that Utahns had built. Ironically, the territory which, except for Nevada, had the least potential for rowcrop agriculture of all the Mountain West provided the eggs, butter, cheese, and vegetables needed to build the mining industries in the nineteenth century.

The Utah example could offer much to those in developing nations around the world today attempting to plan for stable, sustained economic growth. The old Mormon symbols explicitly stated that our economic lives should be as upright as our spiritual lives. It's hard to find examples of such symbols in Utah today, but the enterprises fostered through those symbols built the base that launched Utah into a modern economy. They helped church leaders feed their followers. But, demanding as these material pursuits were, leaders and followers found time to enrich their cultural lives as well.

Cultural Life in Deseret

In the 1940s Sunday band concerts in the park were standard fare in hundreds of towns across the United States. Salt Lake City's Sunday band concerts lingered longer than most—into the late 1970s—the rousing Sousa marches making many a toe tap on the concrete floor of the old green bandstand in Liberty Park. Perhaps the band persisted here because its historical roots are deeper in Utah than in most parts of the country.

The Mormons had a brass band in Nauvoo, led by English convert William Pitt, which stayed intact during the flight west, continuing to cheer the Saints all the way to the Salt Lake Valley. Thomas L. Kane has left this account of the impression its music gave along the valley of the Platte:

Some of their wind instruments, indeed, were uncommonly full and pure toned, and in that clear dry air could be heard to a great distance. It had had the strangest effect in the world, to listen to their sweet music winding over the uninhabited country. . . . It might be when you were hunting a ford over the Great Platte, . . . the wind rising would bring you the first faint thought of a melody; and, as you listened, born down upon the gust that swept past you a cloud of the dry sifted sands, you recognized it—perhaps a home-loved theme of Henry Proch or Mendelssohn. Imagine Mendelssohn Bartholdy, away there in the Indian marches!

The harmony of the various instruments seemed to express a fundamental tenet of cultural life in early Mormon Utah. Cultural expression by these people was to be community expression—that of the group or of ensemble more than the individual. In addition, Pitt's band was to become a symbol of cheerful determination in the most depressing of circumstances. It may well be that the Sunday public concerts were long supported in Salt Lake City because they stirred dim memories in some of the people of a time when their ancestors had a band to cheer them but precious little else.

William Pitt's Nauvoo Brass Band was by no means the only instrumental ensemble in early Utah. In the 1850s Domenico Ballo was converted by missionaries and shortly thereafter came to Salt Lake City. Ballo had studied at the Milan Conservatory and by some accounts had on occasion directed the West Point band. He organized both a band and an orchestra and performed Haydn symphonies for Utah audiences when the territory was barely out of the pioneering stage. Camps Floyd and Douglas likewise had bands in the late 1850s and the '60s, both for parade and recreational purposes. Band music of the time varied, offering arrangements of favorite hymns, such as Eliza R. Snow's "O My Father"; "Home, Sweet Home," "Long, Long Ago," or other popular songs of the day; patriotic songs like "Hail Columbia" or Civil War favorite "When Johnny Comes Marching Home"; and light classical music, including the Mendelssohn that so impressed Colonel Kane on the plains.

The Pitt and Ballo bands played frequently for public holidays. Typical was the report of the 1856 Fourth of July celebration. "The bands under the direction of Major William Pitt, played at the residences of Governor Young, Hon. H. C. Kimball, and Lieutenant General D. H. Wells; after which all the Nauvoo brass band, mounted, and Ballo's and martial bands, in omnibuses, passed through the principal streets discoursing beautiful and harmonious strains of music." The tradition was reinforced in later decades when several of the early mining communities, such as Eureka, Tintic, and Silver Reef, supported town bands at various times. Utah's first full-fledged orchestra was organized in 1877 by Anton Pederson, a native of Norway. His symphony lasted but a few years and was succeeded at intervals by several different organizations until the present Utah Symphony was founded in 1940.

Interior of Salt Lake Theatre. *Courtesy Utah State Historical Society.*

Choral music in Utah began almost upon the arrival of the Mormons, though no doubt the mountain men some two decades earlier had rent the air at rendezvous and winter camps with many a salty tune. Choral performances in the earliest pioneer period were part of church services and held in the first public meeting place — the bowery. It might be appropriate to call the fledgling organization, first directed by John Parry, the Mormon Bowery Choir. Parry continued to conduct after the choir moved into the squat, adobe, Greek Revival building known as the Old Tabernacle. Several conductors succeeded him until 1867 when the choir moved into the new Tabernacle, now well over a century old, which still graces Temple Square.

After that time the choir was directed by a series of conductors, some trained in the finest European conservatories, including Charles J. Thomas, George Careless, and Ebenezer Beesley. In 1929 the choir began regular weekly network radio broadcasts, which have continued to the present. It is perhaps the only church choir to have become an American institution, producing several hit records. The Tabernacle Choir is one of the two or three most widely recognized symbols of Mormon Utah, and rightly so. Its several hundred members from different backgrounds and conditions in life express themselves as a unified, harmonious whole — the epitome of Mormon cultural achievement.

Cultural expression in early Salt Lake City was not limited just to music. The Daughters of the Utah Pioneers Museum at the top of Main Street is a replica of the old Salt Lake Theatre. The Pioneer Memorial Theatre, on the University of Utah campus, is another building honoring the Salt Lake Theatre in its design. The inspiration for both was once one of the great cultural landmarks of the West. It was built in 1861-62, long before the completion of the railroad, as a community enterprise. The workers often accepted tithing scrip or promises of tickets to future performances as pay.

The fact that two buildings in Salt Lake City were built to honor it indicates how important a cultural institution the Salt Lake Theatre was. But Utah's first dramatic performances were held, like those of the first choirs and bands, in the bowery on Temple Square. A play called "The Triumph of Innocence" was presented there in 1849. The next year a Musical and Dramatic Company was organized, moving its performances in 1852 to the old Social Hall, which once stood, appropriately enough, on Social Hall Avenue, between South Temple and First South at State Street in Salt Lake City. A spendid replica was built at Pioneer Trails State Park in 1980. The Social Hall housed musical performances, balls, receptions, and theatrical productions until superseded by the Salt Lake Theatre in 1862. The Deseret Dramatic Association maintained an ambitious repertory schedule, in some seasons performing three times a week such productions as *Othello,* Richard B. Sheridan's *Pizarro,* and *The Merchant of Venice.*

The theatre became one of the most popular cultural activities in Utah. Box offices took scrip as well as cash and even payments in kind — eggs, chickens, or wheat. Mormons and non-Mormons joined in presenting and patronizing the plays. A typical program began with a prayer, followed by a long serious work. The evening was brought to a lively end by a short comedy or farce. After completion of the railroad, notable actors and actresses played in the Salt Lake Theatre while on tour.

Theatre was rivaled in popularity only by dancing. In fact the Salt Lake Theatre was designed so its orchestra seats could be covered by a spring floor to form a large dance hall. British adventurer Richard Burton commented in 1862 that "dancing seems to be an edifying exercise: The

The Charles C. Rich home, Centerville, early 1850s. A rustic adobe adaptation of the Greek Revival style. Now in "Old Deseret," Pioneer Trail State Park. *Dean L. May photograph.*

Prophet dances, the Apostles dance, the Bishops dance." Most holidays ended with a grand ball that often continued until two or three in the morning. Square dances, sedate and ordered, in prescribed patterns like the Virginia reel and very unlike the western square dance of today, were the usual fare, though an occasional risqué round dance such as the waltz was permitted as the century wore on.

Architecture in the city was for the most part spare, practical, and derivative. The ordered, simple style called Greek Revival was as popular in Utah as it had been elsewhere in the United States since the early days of the Republic. It is evident in countless adobe cottages built in the 1840s and '50s as well as in the Social Hall and the Old Tabernacle that stood close to where the Assembly Hall now stands on Temple

The Brigham Young Forest Farmhouse, 1863, originally four miles south of Salt Lake City. A charming Gothic Revival home. Now in "Old Deseret," Pioneer Trail State Park. *Dean L. May photograph.*

The Council House. A Federal Style civic building, built 1864–66, the Council House is similar to those early Utahns had known in the Midwest. *Dean L. May photograph.*

Square. The elaborate Gothic Revival towers of the Salt Lake Temple were not completed until late in the century, though other Gothic Revival buildings, including most notably the Lion House and the reconstructed Eighteenth Ward meetinghouse, now located south and east of the State Capitol, appeared much earlier in the city, along with an occasional pretentious home, such as that of William C. Staines (restored as the Devereaux mansion in the Triad Center). The Federal Style architecture of public buildings the Mormons had known and used in the Midwest was replicated in the Council House, built of sandstone and adobe in 1850 on the southwest corner of South Temple and Main Street (where the Union Pacific Building was later built) and also in the County Court House (1855), an almost identical adobe building on the northeast corner of Second South and Third West. The first City Hall, also similar in design, stood where the Federal Building now is, on the southeast corner of State Street and First South. In the 1960s it was torn down and reconstructed south of the State Capitol where it houses the Utah Travel Council. Most people, however, lived in simple adobe or brick homes built in traditional or pattern-book styles, sometimes reflecting the ethnic background of the owner. Such homes were commonly symmetrical, ornamented according to the combined tastes of owner and builder, and designed to look complete while awaiting the addition of a second story or wing as family needs and means permitted.

The considerable variety and expression of personal taste seen in the houses was contained by a rigid city plan, laid out following principles Joseph Smith had recommended in 1833 in his "plat of the city of Zion." The plan included broad, square-surveyed streets, large city lots and strict rules requiring the adobe, rock, or brick homes to be set back forty feet from the street. Early visitors were invariably impressed with the neatness and order of Mormon towns, always noting, in addition to the homes and buildings, the clear, mountain water that ran in small ditches along the edges of streets and was used both for irrigation and culinary needs. Elizabeth Cumming, wife of the first non-Mormon governor of Utah Territory, was enthralled by her first sight of Salt Lake City on June 8, 1858. It was, she wrote,

> A large, beautiful city, the houses all separate—each with its garden—wide streets, with a pebbly stream running on each side . . . houses mostly about two stories high, built of adobes, which are like bricks in shape and size, but a grey stone color instead of red. The gardens full of flowers & vegetables & promise of fruit. . . . Mountains all around us, looking in the clear atmosphere, but a few *feet* from us—snow on the tops, green below—& the rushing of the water on each side the only sound.

It is clear, then, that there were many cultural opportunities available to city dwellers in Salt Lake, Ogden, or Provo. A resident of any of these growing towns in the pre-railroad days could on a weekend evening have taken in a play, a band or choral concert, perhaps a dance, or attended any number of debating or "polysophical society" meetings. But what of those who lived in Parowan, two weeks by wagon away from Salt Lake City, about as remote a town as one could have hoped to find? As late as 1870 four out of five Utahns lived in towns like Parowan. Without radio, TV, or movie houses, how did these people spend their leisure time? Surprisingly, they spent their time in almost exactly the same way that people in the city did—going to band and choral concerts, to theatricals, or to rollicking dances. The quality of cultural activities available to those in the country was in most cases inferior to that in the cities, but the content was the same. Moreover, what was lost in quality may well have been made up for in opportunity to participate.

For example the Springville band was among six which performed at a celebration in Big Cottonwood Canyon on July

24, 1857. At the time, Springville had no more than 1,000 inhabitants. Parowan, with 861 inhabitants in 1870, had a string band and a brass band, both under the able direction of Thomas Durham. William Bickley led musical endeavors in Beaver, Joseph Coslett in Cedar City, John McFarlane in St. George, and David Edward in tiny Paragonah. These towns had bands a decade or more before the general enthusiasm for brass bands swept the rest of the United States. Choirs were likewise organized in most settlements. The Parowan and Cedar City choirs for years had an intense rivalry. So tough did the competition between churches for choral talent become that Bishop Hughes of Mendon, in Cache Valley, reportedly offered in 1870, "Ten acres of the best land in the settlement . . . for a good basso, tenor, and soprano, who were good members of society and good readers of music, and would settle in Mendon and attend meetings regularly."

Towns in many parts of Utah likewise had dramatic societies shortly after their founding, many meeting in the town "opera house," such as those in Brigham City, Grantsville, and Tooele. Both Parowan and Cedar City had dramatic societies functioning in the 1850s. The Cedar City group had sixty-one members, a high proportion of the adults in the town. During this period, they produced a farce, *Box and Cox,* which had premiered in London only a few years earlier in 1847.

The pace of cultural activity in Deseret was thus worlds away from the drab loneliness Oliver H. Kelly observed at the time on farmsteads elsewhere in the United States. Kelly organized the Grange in 1867 partly to provide a social life for isolated farm families. This need wasn't felt in Utah, mainly because of the unusual layout of early Mormon towns. Church leaders insisted that houses be built together in the typical rectangular-surveyed town, surrounding a square set aside for church and other public buildings. Following the tradition begun by Joseph Smith in his plan for the City of Zion, the fields were outside of town in contiguous plots. The men traveled each day from their homes in town to their fields in the outskirts. Church leaders were acutely conscious of the social consequences of such a settlement pattern. They pointed out in an 1882 letter the "many advantages of a social and civic character which might be lost, misapplied or frittered away by spreading out so thinly that intercommunication is difficult, dangerous, inconvenient and expensive."

But there was a closeness to life in the small Mormon town of the period that some found oppressive. It was difficult to be a dissenter and to go one's own way. Community achievement was more highly prized than individual achievement. And this may explain why there seems to have been less accomplished in painting, sculpture, or creative writing in early Utah, an observation which, if true, says much about the fundamental values of the society. The group activities of music—in band and choirs—of theatre, and of dancing were highly prized in early Utah at the expense of the achievement of the painter, the writer, or the sculptor. The lone individual or eccentric could not help feeling uncomfortable in Zion.

This is not to suggest, however, that there were no fine artists in early Utah. William A. Major, an accomplished painter, came to Utah in 1848. But his brief Utah career, painting mainly portraits and a few landscapes, ended when he left the territory in 1853. C. C. A. Christensen, though trained at the Royal Academy in Denmark, made his living painting inspiring and faith-promoting scenes of Mormon church history, turning his art into sermons. Excellent work was done by Danquart A. Weggeland of Norway, though his talents were mainly employed in the painting of sets for the Salt Lake Theatre and scenes in Mormon temples and meetinghouses. George M. Ottinger also worked extensively with historical representations, portraits, and landscapes. Landscape painting played

a lesser role in Utah art, however, until in the 1890s the LDS church sponsored study in Paris for John Hafen, Lorus Pratt, Edwin Evans, and John Fairbanks, who then returned to devote their considerable talents to painting church scenes adorning the interiors of Latter-day Saint temples. Alfred Lambourne and H. L. A. Culmer were also prominent landscape artists of this later period, emphasizing the romantic qualities of Utah landscapes in a style worthy of the famous Rocky Mountain painters Albert Bierstadt or Thomas Moran.

Early photographers Marsena Cannon, Charles W. Carter, Charles R. Savage, George Edward Anderson, and Elfie Huntington did excellent work, often recording important events as well as everyday scenes in Utah folk life. Their bread and butter, however, was portraiture, as it's always been for all but a few photographers.

There were few writers in early Utah, if one excepts the verses of such notables as Parley P. Pratt, Eliza R. Snow, Hannah Tapfield King, and Sarah Elizabeth Carmichael. Most of their work was devotional poetry, often set to music to become part of the rich repertoire of Mormon hymnody.

Harvest time. Work of early Utah photographer, George Edward Anderson. *Courtesy Utah State Historical Society.*

Newspapers and magazines were published wherever opportunity permitted (including manuscript newspapers laboriously copied by hand and circulated from house to house in smaller towns). The *Union Vedette,* Utah's first daily, served the military and non-Mormon community in Salt Lake City. *Peep 'O Day* for a time served the literary set in the capital. But early Utah newspapers for the most part served to teach and communicate and were not consciously literary in aim. An equally unconscious, though often eloquent literary legacy is in the thousands of diaries and journals kept by individuals, recording the routine of their lives and their interpretation of the world about them.

The only well-known early sculpture was the eagle carved in 1859 by Ralph Ramsey to adorn the entrance to Brigham Young's estate. Mahonri Young, a native son, moved elsewhere to practice his considerable talents as a sculptor.

Cultural life in Deseret, then, was rich,

ambitious, and advanced, considering the poverty of the people and the stage of settlement they lived in. It may have been more conducive to thought and creative energy than our more passive present-day consumption of slick television and flawless professional musical and theatrical performances. It was a rural as well as an urban phenomenon and involved a greater proportion of the country than of the city people. It did tend, however, to favor group over individual accomplishment and the performing arts over the fine arts. The direct influence of Europe, especially Great Britain, was extremely important in the cultural life of Utah as in economic life, bringing well-trained musicians, actors, and artists to Utah and making local band and choral organizations almost an institution here before they had reached many parts of the United States.

Finally, there was one aspect of cultural life in Utah that was fully democratic — open to city dwellers and country folk, to the socially prominent and the unknown, to the schooled and the illiterate. This was participation in Mormon temple ceremonies. There the devout, and this included a high proportion of early Utahns, were taken by means of dramatic techniques on a richly symbolic journey through space and time, designed to communicate clearly man's origins and ultimate promised destiny. Dressed alike in simple, unadorned vestments, Mormons of every class participated in ceremonies that promised to all a glorious celestial future, contingent only upon faithfulness and right living. And the furnishings and appointments of the endowment houses and the temples brought home to men who lived in humble adobe cottages the promised beauty of an exalted life. This was the peoples' theatre, probably participated in by far more Utahns than any of the public cultural offerings and communicating more deeply because of the sanctity attached to it. No doubt poor men and women came away from these services no longer content with

dirt floors and stick furniture — determined henceforth to uplift their lives and attempt to approximate at home the celestial style of life they had glimpsed in the temple.

If it seems strange to see the most sacred Mormon ceremonies as a part of cultural life in Deseret one need only note that in doing so we are only trying to see the world as they would have seen it. For the early Mormons a cultural achievement was a spiritual achievement. And spiritual victories often found a cultural expression. It was Brigham Young, after all, who said, "If I were given the task of civilizing . . . a people, I'd straightway build a theatre for the purpose." In a sense he was, and in a sense he did.

By the mid-1850s the desperate leap of Brigham Young and his followers into the wilderness seemed to have turned out better than anyone would have guessed a few years earlier. Substantial urban centers had been built along the Wasatch Front, and colonies were being established in almost all the promising parts of the region. A rudimentary but workable economy had been built up, combining cooperative endeavor with a healthy dose of American capitalistic enterprise. And withal, the settlers managed to fill the sere and remote landscape with a vigorous program of cultural expression quite unlike anything the American West had hitherto seen. The remainder of the decade would not be as rosy.

For Further Reading:

Histories

Colonizing: The *Atlas of Utah* by Deon C. Geer, Klaus D. Gurgel, Wayne L. Wahlquist, Howard A. Christy, and Gary B. Peterson (1981) has a wealth of information, including splendid maps, on white colonization in early Utah; see especially pp. 89–102. Leonard J. Arrington's *Great Basin Kingdom* (1958) offers perhaps the best readily available study of Mormon colonization in the West, especially in pages 39–228. See also Leonard J. Arrington and Davis Bitton, *The Mormon Experience* (1979), pp. 109–26; Milton R. Hunter, *Brigham Young the Colonizer* (1940); and Joel E. Ricks, *Forms and Methods of Early Mormon Settlement in Utah* (1964). There are several excellent essays on specific topics relating to Mormon colonization in Richard H. Jackson, ed., *The Mormon Role in the Settlement of the West* (1978). Classic studies are Leland H. Creer, *Founding of an Empire: The Exploration and Colonization of Utah, 1776–1856* (1947) and Nels Anderson, *Desert Saints: The Mormon Frontier in Utah* (1942). A powerful study of a specific colonizing effort is David E. Miller's *Hole-in-the-Rock: An Epic in the Colonization of the Great American West* (1959, repr. 1966).

The Mormon Battalion episode is studied in Daniel Tyler's *A Concise History of the March of the Mormon Battalion* (1881), reprinted in 1964. Also very useful is Charles S. Peterson, John F. Yurtinus, David E. Atkinson, and A. Kent Powell's *Mormon Battalion Trail Guide* (1972).

Biographies of Brigham Young range from the highly pejorative and ill-informed *Lion of the Lord* by Stanley P. Hirshson to Leonard J. Arrington's sympathetic, carefully researched *Brigham Young: American Moses (1985).* On these, as on all topics relating to Utah history, the *Utah Historical Quarterly* is a rich mine of information.

Economy: The body of Leonard J. Arrington's work has set the agenda and accomplished to a remarkable degree the study of the early economic history of Utah. Many of his earlier essays were incorporated into his *Great Basin Kingdom: An Economic History of the Latter-day Saints 1830–1900* (1958). Dean L. May's "Economic Beginnings" and "Towards a Dependent Commonwealth" in Richard D. Poll, Thomas G. Alexander, Eugene E. Campbell, and David E. Miller, eds. *Utah's History* (1978), pp. 193–242, provides a brief overview. *Building the City of God: Community and Cooperation among the Mormons* (1976) focuses on communalism in Mormon economic activities, especially the United Order in Utah. There is also an insightful chapter on economic development in Charles S. Peterson's *Utah: A Bicentennial History* (1977), pp. 54–78.

Cultural Life: There is no general overview of cultural life in early Utah. A very valuable resource on the rich Utah folk culture is Hal Cannon, ed., *Utah Folk Art* (1980). Several pieces in the *Utah Historical Quarterly* have helped to fill the void on this topic, including especially the winter and summer issues of volume 43 (1975), the fall 1982 issue and Joseph Heinerman's "Early Pioneer Cultural Societies," winter 1979.

On education see J. C. Moffitt's *The History of Public Education in Utah* (1946), Stanley S. Ivins's "Free Schools Come to Utah," and C. Merrill Hough, "Two School Systems in Conflict, 1867–1890," in the *Utah Historical Quarterly,* October 1954 and April 1960. See also Gary James Bergera and Ronald L. Priddis *Brigham Young University: A House of Faith* (1985) and Ralph V. Chamberlin, *The University of Utah* (1960).

J. Cecil Alter's *Early Utah Journalism* (1938, repr. 1970) is an indispensable guide to the study of the press in Utah. Perhaps appropriately, two studies of the press in Utah examine separately the history of the *Salt Lake Tribune* (O. N. Malmquist, 1971) and the *Deseret News* (Monte B. McLaws, 1977).

George D. Pyper's *Romance of an Old Playhouse* (1929) offers useful information on theatre in the territory. James L. Haseltine has published a useful history of painting, *One Hundred Years of Utah Painting* (1965), and Nelson B. Wadsworth's *Through Camera Eyes* (1975) reviews nineteenth-century photography.

Studies of band, choral, and orchestral music, the dance, and drama in Utah exist primarily in unpublished dissertations and theses that are difficult for the average reader to find. A useful general study, that has some information on Utah is Howard Swan's *Music in the Southwest* (1952). Perhaps the best of the histories of the Mormon Tabernacle Choir is by Charles Jeffrey Calman, *The Mormon Tabernacle Choir* (1979). Bruce David Maxwell's "George Careless, Pioneer Musician," is of interest as is Elmo G. Geary and Edward A. Geary's "Community Dramatics in Early Castle Valley," both in the *Utah Historical Quarterly* (Spring 1985). Laurel B. Andrew discusses some of the cultural implications of Mormon temple building and traces the sources of many of the design elements in *The Early Temples of the Mormons* (1978).

Eyewitness Accounts

Colonizing: Many diaries and journals were kept by white settlers in Utah, and a remarkable number are accessible in special library collections throughout the state. Access to these is through Davis Bitton's indispensable *Guide to Mormon Diaries and Autobiographies* (1977). Among the most widely available that have been printed are Juanita Brooks, ed., *On the Mormon Frontier: The Diary of Hosea Stout, 1844–1861*, 2 vols. (1964, repr. 1982), and Robert G. Cleland and Juanita Brooks, eds., *A Mormon Chronicle: The Diaries of John D. Lee*, 2 vols. (1955, repr. 1983). Parley P. Pratt's *Autobiography of Parley P. Pratt* (1874, repr. 1961) is also readily available and provides a useful eyewitness account. Brooks also edited *Not By Bread Alone: The Journals of Martha Spence Heywood, 1850–56,* detailing a woman's experience during the early white settlement of Utah. Elizabeth Wood Kane's, *Twelve Mormon Homes Visited in Succession on a Journey through Utah to Arizona,* introduction and notes by Everett L. Cooley (1974), provides a perceptive and charming outsider's perspective on life in the Mormon colonies in the early 1870s. Early issues of the *Deseret News* frequently contain letters and reports from newly founded colonies that are revealing and instructive.

Economy: Three narratives by early visitors to Utah that offer fascinating glimpses of aspects of the developing economy are John W. Gunnison, *The Mormons, or, Latter-day Saints, in the Valley of the Great Salt Lake . . . (1852);* William Chandless, *A Visit to Salt Lake and . . . Mormon Settlements in Utah* (1857); and Richard F. Burton, *The City of the Saints . . . (1862).* College and university libraries in Utah will have copies of the Gunnison and Chandless books. The Burton book is widely available in a 1962 edition edited by Fawn M. Brodie. Early Utah newspapers contain many advertisements and announcements that tell much of economic activities. They can be found at least on microfilm in larger libraries.

Cultural Life: Many early visitors to Utah commented on cultural as well as economic life in the territory. They include those mentioned above, especially Burton's *City of the Saints.* In attempting to understand cultural life in early Utah one can hardly do better than to visit local museums, such as the many Daughters of Utah Pioneers relic halls throughout the state, their main museum at the top of Main Street in Salt Lake City, and, also in Salt Lake City, the Utah State History Museum at the Utah State Historical Society and the LDS Museum of Church History and Art. In the exhibits of these institutions the discerning visitor will see musical instruments, scores, posters, photographs, paintings, and arts and crafts, including furniture, that are instructive, enlightening, and often delightful to view as well. Similarly, in a walk down the older streets of almost any Utah town or city one can find a fascinating display of architecture beginning with pioneer adobes. Wadsworth's *Through Camera Eyes,* cited above, provides beautiful examples of the photographer's craft, the content as well as the form of the photographs taking us into the cultural life of our predecessors in Utah. Scores and scripts of music, plays, and recitations performed in the nineteenth century can readily be found at larger libraries. Performing them communicates to us the past with an immediacy hardly attainable in any other way. Early recordings of folk music, such as are found in the two volumes of *The New Beehive Songster,* Okehdokee Records, also take us rather directly back to an earlier generation. They can usually be borrowed from larger libraries.

Wakara in 1854. Portrait by S. N. Carvalho. *Courtesy Thomas Gilcrease Institute, Tulsa, Oklahoma.*

Five

Troubled Zion

The Great Basin was perhaps the most isolated region of the United States when the Mormons settled here in 1847. Yet even that isolation was far from complete. A native American population of 10,000 to 20,000 was already in place when the Mormons arrived. The pioneers of their race had moved in some 600 years earlier. Mexican traders had established trading routes that covered much of the central and southern parts of the area, though they had established no colonies. Working out an accommodation between the old settlers and the new was difficult and costly, especially for the old settlers—the Indians. And just eleven years after the Mormons arrived the federal government founded Camp Floyd, the first federal military post in Utah. Civilian workers and camp followers quickly brought its population to 7,000—the largest settlement in Utah at the time outside of Salt Lake City. Its presence, even in the remote Cedar Valley, was a constant reminder to Brigham Young that the federal government was sovereign in the territory, and most Utahns saw it as the last of a series of plagues visited upon them by enemies bent on their destruction. In the Great Basin they had hoped to distance themselves from American society. That very distance created serious problems of its own, however, and in the end they found

America, having let them leave, would nonetheless not leave them alone.

The Federal Presence

The 1850s had begun optimistically, after successfully weathering a famine during the winter of '48–'49. Visitors in the early 1850s were impressed with the thriving settlements. In August 1850 Calvin Taylor, visiting Salt Lake City on his way to California, wrote:

> The Great Salt Lake City is handsomely laid out. . . . The Streets are of great breadth and cross each other at right angles, forming large squares. . . . To each house is allowed one and a quarter acres of ground which is enclosed and sufficient to produce all the necessary garden vegetables in the greatest profusion. . . . The city is watered from the mountains by means of ditches which convey the water through every part of the city; each principle street having a stream upon each side from which are sluice ways to conduct the water into the gardens for irrigation and other purposes whenever required.

The Jesuit Father De Smet wrote in 1851, "We cannot say what, in the way of colonization may not come to pass in a short time, after witnessing the success of the Mormons, who in less than five years have changed the face of a frightful desert and live there in great abundance." The good father may have exaggerated a bit, as he was wont to do, but it was nonetheless true that future prospects looked rosy in the early 1850s.

In politics the Mormons had not fared as well as they had hoped, but things could have been worse. By the time Brigham Young returned to Utah in 1848 the American conquest in the Mexican War made it clear that the region would be part of the United States. Early the next year a provisional government, called the State of Deseret, was organized. The Deseret legislature met in July and decided to petition for statehood, hoping to preserve the

greatest possible autonomy to citizens of the territory. It was a vain hope. Congress was preoccupied with the seriously divisive question of slavery in the territories. The petition of Utah provided a neat opportunity to balance the admission of California as a free state with that of New Mexico and Utah as territories with the local option of permitting slavery.

A congressional committee named the new territory Utah, after the Indian tribe, and President Millard Fillmore proceeded to appoint Brigham Young governor and Indian commissioner. In gratitude the Mormons named their capital city and a county after him. He filled the next three key posts with non-Utahns, Territorial Secretary (a position of the same level as Lt. Governor) B. D. Harris, Chief Justice Lemuel Brandebury, and Associate Justice Perry E. Brochus. (Brandebury's first name, "Lemuel" was the same as that of one of the more villainous characters in the Book of Mormon, and not likely to get him off to a good start with the Utah population.) The appointees came to Utah expecting to control and profit from court, executive, and Indian office patronage.

When these hopes were thwarted they left—carrying to Washington an official complaint that "almost all the entire population consisted of a people called Mormons . . . the Mormon Church overshadowing and controlling the opinions, the actions, the property, and even the lives of its members." The Mormons responded by singing merrily at their Fourth of July celebration:

> We hail the day Columbia first
> The iron chains of bondage burst;
> Lo! Utah's valleys now resound
> With freedom's tread on western ground.
> Though Brochus, Day and Brandebury,
> and Harris, too, the secretary
> Have gone They went—but when they left us
> They only of themselves bereft us!

The territorial legislature promptly gave the criminal jurisdiction once exercised by the

runaway judges to the local probate courts, an unusual grant of judicial power to be of great consequence in the next two decades.

Brigham Young felt so secure by the fall of 1852 that he asked Orson Pratt to announce publicly the open secret that the Mormons believed in and practiced polygamy, or plural marriage as they called it, defending it as a system socially and morally superior to monogamy.

Though each season brought its share of challenges and problems, the good times continued until 1855. That summer a long drought struck the flourishing territory. One resident wrote towards the end of June that "there has been no rain of any amount, so that the drought was uncommonly great and the streams very low. There is not so much snow on the mountains now, as there was last August." To the drought was added an even worse plague, an infestation of grasshoppers and crickets: "Myriads of grasshoppers, like snow flakes in a storm, occa-

View of Great Salt Lake City in 1853. Frederick Piercy original pencil drawing. M. and M. Karolik Collection (50.3973). *Courtesy Boston Museum of Fine Arts.*

sionally fill the air over this city, as far as the eye can reach, and they are liable to alight wherever they can distinguish good feed." As the winter wore on flour was so scarce that it could not be bought at any price. "Dollars and cents do not count now, in these times," Heber C. Kimball wrote his son, "for they are the tightest that I have ever seen in the territory of Utah."

All of these woes stirred the winds that brightened the fires of the great Mormon reformation—a period of intense soul-searching and recommitment to moral and religious teachings. The reformation began in the little town of Kaysville in September 1856. Great crowds turned out for three days of fiery sermons led off by Jedediah M. Grant, a counselor in the First Presidency of the Mormon church, and mayor of Salt Lake City. At the end of the out-pouring 500 persons presented themselves for rebaptism—a symbol of their determination to reform their lives. From there the reformation spread out to every Mormon town and village. At special meetings strong sermons were given urging adherence to the Mormon food laws, the taking of additional wives, observance of daily prayers, attendance at church meetings, and other evidences of renewed religious zeal. Many of these sermons were excessive and intolerant, particularly some intimating that apostates could get into so vile a state of sinfulness that the voluntary shedding of their own blood might increase their chances of salvation.

As in many similar reformation movements in Protestantism, the enthusiasm could not sustain itself for long, and by spring things had gotten pretty well back to normal. The whole episode was not without its lighter moments. After one session Hannah Tapfield King confided to her diary her unhappiness when Jedediah M. Grant said there was an adulterous spirit in a literary club called the Polysophical Society. "Well, there may be, for he says there is, and probably he understands it. To me it all seemed good and nice, of course a little vanity and folly, and that one sees in the tabernacle and everywhere."

National events were to have their repercussions in Zion as well. Needless to say, Brigham Young's public announcement that Mormons practiced polygamy created a sensation in the eastern press. By 1856 it had become useful in the Republican party's battle against slavery in the territories. They hoped to broaden their appeal by insisting in their campaign rhetoric that Congress had the right to "prohibit in the Territories those twin relics of barbarism—Polygamy and Slavery." When the Democrat James Buchanan was elected he was eager to show that if indulgent towards the one, he certainly did not support both "relics of barbarism."

Events in Utah gave him an opportu-nity to do so. During the winter and spring of 1856–57 a second set of territorial officials—federal carpetbag appointees—left Utah, much as their predecessors had done in 1850. Chief among them was W. W. Drummond, an associate justice of the Utah Supreme Court. Convinced that the Mormons did not respect his authority as a federal official, Drummond left the territory and in March 1857 wrote a letter of resignation to President Buchanan, who had just taken office. He charged that the Mormons had burned court records, were defiant of authority, had a secret band to terrorize dissidents, and hearkened only to Brigham, who ruled in a dictatorial manner over the territory. He recommended that a new set of federal officials be appointed to replace Brigham Young and other territorial officers and that an army be sent to install them. The charges were not wholly unfounded but were extravagantly distorted by Drummond's utter failure to understand the distinctive aspects of the Mormon character.

How were the Saints different? A jingle Mormons of the time sang went:

> For Mormons always vote one way
> And soon a voice they'll get,
> And unison will bless the day
> That shines on Deseret.
> But never mention what we've said
> For this particular reason,
> That if you do we're good as dead,
> Because, you know, IT'S TREASON!

To the Mormons, who valued unity and consensus as supreme social values, their habit of voting one way was evidence of a superior society. To most Americans of the time competition for votes was the only guarantee of an honest political process, and unanimity at the ballot box was, if not treasonous, certainly un-American. Neither group had the imagination to bridge the cultural gap that separated Mormons from other Americans of their time.

Predisposed to action in any case, and taking the report of Drummond at face value, President Buchanan decided to follow the judge's advice. He eventually found a Georgian, Alfred Cumming, who was willing to be governor and following the president's orders the Tenth Infantry Regiment left Fort Leavenworth for Utah on July 18, 1857. The man who would ultimately be commander, Colonel Albert S. Johnston, was not appointed until September 11, when troops were already in the vicinity of Fort Laramie, nearly 700 miles ahead of him.

Mormons in the East had heard the news early in the summer and hastened west to warn Young of the government action. One party—Abraham O. Smoot, Judson L. Stoddard, and Orrin Porter Rockwell—arrived late in July finding the leading citizens, including Young, in Big Cottonwood Canyon, celebrating the tenth anniversary of their arrival in the Salt Lake Valley. Twenty-five hundred people were picnicking, dancing, singing, and toasting the occasion when the riders' message was brought to the Mormon leader. Though Young had known of the government's plans for days, and perhaps weeks, he chose that evening, after the celebration was over, to make the dramatic public announcement.

As territorial governor, and without formal notification of their intentions, Young preferred to see the army as an invading force. He immediately began to mobilize the militia—the Nauvoo Legion, as it was called—as well as the civilian population of the territory. He sent militiamen out on the plains to see to the safety of incoming Mormon immigrants and to spy on the federal troops. He called home colonists from outlying areas, such as San Bernardino and Carson Valley, as well as all missionaries. He ordered fortification of Echo Canyon, the most defensible entry into Utah, remnants of which are still visible nearly 150 years later.

Some Mormons, posing as immigrants, mingled with the troops, getting firsthand information as to the attitudes and intentions of those they spoke to. The reports they brought back represented rank-and-file bravado more than government policy and fed Mormon suspicions that the army planned to destroy them. Men of the Nauvoo Legion under Lot Smith conducted a persistent, guerilla war against the federal troops, capturing 1,400 head of cattle and stampeding others, burning range lands needed to forage the army's remaining animals, and burning three freight trains. Following Young's orders, they employed any means possible short of bloodshed to delay the movement of the army. Faced with winter storms and depleted supplies Johnston decided his troops would have to winter at Fort Bridger. The Nauvoo Legion had preceded them, however, burning all but the stone walls of the Mormon-owned fort and all the buildings of the settlement of nearby Fort Supply as well. His options at an end, Colonel Johnston established a winter camp nearby, which he named Camp Scott. The 2,500 men and officers and several hundred civilian camp followers settled down for a miserable winter on the plains. Only the colonel's vigorous leadership and a relief train from Santa Fe prevented disaster.

The delaying tactics of Young would not be effective beyond winter, and it was apparent that in a pitched battle the Mormon militia would be easily defeated. When the snows melted, an advance by the army into the Salt Lake Valley seemed certain. In February Brigham Young sent an expedition some two hundred miles into the White Mountain country, in the deserts of southwest Utah and southeastern Nevada, to prepare a refuge to which the whole Mormon population could flee if necessary. Later that month, however, hopes for a happy outcome to the stalemate were raised when Colonel Thomas L. Kane arrived in the Salt Lake Valley from California as an unofficial negotiator. An old friend of the Mormons, he had made a daring journey by sea and across Panama, then overland from San Bernardino in an

Camp Scott as sketched by Albert Tracy, 1858.
Courtesy Utah State Historical Society.

effort to avert a calamitous conflict. He encouraged Governor Cumming to come into the Salt Lake Valley under Mormon escort to meet Brigham Young. There Cumming was treated with respect and received as governor, meeting with Young in the William C. Staines home — now known as the Devereaux House. He was amazed to see a mass exodus underway, as 30,000 men, women, and children carried out the evacuation of northern Utah in case the conflict was not peacefully resolved, an apparent first stage in Young's projected flight to the White Mountain region. Cumming and Young agreed that the troops could pass through the city on their way to a permanent campground forty miles to the southwest in Cedar Valley. Young insisted that the city was to be empty, except for men appointed to fire the buildings if the soldiers made a move to molest homes or property.

Kane, ill from his long journey, returned to the East and Cumming returned to the army camps, awaiting the arrival of peace commissioners who were to bring an official pardon to Brigham Young and those "naughty Mormons," as one wrote in his diary. The Cumming party entered the Salt Lake Valley on June 8. Mrs. Cumming wrote of that occasion:

I thought there might be a reception, a *small* one, I knew — for the city was to be abandoned by its inhabitants, until after the army had passed through. This had been agreed upon — but I was *not* prepared for the deathlike stillness which existed. A large, beautiful city, the houses all separate — each with its garden — wide streets with a pebbly stream on each side. . . . The gardens full of flowers & vegetables & promise of fruit — but the doors of all houses closed — not a window to be seen — only boards instead — not a carriage or wagon or mule or horse or man to be seen.

On Saturday, June 26, the army passed through the quiet, deserted city, rolling along South Temple Street and on out of the city to a camp on the Jordan River. Mrs. Cumming wrote,

> On Saturday 26th the army passed through in excellent order. Tired & dusty & hot, yet not a man nor a mule stepped out of place. They encamped about two miles beyond the city—at the Jordan— . . . no wood, bad water & little grass—nothing to be bought in the city at all—for no one is here to sell.

Gradually the Mormons returned to their homes and life returned to normal. Governor Cumming was trusted and respected by the Mormons. Camp Floyd came to be an economic bonanza for the Saints, providing them contracts for goods and services of all kinds. When it was abandoned in 1861 so the men could be called into service in the Civil War, some $4 million in surplus goods and improvements were sold to Utahns for a fraction of their value.

Yet the episode could not be seen as a Mormon victory. The United States had demonstrated its sovereignty over the territory. A large occupation force, though not visible in the Mormon towns, was nonetheless but a day's march away. Moreover, the army made its presence felt and asserted its authority in numerous confrontations on such matters as rangeland and water rights. The year after Camp Floyd was deserted, Fort Douglas was established, this time on the edge of Salt Lake City, keeping the Mormons fully aware of the federal presence from that time on.

The Mormons had at the time a slogan on the masthead of at least one church publication and on placards in public places. "Mind Your Own Business," it said, with an impertinent abruptness. "Saints will observe this. All Others ought to." Unhappily for the Mormons the business they were about did not please most Americans. They had been left alone for a brief ten years in the western haven, but would never be left alone again. Americans of the time would not tolerate a people different in values and aims, even if they lived a thousand miles from the nearest town.

The Mormon War left a legacy more burdensome than just the presence of an occupation army. At the height of the tension, on September 11, 1857, a group of Mormons and Indians in southern Utah, moved by a plethora of momentary fears and passions fell upon a California-bound immigrant company and murdered 120 persons. The only crime in the area exceeding it in magnitude was the Bear River Massacre of 1863, when federal troops under Patrick E. Connor fell upon a band of Shoshone Indians, killing 250. The Mountain Meadows Massacre was far more sensational and is much better known even today, because whites were the victims and the perpetrators.

In the late summer of 1857, a train of California-bound immigrants from Missouri and Arkansas known as the Fancher Party began traveling through Utah along the southern route to California. It was a time of extreme tension, the Mormons fearing that the federal army on the plains intended to destroy them. Moreover, the Utah settlements were on rationing, saving food for whatever dislocation a war might cause. In the circumstances they were distrustful of any strangers among them, refusing to sell them food and staying aloof. This angered the immigrants and according to Juanita Brooks's careful study, the tensions created by the situation were made worse by the delicate relationship between the Indians and the Mormons in southern Utah. The Indians knew that there was tension between the Mormons and other whites, or "Mericats" as they called them, and were spoiling for a fight. The Mormons were anxious to placate the Indians, hoping they would be allies if war broke out. In addition, the Mormons were fearful of retribution by Indians on white settlements if they were not cooperative, as the Indians greatly outnumbered the whites in southern Utah.

The Fancher train made it past all but one of the Mormon settlements and stopped at Mountain Meadows, a favorite resting place for California-bound travelers since early in the century. The difficult Nevada deserts lay ahead of them, but when they sought provisions in nearby towns, the settlers refused to sell. Indians had been threatening to attack the company for days, Mormons in some instances attempting to pacify them with gifts of cattle.

Fearing the situation was getting out of hand, church and militia leaders sent a special rider to Brigham Young on September 6, asking for advice. The next day, however, the Indians attacked, laying siege to the encampment. Before the rider returned the local Mormon leaders, fearful that the immigrants' threat that they would bring back an army from California would be realized, decided they must join with the Indians in assuring that the party would not reach California. Promising protection, they disarmed the immigrants. Then, at a given signal, Indians and whites fell upon them, killing all but seventeen small children. The rider arrived back at the scene on September 13, two days after the massacre, with instructions from Brigham Young that the immigrant train should pass unmolested.

The massacre was first reported to Young as an Indian depredation; it was a year later before he began to learn of white complicity in the matter. Even then the first reports suggested that those involved had been forced to participate by the Indians at the peril of their lives. Fearing that all Mormons would be blamed for an isolated incident with terrible reprisals on the church, Young did not investigate the matter. He urged his successor as governor to do so, but Cumming refused on the grounds that the general amnesty granted by President Buchanan at the end of the Utah War would apply to any whites who might have been involved. As further evidence was brought to light, three local church leaders were excommunicated for their participation and others relieved of church positions. One of them, John D. Lee, was eventually brought to trial and in 1877 executed at Mountain Meadows.

The massacre continues to receive attention and discussion, partly because of its many ambiguities. It was not another of the all-too-common cases of hot-blooded American cavalrymen riding out to stop petty thievery or Indian raids and wantonly indulging in overkill, as at Bear River. This was a much more complicated affair. Interest in the incident, however, is sustained by the fact that Mormons were involved. Some who have written on the subject have claimed the massacre was the predictable consequence of an authoritarian system, where obedience is more prized than exercise of individual conscience. Others have seen in it confirmation of the many tales rampant in the West that there was a band of avenging Mormon terrorists, called Danites, and of implementation of blood atonement doctrines taught during the reformation. To the practicing Mormon it must surely be a matter of grave concern, as it unquestionably was to Brigham Young when he realized the full enormity of the crime.

Yet it would seem that the tragedy at Mountain Meadows was an aberration from the usual Mormon response under pressure. From the time of Joseph Smith to the present, Mormons have persistently taught that the faithful should be full of kindness, patience, and good will. Except for a brief period at Far West, Missouri, the Mormons in their most critical trials had exemplified these qualities. At the death of Joseph Smith, when the inhabitants of towns near Nauvoo were fleeing in terror, the Mormons commanded a powerful well-trained militia, but no act of retribution was undertaken. In numerous other incidents the Mormons have suffered defamation of character, destruction of property and of life, only to turn away and attempt to build anew elsewhere. The Mountain Meadows Massacre was inconsistent with their teachings and nearly all their known acts as a people. How, then, could it have happened?

It could have happened only because in the heat of the moment and with pressures tightening in upon them from many directions a few men panicked. But if the leaders came to the misguided conclusion that they should kill the immigrants, how could they have gotten the rank and file to assent to such a scheme? Some of the men involved at Mountain Meadows could not reconcile the act with their faith and at the last moment fired in the air rather than participate in such a deed. Had more taken the time to weigh the proposed action against the teachings of their faith, the tragedy might not have occurred at all. But then it likewise would probably not have occurred had not President Buchanan chosen to send an army to Utah in 1857. Nor, perhaps, would it have happened had not the Missouri immigrants deliberately provoked the Indians at a time when they were spoiling for a fight. It possibly could have been avoided had the treatment of the Mormons by Americans in Missouri and Illinois years before been different or if the sermons of church leaders during the reformation had been less inflammatory.

But it did happen, and pretending that it did not will not make it go away. Events of the decade made it clear that the Mormons would find no real isolation—no Shangri-la where they could work out their destiny alone. To drought, famine, and military occupation was added a burden of guilt and remorse, made more painful because the act went so utterly against every principle of their faith and the known record of their conduct as a people.

The Indian Presence

The Mormons were relatively more powerful in dealing with the Indians than they were in dealing with Washington. Yet there were limits and restraints, some self-imposed, on what policies they could pursue. The outcome of the confrontation between the two peoples was perhaps predictable, but it was more the unthinking behavior of the white settlers than their conscious policies, that determined that outcome.

One of the happier early encounters between the two groups took place when whites moved into the Sanpete Valley of central Utah in 1849. At the time it was an isolated place—at least four days by wagon from the nearest white settlement. It was isolated, but not lonely. The settlers were surrounded on all sides by Ute Indians who had actually encouraged the whites to settle there. During the first winter a measles epidemic broke out, and the whites used their medicines to nurse the Indians. When supplies ran low, whites and Indians worked together to haul food on sleds through the snow. Yet, there are few signs of that cooperative coexistence evident today. In fact, there is precious little evidence that Indians ever lived there at all, though, every now and then, a fragment from the past turns up—an arrowhead or shard plowed up by a farmer working his fields.

When Manti was settled there were possibly twice as many Indians as whites in Utah Territory. Most belonged to a language group called Shoshonean that had already been in Utah 600 years. During that time they had divided into several distinct groups or tribes. Four of these shared nearly all of present-day Utah when the whites first arrived. Later, in the 1850s, an unrelated group—the Navajo—began to move in considerable numbers into the southeastern corner of the state. But the Shoshonean tribes, the Northern Shoshone, the Gosiutes, the Utes, and the Southern Paiutes, were the principal occupants when the whites arrived in 1847. They did not generally inhabit the mountains or the deserts when given a choice. They preferred the lowlands where water and land combined to produce heavy grasses and abundant game—precisely the areas the white settlers quickly spotted as ideal for the plow. Probably the only thing preventing an immediate confrontation was the fact that the Salt Lake Valley had long been shared by Shoshone and Ute, with neither group putting forward a clear claim to the area.

The white settlers of Manti were among those who did not subscribe to the adage that the only good Indian was a dead Indian. But an appalling number of white Americans did, and, even those who did not nonetheless distrusted and feared the Indians. There were many reasons for this harsh attitude. One had to do with the great difference between white American and native American cultures. Seldom have two cultures clashed so dramatically as when Victorian America came into contact with mid-nineteenth-century native America.

For example, one 1847 company of Oregon-bound immigrants was shocked to see an Indian brave approaching their camp one evening completely nude—except for a tall silk hat and a vest, which he had apparently just acquired from an earlier company. The women were scandalized, retreating in tears to their tents. According to the report, "some of the men, angry that their wives should be insulted, were for shooting the inconsiderate visitor." The Indian carried in each hand two fine fish, and wished to trade them for goods. When this was recognized, cooler heads prevailed, a bargain was made, and the company had a pleasant fish fry that night. It is striking how little provocation it took for some of the whites to seriously consider killing the Indian.

Similar attitudes were evident even in refined people such as Boston-bred Elizabeth Cumming, the wife of Utah's first gentile governor. She described the Utes she saw while traveling into the Salt Lake Valley in 1857: "We passed a tolerable night, and, in the morning, were surrounded by the most disagreeable looking Indians I have ever seen—and we have been surrounded by Indians for several months—so very ugly, and filthy and hideous in expression. I was glad to get away from the creatures." Such attitudes paved the way all across the West for acts of white brutality. Settlers forced removals of Indians from their lands; immigrants killed dozens of Indians for minor offenses, such as petty thievery; U.S. troops indiscriminately slaughtered hundreds on several occasions. Immigrants often saw Indians as "creatures"—less than human—not entitled to the decencies extended to others in normal human relations.

The first whites to settle in Utah were not immune to these attitudes. They had lived for years in frontier areas where most whites despised Indians and their ways. This negative influence was countered by more positive Mormon teachings. The Book of Mormon spoke of a group of once enlightened people of Hebrew descent called "Lamanites." Because of sin, they had fallen into degradation, becoming wild and undisciplined. Mormons assumed that all Indians were descendants of these "Lamanites." They believed that through conversion to Mormonism the Indians would again become a redeemed people and fulfill a special role at the time of Christ's return—a role perhaps even more important than that of white Mormons.

Because of these teachings, the Mormons made extraordinary efforts to befriend and convert the Indians. Their first major mission was to the Indians, undertaken the year the Mormon church was founded. The choice of Jackson County, Missouri, as an early settlement site was made partly because it was conveniently close to Indian territory, enhancing opportunities for missionary work among them. Some of the charges earlier settlers there made against the Mormons were that they openly fraternized with the Indians and claimed that the native peoples would one day inherit the land of Missouri.

After being driven out of Missouri and then Illinois, the Mormons were careful to

Mormons baptizing Shivwits Indians, 1875. C. R. Savage photograph. *Courtesy LDS Church Archives.*

seek permission of the Potawatomi, Omaha, and Otoe tribal leaders before making temporary settlements on Indian land. In doing so, Brigham Young explained that his people, like the Indians, were refugees from the United States and had also suffered white injustices. When, despite promises to the contrary, Indians from these tribes pilfered Mormon camps, Brigham Young warned: "If any of the brethren shoot an Omaha Indian for stealing, they must deliver the murderer to Old Elk to be dealt with as the Indians shall decide."

Later, Young welcomed the opportunity for missionary work among resident Indians of the Great Basin. He advised Jacob Hamblin, one of his principal missionaries: "Continue the conciliatory policy towards the Indians which I have ever commended and seek by works of righteousness to obtain their love and confidence. Omit

promises where you are not sure you can fill them." It is also true that in a message to the territorial legislature he said: "It is manifestly more economic and less expensive to feed and clothe [the Indians] . . . than to fight them." Thus, Mormons shared the widespread animosity of most frontiersmen towards the Indians, but their disposition was tempered by singular teachings and beliefs.

How then, did the more benevolent of these attitudes work out in practice? There were no problems as long as the Mormons stayed in the Salt Lake Valley. But in 1849 and 1850 they moved out to the Sanpete, Tooele, and Utah valleys and into territories long occupied by groups of Indians. They immediately began to fence and plow and offered no payment for the land. They maintained that it, like all land, belonged to God—though once they had claimed it, they showed a lively interest in retaining their own possession.

It did not take long for confrontations to occur, once the Mormons moved into tribal lands. In 1849 Young sent a company of militia to track down several Ute renegades who persisted in helping themselves to livestock. When confronted, the Indians refused to surrender the animals. They then, reportedly, fired upon the militia who returned fire. After a two-hour battle four warriors were killed.

A more clear-cut departure from Young's policy came the next year near Fort Provo, the first Utah Valley colony. Brigham Young sternly warned the colonists to stay aloof from the Indians. But in January three men killed an Indian for stealing a shirt, then tried unsuccessfully to hide the body. The Indians threatened retaliation. Without telling Young of the murder, local white leaders urged the church president to take action against the Utes who, they claimed, were "very saucy, annoying, and provoking, threatening to kill all the men and the women." Young responded by repeating his policy that if any Indians were killed for stealing, the men involved would have to "answer for it." But the settlers persisted in their complaints, claiming they would have to abandon the settlement if something were not done. Encouraged by Captain Howard Stansbury, who was conducting an army survey in the territory, Young reluctantly dispatched a militia force. He authorized them to "exterminate" renegades who would not "separate themselves from their hostile clans and sue for peace." The militia responded with appalling zeal, killing thirty-five in a nine-day campaign and harrying many others from the valley.

Four years later, after learning of the murder that led to the Indian unrest, Young wrote: "These facts, which were hid at the time, explained to me why my feelings were opposed to going to war with the Indians; to which I never consented until Brother Higbee reported that all the settlers in Utah [Valley] were of one mind in relation to it." The white settlers soon learned that they were in peril only if they pursued conflict, and neither Young nor his successors authorized sweeping punitive expeditions after 1851.

In contrast, the first settlers and Indians in Sanpete Valley got along remarkably well, as noted. Perhaps much of their success resulted from the fact that the Sanpete settlement was partly conceived as a mission to the Indians. A leader of the settlers, Isaac Morley, wrote, "Did we come here to enrich ourselves in the things of this world? No. We were sent to enrich the Natives and comfort the hearts of the long oppressed. Let us try the experiment and if we fail to accomplish the object, then say, boys, come away."

Indian-white relationships in Utah were generally characterized by peaceful coexistence. The good feelings were occasionally marred, however, by outbursts of violence. When this occurred, Brigham Young's advice was to "fort up"—that is, to build a protective fort like Fort Deseret. Young encouraged this policy during three outbursts: the Walker War of 1853–54, the

Gosiute War of 1860–63, and the Black Hawk War of 1865–69.

The Walker War was the predictable result of continuing encroachments of whites on the most favorable lands of the territory and their discouraging the Indian slave trade. The conflict was named after one of the most widely known Ute chiefs in the West. Wakara, or Walker, as the whites called him, had taken parties on horse- and slave-trading expeditions as far as southern California. The Ute chief was erratic in temperament but intensely interested in events around him and very much involved in politics, dealing with the whites until his death in 1855. Ironically, it was Wakara who had invited the Mormons to settle in the rich Sanpete Valley in 1849. The Walker War began in Utah Valley and resulted in several skirmishes and in the death of twelve whites and an unknown, but probably small, number of Indians. In May 1854 peace was made at Chicken Creek, near Levan, when Brigham Young met several chiefs assembled by Wakara. Solomon Nunes Carvalho, a member of John C. Frémont's ill-fated fifth western exploring expedition, was present at the peace conference:

> The Governor and council were invited into Wakara's lodge, and at the request of his excellency, I accompanied them. Wakara sat on his buffalo robe, wrapped in his blanket, with the old chiefs around him; he did not rise, but held out his hand to Gov. Young, and made room for him by his side. . . . I made a sketch of Wakara during the time that he sat in council. . . . He looked careworn and haggard, and spoke as follows: "Wakara has heard all the talk of the good Mormon chief. Wakara no like to go to war with him. . . . Wakara no want to fight more. Wakara talk with great Spirit; Great Spirit say—'Make Peace.' Wakara love Mormon chief; he is a good man. When Mormon first come to live on Wakara's land, Wakara give him welcome. . . . If Indian Kill white man again, Wakara make Indian howl."

The calumet of peace was again handed

around, and all the party took a smoke. The council was then dissolved.

The Gosiute War consisted of a series of destructive Indian raids beginning in 1860 on several stage stations along the main overland route across central Utah to California. The raids closed that route (the equivalent in importance of I–80 today) for long periods during the conflict. Richard Burton's skittish progress across Utah to Nevada in 1860 communicates clearly the concern caused travelers by the conflict. On October 5 his party was traveling nervously in a narrow canyon when:

> Suddenly my eye caught sight of one fire — two fires under the black bunch of firs halfway up the hill-side on our left, and as suddenly they were quenched, probably with snow. Nothing remained but to hear the warwhoop, and to see a line of savages rushing down the rocks. We loosed the doors of the ambulance [stagecoach] that we might jump out if necessary and tree ourselves behind it, and knowing that it would be useless to return, drove on at our fastest speed with sleet, snow, and wind in our faces. Under the circumstances, it was cold comfort to find when we had cleared the kanyon that Egan's Station at the further mouth had been reduced to a chimney stack and a few charred posts. The Gosh-Yutahs had set fire to it two or three days before our arrival in revenge for the death of seventeen of their men by Lt. Weed's party. We could distinguish the pits from which the wolves had torn up the corpses, and one fellow's arm projected from the snow.

U.S. troops retaliated massively and the raids ended in 1863. Altogether about 16 whites and over 100 Indians were killed.

The Black Hawk war was a prolonged and costly conflict, extending from 1865 to 1869. It consisted of a series of raids inspired by a young Ute who refused to settle on the recently created reservation in the Uinta Basin. Black Hawk attracted a following of 100 or more militants from the Ute, Navajo, and Southern Paiute tribes. They attacked settlements in Sanpete Valley and in southern Utah, causing the temporary abandonment of at least 25 towns and the death of 70 whites. The territory petitioned federal officials for aid, but were refused. Defense of the area fell entirely on the Mormon militia. According to one account, after four years of hostility and tension, Black Hawk and some of his followers suddenly appeared at Sunday services in the little central Utah town of Fillmore. They told the startled worshippers that they had come to prove "their hearts were good, and that they desired a lasting peace." Black Hawk died in 1870 of tuberculosis. In the funeral sermon, Brigham Young said Black Hawk "was the most formidable foe . . . the Saints have had to encounter for many years." Black Hawk was also the leader of the last major Indian uprising in Utah.

Brigham Young, like other whites in the West, was vexed by the problem of how to deal justly with the Indians. To Young and others it was clear that the only just resolution from the Indian point of view would have been for the whites to leave and let the Indians return to their old ways. Conversely, some whites believed the only solution was to wipe out the Indians completely. Compromises of these extreme viewpoints took two forms: remove the Indians to some place where they might continue their traditional way of life with minimal white interference, or show them there was plenty for all if they would just give up their wild ways and start farming and building like the white men.

Like federal officials confronting the same problems, Young vacillated between the two more moderate approaches. As superintendent of Indian Affairs from 1850 to 1857, Young on occasion advocated both policies. In November 1850 he wrote a letter to the Delegate to Congress, John M. Bernhisel, requesting the Indians be removed "to some favorable point on the eastern slope of the Sierra Nevada where forest, game, and streams are plenty; or to the Wind River chain of mountains, where fish and game abound; or on the Snake River: at neither of which points white men dwell." There was no recorded response to the letter.

More typical were Young's efforts to teach the Indians the white man's ways. One such endeavor was precipitated during the winter of 1848–49. A band of Indians came into the Salt Lake Valley asking to trade two young girls they had recently captured. The practice of slave trading had been going on for many years, but Mormons found the notion repulsive and refused to deal. The leader of the group responded by promptly killing one of the girls in their presence and threatening to kill the other if they did not buy her. They hastily complied. Shortly thereafter Young urged the legislature to pass laws permitting such purchases as "a relief and benefit" to the captives. By taking Indians into their homes, he argued, Mormons "could help the process of civilizing the natives." They could teach them the language and customs of the whites and prepare them for white society. Young himself took in an Indian girl as part of his extensive household. The practice lasted long after the Mexican slave trade was ended. Many Mormons took Indian children into their homes and raised them in hopes of smoothing their assimilation into American society. However benevolent the initial intent, there were no doubt cases when the practice was more an indentured servitude than a "purchase into freedom" as Young had hoped.

Young also encouraged Mormons to speed the process of accommodating Indians to white society by taking Indian women as wives, although no data are available on the extent of such intermarriage. The church president demonstrated similar intentions in recommending the founding of Indian farms as early as 1851. Indian agent Garland Hurt encouraged the idea and several such farms were established near Mormon towns. The settlers had little success recruiting Indians to run the farms,

however. After efforts to secure federal funding were unsuccessful the program failed. The Mormon church founded six Indian farms on its own, and Indians continue to live and farm in these areas today.

Another effort to aid in assimilation took the form of specific Indian "missions"—or colonies. These were founded near substantial Indian populations with the aim of converting the Indians and teaching them to farm and live in settled communities. Most Mormon colonies were charged with this dual responsibility, but particular missions were launched in 1852 at Fort Supply near Fort Bridger, Wyoming; then in 1855 at three sites: Fort Lemhi, on the Salmon River in Idaho; Elk Mountain, near present-day Moab, Utah, and at Las Vegas, Nevada. The Elk Mountain mission failed almost immediately, but the others enjoyed a measure of success for a time.

Federal policies towards the Indians vacillated in a pattern similar to those of Brigham Young. Like Young, the government sometimes settled conflicts with punitive action. In 1863 Colonel Patrick Connor's forces killed an estimated 250 Shoshone men, women, and children at the Battle of Bear River. Two years later, in 1865, the federal government established the Uintah, later combined with the Ouray Reservation, leading to eventual settlement of the Utes on lands in the Uinta Basin. Land south of the San Juan River was incorporated into the Navajo Reservation in 1884.

With the Dawes Act of 1887 Congress reversed its policies by encouraging Indians to give up reservation and tribal life, take up farming, and assimilate into the broader American society. One means of accomplishing this was to break up the tribal lands, assigning or allotting a plot to individual families, who then were to become farmers and ranchers and could buy or sell the lands as private property. Reservation lands left over after the general distribution would be sold to prospec-

Present Indian lands in Utah. *Drafted by Winston Erickson with the assistance of Kathryn L. MacKay.*

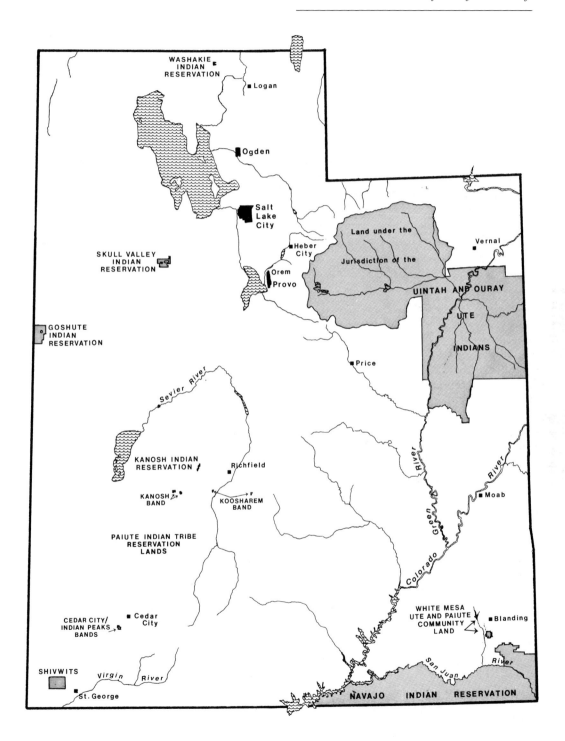

tive white settlers. Thus with whites as neighbors in the newly opened lands and on plots individual Indian families might choose to sell them, the concentration of Indian population would be diluted; the tribal centers, no longer controlling resources as a group, would become irrelevant; and acculturation into the mainstream society would follow.

The Indians immediately saw the implications of the policy and were united in their opposition. One Ute, Happy Jack, explained eloquently, that,

> After the white people come in here they will say "We took your land, now we will take your water, and your house, so you get off this land, go to some other country and find some other place!" . . . You are just like a storm from the mountains when the flood is coming down the stream, and we can't help or stop it.

Allotment in Utah was applied principally among the White River, Uintah, and Uncompaghre Utes living on reservations

Some of the Utes who left for South Dakota in 1906 protesting the loss of their lands. Chief Red Cap is on the far right. *Courtesy Utah State Historical Society.*

in the Uinta Basin. It was attempted on the Uintah Reservation in 1905 and from the start was an utter failure. The Indians knew that many of the whites backing the policy coveted Gilsonite deposits, grazing lands, and other resources denied them by the collective power of tribal ownership. Most Indians did not want to become farmers or stockmen. Fewer wanted to lose their cultural identity, which tribal control over resources had helped them to preserve. Moreover, the parcels of land allotted were often unproductive as farmland and far too small to make a living on. Efforts to develop an irrigation works and clear the land for farming seemed always to result in further losses to the Indians. In 1906 several hundred White River Utes decided to leave altogether rather than stay and see their lands given to white settlers. Their painful, temporary migration to South Dakota, under the leadership of the redoutable Red Cap, was an eloquent expression of their dissatisfaction with the allotment policy.

Interestingly, the effect of allotment on tribal consciousness was apparently the opposite of what its planners had hoped. The Sun Dance, which had originated in the 1770s among the Plains Indians, was taken up avidly by the Utes at the same time the allotment policy was being forced upon them. One superintendent complained in 1912 that the ceremony was causing the Indians to neglect their crops (a powerful comment on Indian priorities). By 1914 the commissioner of Indian affairs banned the ceremony, with no discernible effect upon its continued practice. The peyote religion, which reinforced distinctive Indian traditions, was introduced in 1914 and spread rapidly. The resurgent nationalism occurred during a time when the reservation lands of the three northern Ute groups dropped from 4,000,000 acres to less than 400,000. The number of full bloods declined drastically as well, from 1,854 in 1890 to only 917 in 1930, though such data do not reveal the proportion of the loss due to intermarriage with whites.

The prevailing philosophy of trying to assimilate Indians no doubt helped assure the defeat in 1889 of a bill to set aside a reservation in San Juan County in southeastern Utah for Utes of the three bands living there. The bill would have created a Ute reservation, in addition to lands already established for the Navajo and Southern Paiutes, dividing most of the county between the three groups. The Gosiutes were more successful in bucking the trend, President Taft signing an executive order in 1914 that with additions in 1928 set aside 111,000 acres for the tribe in two parcels some seventy-five miles south of Wendover along the Utah/Nevada boundary. Southern Paiutes, and some Southern Utes, refusing to be resettled onto the Uintah-Ouray or the Moapa, Nevada, reservations, remained near their ancestral homes in spite of the white presence. Various arrangements were made with the Mormon church and with town, state, or federal governments to provide some tenuous measure of tribal attachment to such lands, though these tribes were particularly vulnerable during the federal efforts in the 1950s to terminate special obligations to Native Americans.

Should we in our time return to Manti, scene of early cooperation between the Utes and the new settlers, we could not escape a powerful fact. Those lands were once a favored hunting ground for Utah's Indians. Now only an occasional arrowhead or potsherd is turned up by a farmer tilling the soil. Brigham Young saw what was happening in 1871 and expressed the problem with poignant clarity:

> I will say to our government, if they could hear me, "You need never fight the Indians, but, if you want to get rid of them, try to civilize them." How many were here when we came? At the Warm Springs, at this little grove where they would pitch their tents, we found perhaps three hundred Indians; but I do not suppose that there are three of that band alive now. There was another little band a little south, another north, another further east; but I do not suppose there is one in ten, perhaps not one in a hundred, now alive of those who were here when we came. Did we kill them? No, we fed them. We brought their children into our families and nursed and did everything for them that it was possible to do for human beings, but die they would.

There is ample evidence that the Mormons pursued a more benevolent policy in their relations with Indians than many whites. And, yet, the vexing thing, as Young realized, was that in the long run this benevolence did not make a great deal of difference. In the end, it was not the hatred and distrust of whites that decimated the Indians; it was their plows and fences. The plows and fences of the most benevolent whites were ultimately as destructive as those of the most hateful.

So, the great tragedy of the white man's encounter with the red in America was repeated in Utah. In the clash of cultures neither side was willing to concede. Isaac Morley had his heart in the right place when he said the settlers had "come to comfort the hearts of the long oppressed . . . and if we fail to accomplish the object, then say, boys, come away." But there can be little doubt that the whites did not bring the comfort they had hoped. And when it came right down to it they were unwilling to "come away" and leave the land to the Indians. In Manti today we see fields, fences, and houses; but no Indians.

For Further Reading:

Histories

The 1850s: A general treatment of the period is in Andrew Love Neff's *History of Utah: 1847–1869* (1940). S. George Ellsworth's school textbook *The New Utah's Heritage* (1985) is also very useful as is James B. Allen and Glen M. Leonard's *The Story of the Latter-day Saints* (1976, 1986). Gustive O. Larson's "The Mormon Reformation," in the *Utah Historical Quarterly* (January 1958), is the most readily available study of that topic. The classic study of the Utah War remains Norman F. Furniss's *The Mormon Conflict, 1850–59* (1960). Clifford L. Stott's *Search for Sanctuary: Brigham Young and the White Mountain Expedition* (1984) tells the fascinating and little-known story of Mormon efforts to find a refuge in the Great Basin deserts. The politics of the period is covered in Gustive O. Larson's *The "Americanization" of Utah for Statehood* (1971) and E. Leo Lyman's *Political Deliverance: The Mormon Quest for Utah Statehood* (1985). Juanita Brooks has done the most careful study of the Mountain Meadows Massacre, *Mountain Meadows Massacre* (1950, revised 1962).

Indians: A useful general history of American Indians is Wilcomb E. Washburn's *The Indian in America* (1975). Several short studies of present-day Indian tribes of Utah are in the book edited by Helen Z. Papanikolas, *The Peoples of Utah.* The spring 1971 issue of the *Utah Historical Quarterly,* edited by C. Gregory Crampton, has several articles on Utah Indian tribes. Excellent brief overviews are in S. Ly-

man Tyler's "The Earliest Peoples" and "The Indians in Utah Territory," both chapters of *Utah's History* (1978) edited by Richard D. Poll, Thomas G. Alexander, Eugene E. Campbell, and David E. Miller. On the Gosiutes see *Newe: A Western Shoshone History,* published by the Inter-Tribal Council of Nevada (1976). Ruth Murray Underhill has written *The Navajo* (1971). Also useful is *Dinéjí Nákéé Náahané: A Utah Navajo History* by Clyde Benally and others, published in 1982 for use in San Juan County schools. The Inter-Tribal Council of Nevada printed in 1976 *Nuwuvi: A Southern Paiute History.* A videotape on Southern Paiute history is available through the library of Southern Utah State College. A useful history by James Jefferson, Robert W. Delaney, and Gregory C. Thompson is *The Southern Utes: A Tribal History* (1971). Also see Wilson Rockwell's *Utes: A Forgotten People* (1956). A perspective on Indian-white relations can be gained from Paul Bailey's biography of the Mormon frontiersman, *Jacob Hamblin: Buckskin Apostle* (1948). Also useful is the review of Indian-white relationships in Leonard J. Arrington and Davis Bitton's *The Mormon Experience* (1979), pp. 145–60. Two articles in the summer 1978 *Utah Historical Quarterly* are of value, Howard A. Christy's "Open Hand and Mailed Fist: Mormon-Indian Relations in Utah, 1847–52" and Floyd A. O'Neil and Stanford J. Layton's "Of Pride and Politics: Brigham Young as Indian Superintendent." Brigham D. Madsen's study, *The Mormon Frontier and the Bear River Massacre* (1985) examines that lamentable episode in Indian-white relations in Utah.

Eyewitness Accounts

The 1850s: The richest single collection of descriptions of Utah and the Mormons soon after Mormon settlement is found in the diaries and journals of forty-niners. Most were used by Brigham D. Madsen in preparing his *Gold Rush Sojourners in Great Salt Lake City 1849 and 1850* (1983) and are cited there. Madsen has also edited *A Forty-Niner in Utah: With the Stansbury Exploration of Great Salt Lake. Letters and Journal of John Hudson, 1849–50* (1981). Dale L. Morgan's collection of "Letters by Forty-Niners" was printed in vol. 3 of the *Western Humanities Review* (1949) and thus can be found in larger libraries. Davis Bitton's

Guide to Mormon Diaries and Autobiographies (1977) will also lead the reader to relevant eyewitness accounts.

The famous report by Captain Howard Stansbury, *Exploration and Survey of the Valley of the Great Salt Lake of Utah* (1852), contains general descriptions of Utah society and may be available in larger libraries. William Chandless's *A Visit to Salt Lake* (1857) is likewise of great interest, though difficult to find. Solomon Nunes Carvalho's *Incidents of Travel and Adventure in the Far West*, first printed in 1856, was most recently reprinted in 1954 and is hence more accessible to the average reader. Gene Allred Sessions in *Mormon Thunder* (1982) skillfully uses Jedediah M. Grant's own words to reconstruct what amounts to an unintended autobiography. Grant's sermons during the great Mormon Reformation offer insights into the motivations and course of that period of intense renewal.

The set of letters written by Elizabeth Cumming, wife of Utah's second governor, has been edited by Ray R. Canning and Beverly Beeton and published as *The Genteel Gentile: Letters of Elizabeth Cumming, 1857–1858* (1977). They provide an intimate view of the entire Utah War episode through the eyes of a sensitive and charming woman. A fascinating set of reports published anonymously by a young recruit during the Utah Expedition has been published as *To Utah with the Dragoons and Glimpses of Life in Arizona and California 1858–1859* (1974), ed. Harold D. Langley. The state park at Fairfield (State Highway 73, west of Lehi) preserves a reconstructed commissary building and an old stagecoach inn as well as the Camp Floyd military cemetery. A visit to the site gives one a vivid sense of the setting and flavor of life there in the late 1850s. LeRoy and Ann Hafen edited a collection of documents that offer an "evening news" perspective on the Utah War, *The Utah Expedition, 1857–58: A Documentary Account* (1958). There is a monument at the site of the Mountain Meadows Massacre north of St. George on State Highway 18.

Indians: As noted in chapter two, regrettably few narratives by Utah's Indians (who did not have written language) are available in libraries. *Son of Old Man Hat: a Navajo Biography* is the only one I have found from Indians whose people had a major influence on Utah history. Among collections of legends, which tell much of a people, are William R. Palmer's set of Southern Paiute legends, *Why the North Star Stands Still and Other Indian Legends (1957),* and *Stories of Our Ancestors: A Collection of Northern Ute Indian Tales,* compiled and printed by the Uintah-Ouray Ute Tribe in 1974. There are recordings of Indian songs and dances in most major libraries.

A white's perspective on Utah's Indians is available in Daniel W. Jones, *Forty Years among the Indians* (1890), which can be found in larger libraries. J. Cecil Alter's "The Mormons and the Indians: News Items and Editorials from the Mormon Press," *Utah Historical Quarterly* 12 (1944) documents one perspective. The *Journal of the Southern Indian Mission: Diary of Thomas D. Brown* (1972), edited by Juanita Brooks is instructive. Nearly all diaries by early white settlers contain many references to Indians and vivid eyewitness accounts of relationships between the two peoples, including *On the Mormon Frontier: The Diary of Hosea Stout, 1844–1861* (1964, repr. 1982), ed. Juanita Brooks; and *A Mormon Chronicle: The Diaries of John D. Lee* (1955, repr. 1983), ed. Robert G. Cleland and Juanita Brooks.

The Iron Horse. Art glass depiction by San Francisco artisan Harry
Hopp in Salt Lake City Union Pacific Depot, 1909. *Courtesy Union
Pacific Railroad. Transparency from Utah State Historical Society.*

Six

The Americanization of Utah

The completion of the transcontinental railroad wrought powerful and lasting changes in Utah territory. Few Utahns had any idea at the time how greatly the iron horse was to change their way of life. On that May 10, 1869, much more was tied than steel rails. The event connected a whole series of developments in Utah history that had been taking place over a decade and would add new dimensions to life in the territory. Brigham Young's leadership was now challenged by that of Colonel Patrick Edward Connor. Thousands of Americans and immigrants of all walks of life began to make Utah their home. Tensions between them and the Mormons were to intensify, fired by government efforts in the 1880s to stamp out Mormon distinctiveness— to "Americanize" the territory. The dramatic resolution to that conflict opened the way for statehood in 1896. The tying of the rails was a great event for the nation. It was a well-nigh overwhelming event for Utah.

The Coming of the Railroad

Utah's development before the railroad was unique among the Rocky Mountain states. In a land not particularly fitted by nature to farming, the territory had become a commonwealth of small farming communities. There

Parowan in the early 1850s. From a painting by W. W. Majors. *Courtesy LDS Museum of History and Art.*

was some light industry, and some mining of coal, lead, and iron ore, or at least efforts to do so, but not much precious metal mining. The population was nearly all Mormon, though there were usually a few government officials, merchants, former Mormons, and drifters in the territory.

Most Utah Mormons in the 1860s lived in quiet rural towns. And, allowing for differences in climate and terrain, the towns, or "settlements," as they were called, were remarkably similar. There were wide streets with ditches of clear mountain water running on both sides, used for household as well as irrigation purposes. Lombardy poplars stood in stately rows, breaking the horizontal line of the valley floor. The towns were surveyed in a grid pattern, with streets running north and south, east and west from a central civic square, where the church (always called, significantly, a meetinghouse) and other public buildings were located. Even the names of the streets were the same in most towns, taking a number that indicated their direction (north or

south and east or west) and their distance in numbers of streets from the central town square. Houses were adobe or stone, with many pioneer log cabins still in use as outbuildings. The towns had a canyon nearby which was the source of water and timber and a favorite place for summer outings and picnics.

The Mormon meetinghouse was not just the physical center of the town. It was also the center of the town's social life, serving as schoolhouse, dance hall, public forum, and church. Persons born in a town like this shortly after settlement might have reached the age of fifteen without ever speaking to a non-Mormon, or gentile, as they were called. One man, "Brother Brigham," was the principal architect of that world.

There was another Utah growing in the 1860s, however, and the architect of that

Patrick Edward Connor. *Courtesy Utah State Historical Society.*

Utah had very different aims. It was Colonel Patrick Edward Connor, commander of the Third California Volunteers, a U.S. military company sent to Utah in 1862 ostensibly to keep a watch on the overland mail routes during the Civil War. Connor established Camp Douglas, named after Lincoln's former rival, the recently deceased Stephen A. Douglas, on a square mile of land (later enlarged to 2,560 acres) on the east bench overlooking Salt Lake City. The Mormons suspected, and not without justification, that the troops had been sent to keep a watch on them.

Though Camp Douglas had a smaller staff than its predecessor, Camp Floyd, it was nonetheless more irritating to the Mormon population. It was located right on the edge of the city rather than in a remote valley as Camp Floyd had been. Moreover, its men began in November 1863 to publish the *Union Vedette*, a newspaper

designed "to educate the Mormon people to American views." In addition, Colonel Connor, the commander, was stridently anti-Mormon and took it as his personal mission to reshape Utah into a more American mold. Connor reported to his superiors that the Mormons were "a community of traitors, murderers, fanatics, and whores" and put his mind to devising an effective way of diminishing church influence in the territory. His answer was simple: explore and develop the territory's mineral wealth. If gold and silver were to be found in Utah, the Mormons would be overwhelmed by a flood of gentiles comparable to the California gold rush. This would accomplish the desired end and might even line the pockets of the colonel and his friends in the bargain.

Young's economic policies had favored farming, light industry, and mining for industrial metals. He was strongly opposed to gold and silver mining. Connor, in contrast, encouraged widespread prospecting. After the discovery of silver in 1863 in the Bingham area, the troops of Camp Douglas found silver and gold in several localities. Thus, almost singlehandedly, the colonel opened the precious metal mining industry in Utah, organizing the first mining districts himself in 1863. There was, however, one bottleneck. It was necessary to ship the ore overland by wagon to smelters, which prohibited profitable mining from all but the richest of deposits. Nonetheless, silver and gold production reached $190,000 in 1869, the year the railroad was completed. The next year the Mormons built a trunk line, the Utah Central Railroad, which connected the Salt Lake Valley to the transcontinental line in Ogden. The result was predictable—a seven-fold increase in mining in one year and the launching of an industry that would, true to Connor's prediction, attract thousands of non-Mormons to Utah.

The first mining areas opened were in canyons on either side of the Salt Lake Valley, including Bingham Canyon, Little and

Big Cottonwood canyons and Parley's Canyon. The fabulous Ontario Ledge in Parley's Park was discovered in 1872 and eventually netted its developers, including George Hearst, father of William Randolph Hearst, $14 million. In the 1870s and 1880s mines were opened on the western slope of the Oquirrh Mountains at Ophir, Stockton (named after Colonel Connor's prior home, Stockton, California), and Tintic. The Horn Silver Mine near Milford produced very rich galena ore starting in 1875, leading to the founding of the town of Frisco and completion of the railroad to that point by 1880. Mining began at Silver Reef, near St. George, in the mid–1870s, the sandstone deposits there containing rich deposits of silver — highly unusual for sandstone.

Early in the game Connor discerned the results of all this activity:

> The number of miners of the Territory [is] steadily and rapidly increasing. With them, and to supply their wants, merchants, and traders are flocking into Great Salt Lake City, which, by its activity, increased number of Gentile stores and workshops, and the appearance of its thronged and busy streets presents a most remarkable contrast to the Salt Lake of one year ago.

The completion of the railroad was, of course, essential to development of mining on a major scale; and this in turn led to the changes Connor described.

The arrival of the new Utahns brought by the railroad raised another question that had been quietly brewing for a number of years. The Mormons had taken up their lands with no clear titles — not from the Indians, from the federal government, or from anyone else. They were, like many early western settlers, squatters. Though Brigham Young and others had petitioned on numerous occasions for establishment of a land office, Congress steadfastly refused. In 1865, however, John Pierce, the Denver-based surveyor-general for the area, decided his earlier opposition to the granting of land titles in Utah was due for a

change. He expressed his new view in an official letter. "The true policy of the government in regard to Utah is to encourage the emigration to that territory of a population less hostile to the United States." The "gentile emigration must have the chance of acquiring title to the land, and must be protected in that title." Congress accordingly mandated opening a land office in Utah, which began business in 1869, again, the year the railroad was completed. As a result, Mormons and non-Mormons for the first time were able to gain title to real property in Utah. They did this principally in two ways, through the 1841 Preemption Act, which permitted settlers to purchase their lands from the federal government for $1.25 per acre, or through the Homestead Law, just passed in 1862, which provided land essentially free of charge after settlers made stipulated improvements.

With the discovery of silver and gold numerous boomtowns grew up in the mining districts. These were worlds apart from the farm towns of the Mormons, if not in distance, at least in the life-style afforded their citizens and in physical appearance. The Mormon towns were laid out in symmetrical patterns. The mining towns, in contrast, seemed almost kaleidoscopic, the unpainted wooden structures twisting up a narrow canyon, the main street offering a variety of amusements unknown to the nearby farming towns. The gentiles grew from an estimated 8 percent of the territorial population in 1860 to 21 percent in 1880 and 34 percent in 1890. This, given the high Mormon birthrate, suggests an influx of major proportions and one that went far toward achieving the effect Colonel Connor desired.

In addition to the scattered mining towns growing up in Utah, a group of prominent businessmen decided early in 1869 to take advantage of the proposed railroad route, which passed well north of Salt Lake City. At the crossing of the rail line and the Bear River, north of Ogden, they planned a new capital for the new gentile

Alta—a Utah mining town in the 1870s. *Courtesy Utah State Historical Society.*

Utah that mining and the railroad would bring. The idea caused a land rush to the lower Bear River Valley, and overnight the town of Corinne (first called Connor City) was born.

The "Corinthians," as they liked to call themselves (Mormons called their town "the burg on the Bear"), opened a steamboat service across the Salt Lake, designed to bring ores from the Stockton/Ophir mining areas. But their principal trade was to be in freight bound for Montana mining areas and ores brought from there. Corinne would be a major shipping and commercial center, freighting goods and ores to and from the mining areas of Utah and north to Montana mining areas as well.

Pressured by Brigham Young's insistence that Mormons patronize the newly founded Zion's Cooperative Mercantile Institution (ZCMI) stores instead of non-Mormon stores in Salt Lake City, a good many merchants moved their businesses to Corinne. The boomtown population of the place—teamsters, rail workers, and drifters—sus-tained a lively night life, supporting the nineteen saloons and two dance halls reported there in April 1869. But the next year citizens of another bent built there the oldest Protestant church still standing in Utah.

Trade flourished. Some 3,500 tons of freight were shipped out of Corinne in 1870 and 5,700 tons as late as 1877. But the Utah Northern Railroad, a narrow-gauge built by the Mormons from Ogden to Franklin, Idaho, in 1874, had already begun to cut into Corinne's overland trade. When eastern capitalists and Cache Valley Mormons took over the railway in 1877 and began building it northward, the fate of Corinne was sealed. Freighting ceased, stores and houses were boarded up, and Mormon farmers began to take up lands in the area. A transcontinental traveler stopping there in 1882 asked a farm housewife if there were any Mormons in the town.

Corinne Methodist-Episcopal Church, built 1870. *Courtesy Utah State Historical Society.*

Her answer, "We are all Mormons here," expressed eloquently the abrupt demise of the high hopes its founders once had for "Corinne the Fair."

A good many gentiles remained in Salt Lake City, Ogden, or the mining towns during the 1870s. They tended to fall into three or four fairly well defined groups, each served by a distinctive religious tradition. There was a small but important group of federal government officials and their wives who helped to build an early Episcopal congregation in Utah. These were often persons of considerable cultural refinement and high social standing. The leader of their enterprise was the Reverend Daniel S. Tuttle, who came to Utah in 1867 and remained to serve the Episcopal community for the next eighteen years. He was one of the first ministers to notice that social services such as schooling and hospital care were woefully inadequate in the territory.

The causes of this backwardness were complex. The first law requiring establish-ment of public schools was passed by the territorial legislature in 1851. Actual support of the schools was to come from local taxation, however, and many communities simply didn't do anything about it. Moreover, Brigham Young and other church leaders were fearful that establishment of a secular, territorial public school system would lead to non-Mormon control of the schools. To avoid Washington control, local Mormon congregations held their own ward schools in meetinghouses and failed to support the public (i.e. non-Mormon) schools. A federal judge in Provo expressed the problem of many gentile families when he complained that his wife and three children had to remain in Michigan because there were but six non-Mormon families in the whole town. He complained that "the schools are under the entire control of the Mormons and I cannot think of keeping my children under such influences."

Bishop Tuttle immediately recognized the need for an alternative school for non-Mormons and established St. Mark's Day School in Salt Lake City in July 1867. He founded other schools in Ogden, Logan, Plain City, and Layton, in addition to Rowland Hall Preparatory School for Women, now combined with St. Mark's.

In health care as well the Mormons tended to provide for their needs within their own system and to be unaware that the needs of non-Mormons in the territory were not being met. The Mormons were distrustful of the medical establishment, preferring to fight illness with prayers and the use of herbs and home remedies. Again Bishop Tuttle recognized a need, founding St. Mark's hospital in 1872 in a small adobe building, the first hospital in Utah.

While seeing to a wide range of social needs of his congregation, the bishop did not neglect his religious calling. He founded congregations in many towns and supervised construction of St. Mark's Cathedral in Salt Lake. The cathedral was completed in 1871 and remains one of Utah's finest nineteenth-century church buildings. Bishop Tuttle was succeeded by Bishop Abiel Leonard, who continued the effort of his predecessor to fulfill both religious and social service needs, extending the work to more towns, including establishment of a church and mission on the Uintah-Ouray Reservation in 1895.

A less elite group of early Utahns were soldiers and railroad and mine workers. Most of them were Roman Catholic. Priests passing through Utah celebrated masses at Camp Floyd and Camp Douglas in the 1850s and early 1860s. The first to stay any length of time was Father Edward Kelly, who came to Utah for a brief time in 1866, holding services in the Old Tabernacle on Temple Square and in Independence Hall. He secured property for a church building and then returned to San Francisco. After two years the Reverend James P. Foley came to Utah, later joined by Patrick Walsh. They constructed an adobe church on the site Father Kelly had secured, and in 1871 replaced it with the brick church of St. Mary Magdalene.

Their successor, Lawrence Scanlan, was one of the most beloved and vigorous of Utah's religious leaders. He directed Catholic activities in Utah for 42 years, from his arrival in 1873 until his death in 1915. Like Episcopal Bishop Tuttle he saw to the building of schools, orphanages, and hospitals as well as churches. The Cathedral of the Madeleine was completed under his supervision in 1909. Since most of his communicants lived in mining or railroad towns he spent much of his time on the road, riding or walking to Ophir, Stockton, and even Silver Reef to hold services for his widely scattered flock.

In 1869 a number of Jewish merchandising and trading families, including the Auerbachs, moved to Utah. Shortly thereafter the first Jewish services were held. The first congregation, B'nai Israel, was organized in Salt Lake City in 1881, building their synagogue in that year and their B'nai Israel Temple in 1891. In 1889 a conservative congregation was organized, building its own synagogue after the turn of the century.

The Catholic, Jewish, and Episcopal churches served mainly a population of their faith already living in Utah. At about the same time a number of evangelical and other Protestant churches sent ministers to Utah, not so much because they had members here needing pastoral care, but rather as a mission to convert the Mormons. They came pretty much as missionaries at the time went to "heathen" China or "darkest" Africa, hoping to convert and build congregations after their arrival. For most the work was discouraging. After moving into small towns that were nearly 100 percent Mormon, they found themselves isolated and without a support base for their labors. Sunday services might at best be attended by two or three persons.

They then took a leaf from the work of Bishops Tuttle and Scanlan and began to build schools. Their schools, however, were not so much to provide education for gentiles—quite the opposite in fact. They hoped to provide a better education for Mormon youth than they could get in the local ward school and at the same time perhaps woo them into a more traditional form of Christianity. Generally the missionaries were better educated than those teaching in the wards and provided a superior education. Moreover, tuition was kept low and in some instances was free for Mormon children, even when non-Mormons had to pay.

The result was a vigorous education program of considerable dimensions. Congregationalists arrived early under sponsorship of the ubiquitous Colonel Connor. Later, Baptists, Lutherans, and other Protestant denominations came. The Presbyterians and Methodists both began missionary work in Utah in 1869, the year of the railroad, and over a period of twenty-five years had opened seventy-five schools and fifty-three churches, expending well over $1,500,000 in their effort.

By the 1890s, several forces had led to the decline of church schools in Utah. Mormon leaders had concluded that public schools were preferable for Mormon youth to Protestant schools. In 1890 the territorial school system began to provide free, tax-supported education throughout the territory. Shortly thereafter, the depression that followed the Panic of 1893 dried up contributions from Protestant congregations in the East, and the mission boards began to have doubts about continuing the Utah missions.

Finally, the common hope of educating the children out of their Mormon ways was not realized to any great extent. A Methodist committee reported that "if two hundred real Mormons have been changed into real evangelical Christians . . . we have been unable to discover them." Mission and school activity gradually declined until there were only a few survivors, such as Wasatch Academy in Mount Pleasant, Westminster

College in Salt Lake City, and Judge Memorial High School and Rowland Hall-St. Mark's. These have continued up to the present, maintaining a tradition of excellence in education.

All told, the investment had been enormous—and with a generally positive effect. Mormon youths who in some cases had never spoken to a gentile, were given the opportunity to broaden their experience. The quality of education in the territory was improved, and numerous social services, such as hospitals and orphanages, were founded. Moreover, the Mormons, who had tended to handle such needs within their church system, began to open hospitals, schools, and colleges of their own, increasing the extent and variety of such institutions available to Utahns.

There were, over the years, many highly dedicated—even heroic—missionaries, such as the Reverend and Mrs. George W. Martin, who cheerfully continued a difficult labor for the Presbyterian church in Manti for forty years. Claton Rice arrived in Cedar City in 1913 to find a non-Mormon minority consisting of a newspaperman, a plumber, and two families who were sheep ranchers. He regularly walked the eighteen miles to Parowan on Saturday afternoon, held church school there Sunday morning, and then walked back to Cedar City, arriving at 5:00 P.M., in time for church school and a preaching service at 7:30. Remaining in this labor five years, Rice reflected on his experience:

This strange eddy into which they had been drawn for the time being held them fast, as I saw it; but when the great stream of ongoing American life rushed in upon them, as it would eventually, I felt sure that they would become more aware of what separation of Church and State means in our republic.

As one might expect, the Utah problem of separation of church and state was most evident in the field of politics. Until the coming of the railroad, elected officials in Utah were nearly always men who were also prominent church leaders and were usually chosen from a single slate of candidates approved by the church hierarchy. This was consistent with the Mormon idea of leadership and authority. The best and most inspired men, they felt, had been chosen for church leadership—why not have such men take care of other affairs as well? One meeting of the territorial legislature was proud to have gone through an entire session without a single dissenting vote. The Mormons did not stop to consider that some might not share their confidence in the political and economic wisdom of the church leadership. In time, however, as the non-Mormon minority grew, this effective disfranchisement of the gentiles became a greater problem.

A group of prominent Mormon dissidents led by William S. Godbe saw that the railroad would set in motion forces that would demand an end of one-party rule in the territory. In February 1870 these "Godbeites," as they were called, met in Corinne with Connor and other leading non-Mormons to found the Liberal party. The Mormons had for some time called their political system the People's party. The *Mormon Tribune*, which had been founded by the Godbeites when they were within the fold, became the *Salt Lake Tribune,* a stridently anti-Mormon paper. It supported year after year a slate of Liberal party candidates, who year after year were doomed to defeat because of the overwhelming Mormon majority. Though the Liberal party did not do well in balloting, its members were nonetheless of great influence. They had better connections with Washington and the broader American people and ready access to the great mineral wealth of the territory. They used these assets effectively and by 1890 had become a nearly equal match for the Mormon majority in Utah.

Brigham Young had welcomed the railroad. He had no doubts that it would bring great changes to the territory, some of which he welcomed, others he wished to avoid. He could not have been happy, for example, over the fact that Salt Lake City, which had three saloons in 1869 had thirty-eight in 1874. On the other hand, the enormous efforts he had expended in helping the Mormon immigration to Utah were almost at an end; equally important, Utah products could henceforth be marketed in California and the East at much less cost. As early as 1853 Young had maintained that he "never expected that this community would be composed entirely of Latter-day Saints." He nonetheless was concerned about the size of gentile influx the railroad and mining would bring. He likewise feared that the railroad would destroy Utah's independence by integrating the economy too greatly into national patterns. Part of his effort to counter this was the cooperative movement, which led to the founding of many local industries and of the giant retailing network now known as ZCMI—Zion's Cooperative Mercantile Institution.

Not satisfied that the Saints were as united in temporal and spiritual affairs as they should be, in 1874 Young began the United Order of Enoch. Under church planning and direction, producers' cooperatives were founded in various forms in more than 200 Mormon towns and villages. Some communities, such as Orderville, ate at a common table, wore common homemade clothing, and shared the work and rewards of their cooperative labors equally. Others, such as the Salt Lake City Nineteenth Ward, simply founded a cooperative factory, continuing to live and work pretty much as they had in the past. Several of the United Orders were financial and spiritual successes for a considerable period of time, though most failed within the year.

The movement did not insulate the Mormon commonwealth from that of the nation as Young had hoped, for the larger economic forces at work were inexorable. It nevertheless did have important long-term consequences among the Mormons, implanting a notion that a heavenly economic order would be one where, under God's direction, cooperation would replace competition; simplicity, ostentatiousness; stewardship, private acquisitiveness; and sharing, selfishness.

In the final year of his life, the Mormon leader no doubt had cause to contemplate the important changes the railroad had brought to his Great Basin kingdom. There were by this time Protestant churches in many Mormon towns. Mormon children were attending schools in these buildings in considerable numbers. There were visible signs of a cosmopolitan urban life in Salt Lake City and Ogden, with all the opportunities and vices urban life affords. Wide-open mining towns now dotted the landscape, dramatically different from the quiet farming communities Young had founded.

For a time, Brigham Young's Utah and that of Colonel Connor would coexist, touching occasionally, but keeping for the most part a discreet distance. The most bitter phase of the struggle between their competing visions of Utah's economic, social, and religious future would take place in the '80s, after Young had passed from the scene. The nature of the resolution that tempered the conflict is still a matter of debate.

The Raid

Salt Lake City's Sugar House Park was the unlikely setting for much of the conflict that arose between Mormons and others in the 1880s. Today a Sunday stroll though the park takes one past picnics, kite-flying contests, soccer games, and a perpetual train of joggers. But the area was long the site of the territorial prison, completed in 1854. There were forty-seven inmates by 1880, only seven of them native sons. But shortly thereafter, the prison population began to boom. It had reached sixty by 1884, and grew so rapidly thereafter that within four years a new building had to be built. The new facility was already

too small to house the burgeoning population when completed in 1888, and another addition was made by 1891.

The flood of new inmates of the late 1880s was surely one of the most unusual prison populations in the history of penology. One of them, Joseph Bywater, wrote, after being assigned a cell: "Brother Harper was my cell mate, and we decided to keep our cell pure and free from pollution; so in the evening we arranged that we would dedicate our cell for our home and unto the Lord." Among the prisoners were members of the Mormon First Presidency, apostles, and dozens of stake presidents and bishops. A federal official complained bitterly that some, having served their time,

> have . . . been met at the prison doors by brass bands and a procession with banners, escorted to their homes to be toasted, extolled, and feasted as though it were the conclusion of some brilliant and honorable achievement, rather than the expiration of a sentence, an expiation for a crime committed against the laws of the country.

Hard words. But these were hard times for Utah's Mormons. And though most were born in America their critics considered them decidedly un-American. The problem that led to the burgeoning of Utah's prison population in the 1880s was clearly expressed by a federal judge when sentencing John Nicholson, associate editor of the *Deseret News* in 1885. "If you do not submit, of course you must take the consequences; but the will of the American people is expressed and this law will go on and grind you and your institution to powder!"

The Mormons and the American people had by 1885 reached an impasse. With the Civil War ended and the Reconstruction of the South completed, a U.S. Congress, heady from unrestrained exercise of its power in the conquered provinces of the South, now turned its full attention to what was called "The Mormon Question." Congressional interest in the Mormon question went back at least as far as the 1850s. In the presidential campaign of 1856 the newly founded Republican party promised to stamp out the "twin relics of Barbarism"—slavery and polygamy. Their candidate, John C. Frémont, lost to a Democrat, James Buchanan, who promptly set out to show that he could be as tough as anyone else on at least *one* of the relics of barbarism.

Buchanan sent the Utah Expedition in 1857, to assert federal authority in the territory. The Republicans for their part passed the first federal anti-polygamy law, the Morrill Act, in 1862, shortly after they gained power. However, President Lincoln, with the Civil War on his hands, had little interest in enforcing it. He reportedly explained that as a boy on the farm they sometimes came upon a log that was "too hard to split, too wet to burn and too heavy to move, so we plowed around it. That's what I intend to do with the Mormons."

And that was pretty much what he did. Congress might likewise have looked the other way had it not been for the fact that there were two parties in Utah, both with solid Washington connections, who spared no effort in keeping the question alive. The first of these was a rapidly growing community of gentile businessmen and federal officeholders. It was difficult for white Anglo-Saxon Protestants, accustomed to power, to adjust to being a minority in an American territory. Moreover, the Mormon majority was so self-contained that it often ran roughshod over such minorities, leaving them disfranchised and without an effective voice in local politics. The main source of power for the non-Mormon minority was better connections with Washington, and this would be helpful only as long as Utah remained a territory.

They therefore vigorously opposed statehood, reminding Washington officials on every possible occasion of the un-American Mormon practices of cooperative economic development, consensus politics, and polygamy. Their tactic was effective. Six

times between 1849 and 1887 the Mormon-controlled territorial legislature petitioned Congress for statehood and each time that petition was rejected. Utah settlement had begun in 1847, long before any of the surrounding states, yet Utahns watched helplessly for almost half a century as other western areas were settled, given territorial status and then statehood, often taking territory that had been part of Utah.

Oregon became a state in 1856; Nevada in 1864; Colorado, 1876; Montana, 1889; Wyoming and Idaho, 1890. Frequently the neighboring states had far fewer people than Utah. Among the new states in 1890 was Montana with 132,000, Idaho with a population of just over 84,000, and Wyoming with but 61,000. In that same year Utah had a population of 208,000.

The second lobby important in influencing Congressional policy toward Utah was that of the Protestant churches. Congress had long been responsive in its China policy to the requests of missionaries for legislation supporting their activities in the Far East. It is perhaps useful to see Utah as an eddy in this stream of thousands of selfless, dedicated missionaries who labored in China and Japan towards the end of the last century. They quite honestly saw Mormonism as a heresy, at least as pagan as Buddhism or Shintoism and perhaps more destructive because it claimed to be a Christian religion. Indeed, their perception of the Mormons as somehow akin to the Orientals did not stop there. The hierarchical system of church government they saw as a form of Oriental despotism, using any means, including terror if need be, to keep the rank and file ignorant, superstitious, and hence responsive to the will of the leaders. The practice of polygamy was confirming evidence that Mormonism was a bizarre mutant, somehow transplanted to the desert places of America but wholly incompatible with American religious and political institutions.

"It is the object of the Mormons," wrote Senator George F. Edmunds in an 1882

Harper's Magazine," to set up for them-selves and maintain an exclusive political domination in the Territory of Utah. . . . The problem must now or in the near fu-ture be resolved and the irrepressible con-flict between polygamous Mormonism and the social and political systems of the people and the rest of the United States must have a decided issue." In retrospect these charges seem wild and extravagant. Was there any truth at all in them, or were they pure inventions of people who for sec-tarian or other reasons wished to destroy Mormonism? Though grossly exaggerated in some instances, there was a good deal of truth underlying them. In fact, one could plausibly argue that these hostile crit-ics understood the Saints better than they understood themselves.

Take for example the problem of gov-ernment in a democracy. The Mormon sys-tem, according to Joseph Smith, was a "theo-democracy." James B. McKean, chief justice of the territory in the early 1870s, called it a "polygamic theocracy." Neither term tells us much, but the record gives us some sense of how it worked. It is imme-diately obvious that the church government was hierarchical, ascending through priest-hood offices to the Quorum of Twelve and the First Presidency, with the prophet or president over all. One could be given a higher office only at the initiative of those above him. Moreover, the Mormons be-lieved in and tried to practice consensus government. When a problem arose in Mount Carmel in the 1870s over economic issues the question was first discussed at length with the rank and file. But when a vote was taken on the matter it was ex-pected that it would be unanimous and that all who thus voted were thereby bound to support the policy, even if they had mis-givings. The voting was a symbol of com-mitment to a consensus already reached, not a means of making decisions. In this case, the vote was not unanimous and the only solution was for the dissidents to pull away and form their own town, Orderville.

Only then could the two communities continue to function. There was no con-cept in the Mormon system of a loyal op-position.

When Mormons set up civil government in early Utah they simply nominated those whose aptitude had already been sanc-tioned by divine call to church positions, normally one candidate for each office, and then elected them. Moreover, as the elected officials met in legislative or other bodies their decision-making process often fol-lowed closely that which they followed in church councils. Indeed, they made little distinction between religious and secular aspects of their lives. A dispute over water brought before a county court in Taylors-ville in 1855 was referred by that court to a church High Council!

This was utterly alien to the American way of doing things. American politics in the 1880s was a wild and raucous affair, with the most virulent of charges and coun-tercharges exchanged between candidates and a great hoopla of bands, posters, speeches, and promises essential to the pro-cess. Never did the election of one party lead, as Jefferson long before had hoped, to the end of party and faction. The losers always began shortly to make plans for their ultimate triumph.

The political process was but one aspect of the Mormon question. Equally impor-tant was the question of what the end of politics was to be. The Mormons believed that their church, which they called the Kingdom of God, was the stone the Prophet Daniel said would one day roll forth to fill the whole earth and subdue all kingdoms. They expected that all civil government would one day fail and that when that happened their ecclesiastical gov-ernment would step in to fill the void. When the Civil War broke out they saw the collapse of the American government as imminent and made preparations to gov-ern themselves. In 1862 they drafted a con-stitution for a proposed state of Deseret, elected a full slate of candidates, and petitioned Congress for statehood. When the petition was rejected the legislature of the state of Deseret continued to meet until 1870, reenacting the legislation just passed by the territorial legislature. As Brigham Young put it, "We should get all things ready, and when the time comes, we should let the water on the wheel and start the machine in motion."

In addition, the Council of Fifty, a clandestine body of notables, met at various times during the period, feeding rumors that the territory was actually ruled by a small group responsive to the church leaders rather than by elected officials responsible to the voting public. In fact, the Council did not wield a powerful influence in the late 1800s. But all things considered, a gentile in Utah at the time would justifiably have felt he was not being represented in a democratic fashion in the territorial legislature and that some action was needed to bring democracy to Utah.

What about the charge that the Mormons were un-American in their economic activities? It is important to remember that this was what Mark Twain called the "gilded age" in America, when John D. Rockefeller and Andrew Carnegie were heroes and Horatio Alger in countless popular stories taught that with a little luck and pluck the poorest bootblack could, in America, become a millionaire. It was also the age when most people believed that the government should have no voice in economic decision making, leaving the economy solely to the invisible hand of the marketplace and the unhampered decisions of investors and industrialists.

This contrasts powerfully with the central direction given Utah's economy through the cooperative principles that were part of the founding of the ZCMI system, the United Order, and later Zion's Board of Trade, which regulated prices and wages. The Mormons' fundamental proposition was that all property belongs ultimately to God. Men may use it and the fruits thereof but not without entailing obligations

through that use. The Mormons taught that cooperation and sharing were ultimately more ethical than the competition and individualism that are central tenets of capitalism. These principles of economics were noted and commented on by non-Mormons at the time. Prominent reformers pointed to the cooperative industries of the Mormons as models for the greater society, and Edward Bellamy spent time in Brigham City, observing its economy and discussing it with Lorenzo Snow, before writing his critique of American society, *Looking Backward,* in 1888. Thus, from the point of view of the gentile capitalist in Utah in the 1800s, the Mormon system, would have looked quite un-American.

Recognizing all these differences, those opposed to the Mormon church nonetheless agreed that the most valuable strategy in their effort to Americanize Utah was to attack polygamy. Polygamy had been introduced secretly by Joseph Smith in the early 1840s and had been controversial and divisive, even among Smith's inner circle of loyal followers, from the beginning. The revelation commending plural marriage (as the Mormons called it) to faithful Mormons was recorded in 1843. The practice was publicly announced and defended in 1852, shocking and outraging the sensibilities of middle-class Victorian America.

Though only men of upright character and reasonable means, who could get the permission of the earlier wife or wives, were to take plural wives, polygamy was more widespread than has often been thought. The author's study of the number of polygamous families in Kanab in 1874 found that about 10 percent of the married men had other wives in the town at the time. Sixteen percent of married women had sister wives in the town. Nearly 25 percent of all men, women and children were in polygamous households. Those who did not were in many cases committed to the broader system of which it was a part and helped to defend it.

Seeing polygamy as a moral issue, like

slavery, that could be used to unite the American people against the Mormons, the gentiles of Utah spared no effort to publicize the problems it created and to enlist the help of the nation in eliminating the institution. Their efforts led to a renewal of national interest in the early 1870s. An extremely harsh measure was introduced in Congress in 1870—the Cullom bill. Debate on the bill raised a storm of protest in Utah, including a mass meeting of some 5,000 Mormon women in the Tabernacle who shocked suffragettes around the nation by defending their right to practice polygamy in the name of women's rights. The bill was ultimately defeated, partly because of opposition by the railroad lobby and southern congressmen who opposed excessive federal involvement in local affairs. Most of its provisions, however, were to be passed as part of subsequent antipolygamy statutes. The first of these was the Poland Act of 1874. Federal judges had found it almost impossible to get a conviction against polygamists in the probate courts, which were under locally elected judges. The Poland Act moved jurisdiction in criminal cases from the probate courts to the federal courts, thus opening the way for vigorous prosecution of the law.

In the meantime, the Mormons protested all such action, claiming that the antipolygamy laws interfered with their First Amendment rights of freedom of religion. Finally, in 1879 they managed to bring a case before the Supreme Court. The court held that George F. Reynolds, once Brigham Young's secretary, had been rightfully convicted under the Morrill Act. Congress, it claimed, could not regulate religious belief but could regulate religious practice. With momentum thus established, and with the full support of President Ulysses Grant who had visited Utah in 1875, the campaign continued. The next step was the Edmunds Act of 1882. Designed to strengthen the Morrill Act, it declared the contracting of polygamous mar-

riages a felony and cohabitation, or living with polygamous wives, a misdemeanor. Sentences could range from $300 and six months in prison for cohabitation to $500 and five years in prison for polygamy. The act denied polygamists the right to vote, hold office, or serve on a jury. Regular election procedures were eliminated, and an election commission was established to oversee politics in Utah. The Utah Commission, as it came to be known, arrived in 1882 and shortly began applying the law as broadly interpreted by them and the federal judges.

Under the vigorous leadership of Chief Justice Charles S. Zane, the whole federal apparatus was committed to the tasks of rooting out polygamy and destroying Mormon political influence in the territory. Posters announced substantial rewards for information leading to the arrest of prominent Mormons, and twelve to twenty dollars for the arrest of any polygamist. Zane dispatched federal marshals to all parts of the territory, sometimes disguised as itinerant peddlers or laborers, to track down the offending parties.

On March 31, 1885, LDS President John Taylor gave his last public sermon, then went into hiding. For two and one-half years, until his death, he was forced to move frequently from place to place, dared not visit his wives and families, and could meet only occasionally with other leaders. The Mormons worked out an elaborate system of surveillance and underground transportation, building hiding places in houses, barns, and attics, and communicating through prearranged signs and codes. Many moved to Mexico and Canada, establishing colonies for polygamists under a gentlemen's agreement with local officials despite national anti-polygamy laws in the two countries.

Even with all these precautions the marshals arrested and imprisoned 1,035 men under the legislation, swelling the population of the territorial penitentiary at Sugar House. With a high proportion of the lead-

ing Mormon men on the underground, many church programs were temporarily dropped and the United Order movement abandoned. Still, the church continued to function, and the People's party maintained its political control. Some observers began to wonder if all the zeal had been misplaced. "Not polygamy but the power of the Priesthood is the real danger," claimed the editors of the Springfield, Massachusetts *Union*; "the essential principle of Mormonism is not polygamy at all but the ambition of an ecclesiastical hierarchy to wield sovereignty: to rule the souls and lives of its subjects with absolute authority, unrestrained by any civil power."

Responding to such sentiments, Congress passed in 1887 the Edmunds-Tucker Act, designed to destroy the Mormon church economically and politically. It abolished women's suffrage in the territory and authorized the Utah Commission to administer an oath to all prospective voters, jury members, or officeholders, requiring that they affirm obedience to and support of

Cohabs in front of territorial prison at Sugar House, 1888 or 1889. Holding a bouquet in the center of the photograph is George Q. Cannon, First Counselor in the Presidency of the Latter-day Saint church. *Courtesy of Utah State Historical Society.*

all antipolygamy laws. It disbanded the Perpetual Emigrating Fund Company, which, it was felt, brought ignorant aliens directly into the Mormon system without their ever having an opportunity to learn American principles of government. The act also removed the remaining obstacles to prosecution of polygamists by requiring compulsory attendance of witnesses at trials and permitting wives to testify against their husbands. Finally, the law disincorporated the church and provided that all its property in excess of $50,000 would be taken over by the United States.

Realizing that full enforcement of the law would bring the church to its knees, the new church president, Wilford Woodruff, encouraged the submission one more time of a petition for statehood. The proposed constitution outlawed polygamy and "union of Church and State" or domination of the state by any one church. The petition was ultimately denied. In the meantime, church officials had tried to soften the attack against the Mormon vote by sponsoring non-Mormons for political office. The Utah Commission was unimpressed, and, in addition to requiring the test oath for all elections, began to redraw voting districts to lessen Mormon influence and to appoint non-Mormons almost exclusively as registrars and judges of elections. They further recommended that Congress pass legislation barring Mormons from voting whether they practiced or believed in polygamy or not. Such a law had already been passed in Idaho and was sustained by the United States Supreme Court in February 1890. That same month local elections brought a victory to the Liberal party in Salt Lake City and in Ogden. Spurred on by the cheering news, Congress proceeded to draft the Cullom-Strubble bill, which, as one judge put it, "Stripped of its serpentine verbiage . . . is simply a bill to disfranchise all members of the Mormon Church."

While Congress proceeded to consider the Cullom-Strubble bill and federal agents began to take over church properties, Wilford Woodruff considered his options. Finally, on September 25, he wrote in his diary, "I have arrived at a point . . . where I am under the necessity of acting for the temporal salvation of the Church. The United States Government has taken a stand and passed laws to destroy the Latter-day Saints on the subject of polygamy, the Patriarchal order of marriage, and after praying to the Lord and feeling inspired, I have issued the following proclamation which is sustained by my counsellors and the Twelve Apostles." In the proclamation, which came to be known as the Manifesto, the church president maintained that no plural marriages had been contracted in Utah during the last year and advised

Latter-day Saints "to refrain from contracting any marriage forbidden by the laws of the land."

It was at least the beginning of the end for the bitterness and anguish the last decade had brought. The following year the church encouraged Mormons to join one of the national parties. To achieve a reasonable balance they especially urged the Democratic-inclined church membership to support of the Republican party. A month later they disbanded the People's party. The Liberal party members feared that if they disbanded, their voting strength would be split between the two national parties. They continued to field candidates until 1893, then moved en masse to the Republican party, which they found to their discomfort already dominated by a number of prominent Mormons.

In 1893 and 1894 Presidents Benjamin Harrison and Grover Cleveland granted amnesty and pardon to all who had refrained from cohabitation since November 1, 1890. New plural marriages, though strictly forbidden by federal officials, continued to be secretly authorized sporadically by church leaders until 1904. Polygamists were likewise forbidden by the amnesty to live as husbands with former plural wives, but it was understood locally that they would not be prosecuted for doing so and that with no new marriages the institution would gradually die out. Congress voted to restore church property seized by the government and the next summer passed Utah's Enabling Act, providing for the election of delegates to a constitutional convention. The most significant debate in the convention was over women's suffrage, and a constitution was finally written that gave women the vote and rights equal to men, outlawed polygamy, and provided for separation of church and state. On January 4, 1896, President Grover Cleveland issued the proclamation admitting Utah as the forty-fifth state of the Union.

Monday, January 6, 1896, was inaugu-

ration day for the state of Utah. The ceremonies were held in the Tabernacle on Temple Square. The building was extravagantly decorated for the occasion. The old territorial secretary conducted the exercises. George Q. Cannon, the leading strategist in the Mormon quest for Utah statehood since the 1860s, read an opening prayer prepared by Wilford Woodruff, who was too ill to do so himself. In attendance were Mormon church officials, including Woodruff, military officers from Fort Douglas, and an overflow crowd. The new Governor, Heber M. Wells, spoke in his inaugural of the need to heal old wounds. After the Tabernacle Choir sang "America," the benediction was given by the Reverend Thomas C. Iliff of the Methodist church. Even for the people in remote Kanab it was a day for rejoicing. An aging widow, Rebecca Howell Mace, described the event:

On the 6th—Monday, the officers of the new State, . . . was inaugerated, the day be-

Statehood Day in Utah. *Courtesy Special Collections, Marriott Library, University of Utah.*

ing set apart as a holiday to be remembered as such forever. It was enjoyed to the utmost.

Guns were fired at daybreak. 10:00 a procession was formed, lead by the Band of Home Guards—followed by citizens, also a juvenile corps, or Bell Brigade.

At two o'clock the citizens met in the Social Hall and partook of a Pic Nic Dinner, then followed speech and Song, closing the day with a grand Inaugural Ball.

The day was all that could be desired. The weather was pleasant and all enjoyed themselves, there was nothing to mar the occasion, and it will be a day long to be remembered by the inhabitants of Kanab both old and young.

It would seem that both parties to the conflict ended by this happy occasion had only a vague notion of what had happened. The Mormons had rather blithely failed to open political processes in the territory to the new populations coming in. Whether intended or not, they had, in effect, denied civil rights to the minority group. The response, nonetheless, seems to have been extreme. Under prodding from some of Utah's 21,000 non-Mormons the U.S. Congress was quite willing to countenance denial of most civil rights to all of the 120,000 Mormons in the territory. And more than this, they proceeded systematically to eradicate the outward practices that highlighted Mormon distinctiveness—polygamy, cooperative enterprise, and consensus politics. The Mormons, they felt, had to be thoroughly "Americanized" and thus prepared to assume the responsibilities of citizens in the newest state in the Union. Congress had changed, however, only the most visible symbols of Mormon distinctiveness. At the heart of the matter was a cultural difference neither Mormons nor non-Mormons fully understood. Both saw the matter as far more simple than it really was.

There is profound irony in the fact that Utah's first white settlers, who had felt the solution to their Indian problem was to get the natives to adopt white ways now suffered from outsiders who tried in the same way to solve their Mormon problem. But people adhere with remarkable tenacity to their old ways. The persistence and even resurgence of tribal traditions among the Indians in recent years is impressive. And there is much evidence that the Mormons similarly have held to a value system greatly at odds with that prevailing in America.

Perhaps the real lesson of the "Americanization" of Utah is that it is far less costly to tolerate the different life-styles of others than it is to try to change them. Americans have perhaps finally begun to learn that their notion of what is to be American should be elastic enough to accommodate people different from themselves. This is not to suggest that the changes brought by the railroad and the antipolygamy raid were of little conse-

quence. But the waters of cultural difference run deep. It could be plausibly argued that despite protestations and outward demonstrations of patriotism, many Utahns to this day have successfully and happily eluded "Americanization."

For Further Reading:

Histories

Railroad: The problems and consequences of transportation to the Far West, including the railroad, are skillfully presented in Oscar O. Winther's *The Transportation Frontier: 1865–1890* (1964). The winter 1969 number of *Utah Historical Quarterly* has several worthwhile pieces on the joining of the rails, most focusing on the physical task of building the road and the ceremonies attending its inauguration.

The most readable study of Mormon village life is Nels Anderson's classic *Desert Saints: The Mormon Frontier in Utah* (1942). Lowry Nelson's *The Mormon Village: A Pattern and Technique of Land Settlement* (1952) is a very important study, but not as readily accessible to the average reader. Wallace Stegner's *Mormon Country* (1942) offers a delightful and informative perspective on rural Utah life in the 1940s with a good many resonances from an earlier time.

E. B. Long's *The Saints and the Union: Utah Territory during the Civil War* (1981) touches on many events discussed in this chapter, including the relationship between Brigham Young and Colonel Connor. Leonard J. Arrington's *Brigham Young: American Moses* (1985) is probably the best biography of the Mormon leader in print.

Problems of landholding and titles are treated in Gustive O. Larson, "Land Contest in Early Utah," *Utah Historical Quarterly,* October 1961, and Laurence R. Linford, "Establishing and Maintaining Land Ownership in Utah Prior to 1869," *Utah Historical Quarterly,* Spring 1974.

There are a good many histories of particular mining towns and districts, most of them printed in the *Utah Historical Quarterly,* but there is no general history of mining in Utah. hilip F. Notarianni's *Faith, Hope, and Pros-*

perity: The Tintic Mining District (1982) is a useful recent book-length study of one area.

Brigham D. Madsen's *Corinne: The Gentile Capital of Utah* (1980) is especially germane to this chapter. Robert J. Dwyer's *The Gentile Comes to Utah* (1941; 1971) and A. J. Simmonds's *The Gentile Comes to Cache Valley* (1976) illuminate particular aspects of the lives of early non-Mormons in Zion. *The Peoples of Utah* (1976), ed. Helen Z. Papanikolas, has chapters dealing with early Utahns who came to work for mines and railroads.

A readily available overview of non-Mormon religious activities in Utah is in T. Edgar Lyon's "Religious Activities and Development in Utah, 1847–1910," *Utah Historical Quarterly,* fall 1967. A brief biography of Bishop Scanlan by Robert J. Dwyer, "Pioneer Bishop: Lawrence Scanlan, 1843–1915" also was printed in the *Utah Historical Quarterly,* April 1952. See, in addition, Jerome Stoffel's "The Hesitant Beginnings of the Catholic Church in Utah," *Utah Historical Quarterly,* winter 1968, and Louis J. Fries, *One Hundred and Fifty Years of Catholicity in Utah* (1926).

"An Outline History of the Protestant Churches in Utah" by Herbert W. Reherd is in Wain Sutton, ed., *Utah: A Centennial History* (1949), and can be found in most larger libraries. An overview of Episcopal churches, including the work of Bishop Tuttle, is in James W. Beless, Jr., "The Episcopal Church in Utah," *Utah Historical Quarterly,* winter 1968. Presbyterian activities are detailed in Ruth Walton, *A Century of Service in Utah, 1869–1969* (1969). Methodists are treated in Henry Martin Merkel, *History of Methodism in Utah* (1938); Congregationalists in *History of the Congregational Church, 1865–1965* (1965); and the mission schools in Brumitt Goodyear, *Home Missions on the American Frontier* (1939), and D. H. Christiansen's "Mission Schools in Utah," *Utah Education Review* (March 1915). Early Jewish communities in Utah are described in Leon L. Watters, *The Pioneer Jews of Utah* (1952), and in Juanita Brooks, *The History of the Jews in Utah and Idaho* (1973).

Ronald Walker has outlined the history of the Godbeite movement in "The Commencement of the Godbeite Protest: Another View," *Utah Historical Quarterly,* summer 1974. The history of Mormon communitarianism, especially the United Order, is explored in *Building the City of God: Community and Cooperation Among the Mormons* (1976) by Leonard J. Arrington, Feramorz Y. Fox, and Dean L. May.

Americanization: A solid and useful study that takes into account recent research on Mormon polygamy is Richard S. Van Wagoner, *Mormon Polygamy: A History* (1986). The best book on the origins of Mormon polygamy, placing the institution into the broader perspective of nineteenth-century innovation in family structure, is Lawrence Foster's *Religion and Sexuality: The Shakers, the Mormons, and the Oneida Community* (1984). D. Michael Quinn has thoroughly studied post-Manifesto plural marriage in "L.D.S. Church Authority and New Plural Marriages, 1890–1904," *Dialogue: A Journal of Mormon Thought,* spring 1985.

The difficult process of gaining statehood for Utah, especially the antipolygamy campaign, is studied in Gustive O. Larson's *The "Americanization" of Utah for Statehood* (1971). Political aspects of the same process are the focus of E. Leo Lyman in *Political Deliverance: The Mormon Quest for Utah Statehood* (1986). The classic study of the Council of Fifty is Klaus J. Hansen's *Quest for Empire* (1967), though D. Michael Quinn suggests convincingly that Hansen may have overstated the importance of the council during the Utah period in "The Council of Fifty and its Members 1844–1945," *Brigham Young University Studies,* winter 1980.

Eyewitness Accounts

Railroad: A visit to the Golden Spike National Historic Site effectively communicates the epic importance of the completion of the transcontinental railroad to Utah. There one can see splendid replicas of the engines that touched during the May 10, 1869, celebration, travel over portions of the original roadbed, and see films that review the history of the railroad's coming to Utah. On May 10 of each year, starting at 10:00 A.M., a colorful reenactment of the driving of the golden spike is presented. A good many folksongs about the railroad and Mormon/gentile relations were sung in the nineteenth century, some of which can be heard in recordings on albums titled *The New Beehive Songster,* 2 vols., Okehdokee Records; and *Songs of the Mormons,* Library of Congress,

Division of Music. Both would be available in larger libraries.

The observations of early visitors to Utah cited in previous chapters provide insights into Mormon village life. Perhaps the best of the lot is Elizabeth Wood Kane's *Twelve Mormon Homes*, originally printed in 1874 and reprinted in 1974, ed. Everett L. Cooley. There is a highly readable essay — part study and part memoir — by Edward Geary, "The Town on the Prickly Pear Flat: Community Development in Castle Valley," in Jessie L. Embry and Howard A. Christy, eds. *Community Development in the American West: Past and Present Nineteenth and Twentieth Century Frontiers* (1985). Much can be gained from a visit to Pioneer Trail State Park, near the Hogle Zoo in Salt Lake City, which re-creates a Mormon village prior to 1869. One can imbibe more directly the flavor of early Mormon village life by visiting rural towns, such as Spring City, Panguitch, Midway, La Verkin, or several dozen others. In such towns the physical setting and much of the cultural setting of

an earlier time is still evident to the close observer. The remains of the abandoned farm town of Grafton, near Rockville, are also evocative. Many reports from the people of early Utah towns are printed in the *Deseret News* of the period, which can be found on microfilm in larger libraries.

Visits to older mining towns, such as Eureka, the ruins at Silver Reef, and in a curious way, even modern Park City, can help one to recapture a sense of life in early gentile Utah. A helpful guide to such visits is Stephen L. Carr's *The Historical Guide to Utah Ghost Towns* (1972).

At the Fort Douglas Military Museum are exhibits re-creating life there in the nineteenth century. The cemetery contains the graves of a number of early military personnel including Patrick Edward Connor. The *Union Vedette* can be read on microfilm in some college and university libraries in the state, as can the back issues of the *Salt Lake Tribune*. Criticism of Brigham Young's leadership by the dissenting

Godbeites is evident in the *Utah Magazine* (1868, 1869) and in T. B. H. Stenhouse, *The Rocky Mountain Saints* (1872). Both can be found in college and university libraries.

Episcopal Bishop Daniel S. Tuttle's reminiscences were reprinted in 1987 by the University of Utah Press as *Missionary to the Mountain West: Reminiscences of Episcopal Bishop Daniel S. Tuttle, 1866–1886.* Several other useful sets of observations by other non-Mormons of the period are printed in William Mulder and A. Russell Mortensen's *Among the Mormons* (1958), especially chapter four. Though from a somewhat later period, Claton Rice's reminiscences of life as a Protestant missionary in Cedar City are valuable, printed as *Ambassador to the Saints* (1965). Visits to St. Mark's Cathedral and the Cathedral of the Madeleine in Salt Lake City and to the charming nineteenth-century Protestant churches still standing in such towns as Corinne, Manti, Richfield, and Monroe help one to understand and appreciate the dedication of those committed to religions other than Mormonism in early Utah.

Americanization: Valuable, though often acerbic, non-Mormon perspectives on the struggle for statehood are in R. H. Baskin's *Reminiscences of Early Utah* (1914) and Frank J. Cannon and Harvey J. O'Higgins's *Under the Prophet in Utah* (1911). Both can be found in larger libraries. A different view is evident in M. Hamblin Cannon, "The Prison Diary of a Mormon Apostle," *Pacific Historical Review*, November, 1947. A poignant memoir of an unhappy marriage during the later years of polygamy is Annie Clark Tanner's *A Mormon Mother* (1969). *Dear Ellen: Two Mormon Women and Their Letters* (1974), ed. S. George Ellsworth, offers another perspective on life in polygamy as does *Not By Bread Alone: The Journal of Martha Spence Heywood 1850–56* (1978), ed. Juanita Brooks. Lively descriptions of the first Statehood Day, January 6, 1869, are found in the *Deseret News* and the *Salt Lake Tribune* under that date.

New Pioneers Joseph Sargetakis (on the right) and his work partner
coming out of Castle Gate Mine No. 2. Sargetakis died in the explosion in this mine, March 8, 1924. *Courtesy Steve Sargetakis and Utah
State Historical Society.*

Seven

The New Pioneers

The iron horse is a compelling and powerful image for Americans. Besides the drama of the locomotive itself, belching steam and bellowing across the plains, the railroad has been a unifying force, tying ocean to ocean, East to West, North to South. In addition, it was among the forces pulling thousands of emigrants from Europe in the nineteenth century—offering jobs and new vistas and moving these people into the very heart of the continent.

Railroad building in Utah began in the late 1860s, and major lines were being added from that time until 1910. It took an army of workers to lay all those miles of track and work the mines and smelters the railroad served. Utah's farm population simply didn't have the time or inclination to undertake the full burden. The scarcity of help drove up wages and made it profitable for the companies to import workers from abroad. In northern and southern Italy, in the Slavic provinces of the old Austro-Hungarian Empire, in Crete and mainland Greece, advertisements and agents plied the local populations with promises of high wages. Driven by poverty, war, and persecution they came and with remarkable fortitude shouldered the burden of labor required by the railroad and mining industries of Utah. Many stayed, pioneering a new life here. In the process they changed the face of the territory, bringing a variety of cultures and a way of life that made Utah more like the rest of America than she had ever been.

The Coming of the New Pioneers

Utah's new pioneers were part of a great migration of people from eastern, central, and southern Europe to come to America at the end of the 1800s and in the early years of this century. Between 1901 and 1910, over 6,000,000 immigrants came to the United States from Europe — more than in any other decade in the nation's history. Most came seeking jobs. American industry was burgeoning and industrialists needed a plentiful supply of labor. The "new immigrants" settled mainly in cities such as Chicago, Cleveland, or New York City, where unskilled factory work was plentiful. There, living in crowded tenement houses, they concentrated in sufficient numbers to virtually create a colony of the homeland, forming mutual aid societies, religious congregations, and trade and communications networks closely linked to each other and to home.

A good many had no intention of staying in America. But once here most chose to stay, whatever the problems of their new life. It was far more common for workers to use their savings to bring family members one by one to the golden land, or even to return, acquire a bride, and bring her back, than it was to return for good.

The new immigration brought out many fears and prejudices among the older immigrants — the northern Europeans. Language, religion, stature, and sometimes complexion, set them apart. Thrown back on their own resources they gained power through urban political machines that seemed to established Americans decidedly undemocratic. Worse, in the eyes of some, they often joined and supported the labor union movement, participating in strikes and protests when wages were cut or new ethnic groups were brought in to work more cheaply than the old. Many were Jews, who

suffered from prejudice in America as they had in Europe for hundreds of years.

As the stream grew, some Americans had grave doubts about the ability of the Republic to survive. An evangelical minister, Josiah Strong, published in 1885 a book called *Our Country* that became an immediate best-seller. In it Strong listed the "seven perils" facing the nation. The list began with "Romanism," but proceeded quickly to Mormonism, intemperance, socialism, wealth, and immigration. The last was "the city," which, he maintained, provided the base for "an army twice as vast as the estimated numbers of Goths and Vandals that swept over Southern Europe and overwhelmed Rome."

But not all of the new immigration settled in the cities. A good many, perhaps out of inclination or perhaps because they happened to respond to an agent supplying western labor needs, came west to work on railroad crews or in mines. They landed at Ellis Island, like others, and were processed there. Often speaking no English and with only a slip of paper showing their ultimate destination as Salt Lake City, they were directed to a train that brought them to Utah. The proportions reaching Utah were comparatively small (16.9 percent of 373,351 Utahns were foreign born in 1910). Yet the new pioneers eventually had a considerable impact, as the established population wasn't all that large itself.

But not at first. The new arrivals were initially shuttled from Salt Lake City to Bingham Canyon, Helper, or perhaps to the smelters of Murray — right into a society where they could find kinsmen or countrymen and a few of the pleasures of home. There, they lived quite apart from the rest of Utah, pioneering a way of life that was dramatically different from that in the Mormon farming towns; one that had never been tried in Utah before.

The first Italians to arrive in Utah came in the 1870s, preceding the new immigration by two decades. Protestants from northwest Italy, and converts to Mormonism, they

settled as farmers near Ogden and Logan. Italians of the new immigration began to make their way to Utah as early as 1893, when the Building Trades Congress passed a resolution asking the city council to assure that companies hire "white men" rather than "dagoes." By the late 1890s a strong tide of immigrants was settling in Carbon County where they were employed by the Denver and Rio Grande Railroad as coal miners or railroad maintenance men. The arrival of Italians in eastern Utah was still news in 1899 when the *Eastern Utah Advocate* reported (November 30) that "about fifteen to twenty Italians have arrived in town, presumably to work in the mines here [at Castle Gate] or at Sunnyside."

The historical record does not tell us how they first happened to come—whether through a padrone, an Italian labor agent, a coal company agent, or by some other contact. Their arrival in groups suggests that possibly an employee of the coal companies recruited them in East Coast cities with arguments like those that attracted

Foreman Joe Bonnaci's Italian section gang. *Courtesy Utah State Historical Society.*

the father of Angelo Calfo, "I don't recall the very first, but I believe that it was back in 1894, '95 or something like that. . . . Well, he came to New York and from New York he heard the West was better conditions, it was better, it was new and he came West here." Once a nucleus was established through such means, personal ties to the homeland helped to bring others to the coal camps at Clear Creek, Winter Quarters, Castle Gate and Sunnyside.

Italian neighborhoods also sprang up in copper and precious metal mining areas, such as Bingham, Stockton, Ophir, and Mercur—so many in Mercur that a Catholic church was built there in 1904. Smelters in Magna, Garfield, Murray, and Tooele also offered jobs that Italians were willing to fill. Residents recalled that as late as 1914 Magna's "Little Italy" was "just a bunch of shacks that they built themselves. . . . The copper company let you build your shack there. . . . No bathrooms, of course, we had to use the number three tub." Still others worked for railroad companies in Ogden, some eventually establishing farms and dairies in the North Ogden area.

The Italians, with other ethnic groups in Utah, were often vilified in street talk and print and denied respect as individuals because of prejudice. Discrimination became organized when the Ku Klux Klan appeared in Utah in 1921, growing rapidly in 1924 and '25. The Klan burned crosses in Salt Lake City and in Helper. Klansman paraded openly in the streets of Magna, and Price Klansman in 1925 murdered, by lynching, a black, Robert Marshall. Some immigrants at the time suspected Mormon involvement in the Klan and subsequent historians have at times supported that view. Larry R. Gerlach's study, however, has conclusively shown that the strong official opposition of the Mormon church leaders against the Klan was effective in keeping the great majority of its members from associating with the organization.

Masons (who excluded Mormons from membership) were the principal leaders of the Klan in Carbon County. Leaders and members throughout Utah were from the more established non-Mormon population of the state. Gerlach concluded that "the single greatest obstacle to the development of the Klan in the Beehive State was the Mormon church." Thanks, in part, to such opposition the Invisible Empire was never a great influence in Utah and was all but dead by 1926. There is no record of Klan activities from 1932 to 1979, when an apparently ephemeral resurgence occurred in some areas of the south Salt Lake Valley. Nonetheless, the Klan was destructive, heightening the tensions, fears, and mutual distrust that arise when different societies and value systems are brought into close contact.

Even in the face of poverty, bigotry, and labor strife, the Italo-Americans maintained courage and dignity and, more remarkably, a hold on distinctive aspects of their native society. Italian-language newspapers were published sporadically in Utah between 1908 and 1917. Fraternal organizations and mutual aid societies were founded in most towns where Italian immigrants settled. And, as Philip Notarianni has observed, they

> kept aspects of life with which they were most familiar. Language, customs, basic religious beliefs, family life, and food were important. . . . Customs such as *boccie* (played on courts in Helper, Bingham, and Salt Lake); the art of wine-making and sausage-making; and nightly promenades by husband, wife, and family, as well as frequent visits to homes of friends and relatives characterized early Italian life. The Italian community also had midwives and folk cures.

Italo-Americans are less evident in Utah today. As with other ethnic groups, many of the immigrants and their children eventually moved to the cities, distributing themselves among established neighborhoods in such a way that they lacked the critical mass needed to sustain such highly visible and self-conscious communities as one sees in Boston's North End.

Shortly after the Italians, others of the new immigration began to arrive in Utah— including Serbs, Croats, and Slovenes. Since many were from the old Austro-Hungarian Empire they were often referred to as Austrians in the official records, but were of Slavic, rather than Germanic stock. In a migration pattern very similar to that of the Italians, their neighbors across the Adriatic, they came to work for what seemed at the time high wages in the mines, smelters, and railroads of the West.

First to arrive were the men. Many made the long journey several times, working a year or two and then returning to their native village. Sometimes the process of immigration occupied a full generation, the sons following the fathers, first as migrants and eventually as immigrants. Mile Dagosava, a Serb who came to Utah before he was sixteen, explained the process:

At that time people just started to come over to this country and everybody said that there was wealth here and you make fast money and all that. My father was already here and come back. He was working down here in Midvale smelter and he came back to the old country. . . . But that was hard life when I come here and start working and wasn't easy like now.

Somehow, the men found time away from their back-breaking labors to join in fraternal organizations where they could replicate at least a part of the homeland and enjoy socializing in traditional ways. The first Croatian lodge in Utah was founded in Bingham in 1908. Some continue to function in Midvale, Murray, and Carbon County.

Gradually some of the men began to wish for a more complete family life and brought wives or sweethearts to Utah from the old country. The first women to arrive created something of a sensation among the bachelor societies. Joseph Mikic, a Serb from Midvale, recalled that

They had saloon there in Midvale and some Serb used to run saloon there. First woman come there. His wife come there. . . . God, well, you know, we crazy. See her, first woman from, come from Yugoslavia. We give her $800 that night. Wedding present. . . . You know how people use to marry. They never give anything but money.

With the formation of families and the birth and death of loved ones a gradual commitment to remaining in the new land was made. I recall, however, meeting some years ago in a tiny Lebanese village an old man who had spent most of his working life in Chicago and then retired to his native home on Social Security, living in considerable comfort. He greeted me like a long lost brother, regaled me with food and embraced me with tears in his eyes as I drove away from his village. There were no doubt also Yugoslavs who felt them-

Croatian-Americans Martha Padjen and Sophia Lovrich Piedmont playing the tambura. *Courtesy Utah State Historical Society.*

selves strangers here all their lives and retired happily to the surroundings of their youth in the old country, but not without fond memories of America. Most, however, while enduring heavy labor and humiliating epithets such as "Bohunk" and "No-name-o-vitch," carved out a niche in Utah and stayed to raise their children and grandchildren in their adopted America.

Hard on the heels of the Yugoslavs came the largest and perhaps most visible of all Utah's new pioneers, the Greeks. Their homeland had long suffered from political turmoil, depriving the people of political control, limiting educational opportunities, and relegating them to poverty. In 1907 drastic failures in the staple crop of currants caused many young men to look abroad, and Greek immigration to Utah began in earnest. Leonidas Skliris, the "Czar of the Greeks" was the principal agent for

Greek laborers in all of the West, enriching himself by the fees he charged the workers he placed in employment. As with the South Slavs, most Greeks expected to work for a time, save enough to acquire a store or business, and then return. Intensely nationalistic after hundreds of years of foreign rule and influence, they often brought with them a vial of soil from the native land, so if they should die as exiles the priest would sprinkle it over them at burial.

Many more of them died as exiles than intended—taken by industrial accident or disease. Others simply had too much inertia, once settled into American life, to pull up roots again and return home. Altogether some 60 percent of those who came lingered in America, enough to cause Greek officials some concern, especially as stories of harsh living and working conditions, accidental maiming, and persecution began to be circulated back home. The Greek government sponsored in 1914 a tour of America by an educated and cultured Greek, Maria Economidou to investigate the re-

Greek funeral in Salt Lake City, 1914. *Courtesy Utah State Historical Society.*

ports. Helen Z. Papanikolas described her remarkable visit to miners in remote Carbon County:

> She traveled into the Clear Creek, Utah, mine three miles in blackness until coming to shadowed men. Narrow shafts of light shone from the carbide lamps on their caps. They stood in icy water, rhythmically swinging pickaxes against a wall of coal.
>
> She called, "Have life, young Cretans! May the God of Crete be with you!" Startled by the unearthly feminine voice speaking their language, they dropped their picks and approached warily. The voice had seemed to come through the roof of coal from the sky. When light from their lamps fell on her face, they were astounded. A six-foot youth wept.

Observing the pitiful housing conditions, tyranny of company officials, and callous disregard of health and safety for the miners, she complained to the manager of the

Utah Copper Company, R. C. Gemmel. He shrugged off her pointed observations by explaining that the men preferred such conditions and would not accept better if provided.

Despite such indifference, the Greek community grew until it reached 4,000 in 1910, about 1,000 more than there were Italians. There were only 10 women, however, among the whole 4,000, hardly enough to replicate to any great extent the home society. The void was filled over the years by picture brides, journeys home in search of a spouse, and occasionally by marriage to a local girl. In time, as a more balanced replica of the home society was achieved, the one-time industrial workers became shopkeepers, their sons moving to positions of considerable importance in Utah's business and professional community.

The Greek-Americans have retained their identity and culture more successfully than some ethnic groups in Utah. Greater numbers gave their community the critical mass others lacked, offering a broader and more concentrated segment of the home society to sustain pride and identity in the face of the "toil and rage" Helen Papanikolas so eloquently documented and described. Moreover, their church was more exclusively a national church than Roman Catholicism was for the Italians. Beginning with the Holy Trinity Church, built in Salt Lake City on Fourth South between Third and Fourth West in 1905, the Greek Orthodox churches and the priests who served in them provided a focus for Greek nationalism and ethnic identity that has preserved the distinctiveness of their community in Utah for nearly century.

There were other, smaller, groups who were not precisely part of the new immigration from southern Europe. Some preceded the new immigration and some came later, yet all but the Jews began their new lives working in railroad, mine, and smelter.

The first were the Chinese, who like the others, came not to stay, but to earn cash sufficient to enhance their position at home. Utah's Chinese, like those in other parts of the West, came almost to a person from one province— Kwangtung—in south China, with Kwangchow (Canton) the capital city. Floods, typhoons, and natural catastrophes on the Pearl River delta along with political corruption and onerous taxes had long limited opportunities in the region. Eager to supply labor needs in America, businesses worked out a "credit ticket" system that advanced the forty-dollar passage to the West Coast. Thus encouraged, they came in great numbers to work in Gam Saan—the Golden Mountain. About 100,000 eventually landed in San Francisco alone between 1840 and 1880. The first to come to Utah worked for the Central Pacific Railroad in the late 1860s, gaining an enviable reputation for industry, skill, and courage in laying the most difficult sections of the transcontinental railroad line. Some remained after completion of the railroad to man section crews. A young man who grew up in railroading recalled:

> After they used them in the construction of the central Pacific roadbed, then about every twelve or fourteen miles they had a section house along to keep the track up after it was built, and at each one of these section houses they had a section boss and he was usually a big, burly Irishman, and then he usually had about thirty Chinese coolies working under him as section hands, and that was the set up all the way from Ogden to Roseberg, California.

Some of these men eventually found the means to open laundries and restaurants; others worked as cooks in mining camps. American observers were intrigued to watch such workers "writing long letters back home to China . . . [using] little paintbrushes to make their Chinese hieroglyphics." Others noted "little huts adorned with signs, vouching for 'good washing and ironing done here.' " Though primarily a male society, like that of the other new pi-

oneers, a wedding was reported in 1870 of "Mr. John Tip to Miss Ma Choy both of the Flowery Kingdom, but now residents of Corinne."

Utah's earliest Chinese community was first concentrated in Box Elder County. The Chinese Exclusion Act, passed by the U. S. Congress in 1882, led to a great reduction of their numbers, opening jobs for the Italians, Slavs, and Greeks who were to follow. A number of Chinese remained, at least 106 residing in Ogden in 1890. After 1900 most Utah Chinese moved into urban areas, especially Salt Lake City. Plum Alley (running north and south from First to Second South between Main and State streets) became for a time Utah's principal "Chinatown," though Ogden and Park City retained visible communities as well. Salt Lakers recalled that in the 1890s "a prominent feature of nearly all New Year parades was a huge Chinese dragon two hundred feet long which progressed along the street like a gigantic centipede."

Remnants of the earlier immigrants have

Chinese workers on Central Pacific Railroad. *Courtesy Utah State Historical Society.*

combined in recent years with Chinese who moved to Utah after the Exclusion Act was repealed in 1952, bringing the present population to something over 1,000. Somehow, in spite of prejudice and persecution, resulting in a seventy-year period of exclusion, the Chinese seem a natural part of Utah and the West. Perhaps this is because they came here early and have tenaciously maintained ever since a presence and place among the peoples of Utah.

The Japanese came after the Chinese. Their migration to the Mountain states reached a substantial flow in the 1880s. As anti-Chinese sentiment grew in the West many Chinese fled to San Francisco, leaving a void Japanese labor agents were quick to fill. One of the earliest in Salt Lake City was Yozo Hashimoto, who was running a labor agency in Salt Lake by 1890. His nephew, Edward Daigoro Hashimoto, rose as a young man to great prominence in the business, supplying labor to the Denver and Rio Grande and the Western Pacific railroads and other industries in the West. His business and commercial connections were of considerable importance in the area, and Salt Lakers were by 1904 calling him the Mikado of the city. He continued to be a major figure throughout the West but retained Salt Lake City as his base, building a comfortable home there in a fashionable neighborhood in 1912.

Though most Japanese came to Utah as railroad workers, many later purchased land and became highly successful farmers. Utah's celery and strawberry crops were known nationally in the early decades of the twentieth century and were largely the product of Japanese farmers in Box Elder, Weber, and Salt Lake counties.

As with the Chinese, a small, but highly visible Japanese American community established itself in Salt Lake City, comprised mainly of refugees from the many "Jap" town sections of mining and smelting areas. In 1907 a Japanese Noodle House was opened on West Temple Street. The next year a remarkably persistent and flourishing tradition of Japanese-language newspaper publication began, when Shiro Lida started printing the *Rocky Mountain Times,* which continued until 1933. The *Times* shared the Japanese market after 1916 with the *Utah Nippo* (still in print), begun by Uneo Terasawa, and with K. Hirasawa's *New World,* which was published only in 1918. In Ogden, T. Kameyama printed a daily, the *Japanese News,* through 1914 and '15.

By 1912 there were well over 2,000 Japanese Americans in Utah, enough to build the first Buddhist church. As the population grew, a variety of specialized businesses, including even a tofu bean-cake factory, were founded. The population reached 3,000 by the early '20s. But in 1924 they, like the Chinese before them, were excluded from immigration and denied citizenship by the U.S. Congress. The prejudice that fed such laws was evident in Utah as well, where Japanese Americans were excluded from more exclusive restaurants and permitted only balcony seats at theatres. Despite such indignities the community survived and even grew, maintaining its cultural and social center in the Salt Lake City downtown area even when construction of the Salt Palace in 1966 and subsequent expansion destroyed many familiar landmarks, including the Buddhist church built in 1912.

As the Japanese began to move toward farming, shopkeeping, and commercial pursuits, Hashimoto became labor agent to Mexicans, bringing them into Utah as strikebreakers during labor disputes in 1912 and subsequent years. Prior to that time, despite the historic relationship of Utah to the Southwest, there were few Spanish-speaking people in the area—only 40 in 1900. At the turn of the century some Hispanic peoples began moving into the southeastern corner of the state from New Mexico and Colorado, where they worked as ranch hands and sheepherders, some buying land and beginning operations on their own. They were soon to be outnumbered, however, by the Mexican-born, brought by the labor contractor, Hashimoto. In 1918 and 1919 large numbers of Hispanics appeared on the employee lists of the Utah Copper Company. The experience of Santos Cabrera was not atypical:

> Yes, I came up from Texas in 1918, while the war was still on in Mexico, and there were very few families in Salt Lake City. A few from Old Mexico, and a few from Colorado and New Mexico, but very, very few families . . . here in this area when you saw a Mexican woman, it was like seeing your mother.

Their numbers grew rapidly. By 1923 nearly 20 percent of the section crew workers on the Los Angeles and Salt Lake Railroad had Spanish surnames. By 1930 the Mexican-born alone in Utah numbered 4,000 and as the century wore on the constant ebb and flow of migrants seeking farm labor left from each tide a proportion who found a permanent niche and became citizens.

These new pioneers, like their predecessors, founded social organizations, mutual aid societies, and churches to help them cope with the isolation and frustration of living in an alien world. A Mormon branch was organized in 1923. In 1927 a Roman Catholic mission was launched, which came to be known as the Mission of Nuestra Señora de Guadalupe. A moving force in its success was Father James Earl Collins, who worked tirelessly to provide a social and religious center for the community. The mission had a parish song that bespoke both the spirit and poverty of the enterprise:

> We're down on Fourth South,
>   far from luxury,
> Down where the viaduct spans
>   the D& RG.
> Most unpretentious, but somewhat
>   quaint
> With Guadalupe as our patron Saint.

Though many, including some U.S. citizens, were deported to Mexico during the Great Depression, the Spanish-speaking community by the 1960s and 1970s had become a highly self-conscious and articulate group and the largest of Utah's ethnic minorities.

Blacks have been in Utah since the time of the mountain men. James Beckwourth, one of the best known of the early trappers, was a mulatto. There was a black, Jacob Dodson, in John C. Frémont's 1843 expedition. Three black men were with the advance company of 1847 pioneers, Green Flake, Oscar Crosby, and Hark Lay. Blacks came to Utah during the pioneer period both as freedmen and slaves, some Mormon and some non-Mormon. An 1852 act of the legislature legalized slavery in the territory, and there were some exchanges, sales, and purchases of blacks until emancipation a decade later.

According to prominent black pioneer, Alex Bankhead, that event led to a con-

Don Freeman Bankhead, early Utahn. *Courtesy Utah State Historical Society.*

siderable exodus as the freedmen "left Salt Lake City and other sections of the Territory, for California and other states." Bankhead, a devout Mormon, remained with other blacks of his faith, but celebrated emancipation by naming his newborn son Don Freeman Bankhead.

Black soldiers were stationed at Fort Duchesne in 1886 and at Fort Douglas in 1896 and 1899. Thanks in part to the work offered by railroads, there were enough by the late 1890s to found the Trinity African Methodist Episcopal Church and to support several newspapers. *The Democratic Headlight* appeared briefly in 1899 under the editorship of J. Gordon McPherson. *The BroadAx* was published by Julius F. Taylor from about 1895 to 1898 and the *Plain Dealer,* from 1896 to 1909, under the editorship of another Taylor—William W. A Salt Lake City branch of the National Association for the Advancement of Colored People was founded in 1919.

The migration of substantial numbers of blacks into Utah did not take place, however, until the 1920s and 1930s. As they moved into the Beehive State they suffered like other immigrants from prejudice and discrimination, perhaps exacerbated here by a Mormon practice that prior to 1978 did not permit blacks to hold the priesthood—a privilege extended to men of all other races. Employment, housing, and public accommodations were formally or informally restricted for blacks as elsewhere in America. Marian Anderson, Harry Belafonte, Ella Fitzgerald, and Lionel Hampton were among many leading blacks who were denied lodging in major Salt Lake City hotels into the 1960s. (Anderson was permitted to stay at the Hotel Utah if she used the freight elevator.) Prior to 1950 blacks were not permitted at Lagoon amusement park except for one day after its "public" closing on Labor Day. The courageous and determined efforts of Robert E. Freed after he leased the park in the late '40s finally opened Lagoon to all races. There were lynchings in Utah, as well, among the victims a black who was shot and hanged at Uintah in Weber County in 1869 because "he is a damned Nigger" and Robert Marshall, murdered in Price in 1925.

Progress in combating prejudice has come slowly to Utah, and in response primarily to the great struggle for dignity and freedom that took place on the national level in the late '50s and the '60s. Yet progress there has been, and though blacks remain few in Utah and the West, their continued presence and increasing acceptance is a tribute to those who for a century and a half endured discrimination far greater than that afflicting any of the new immigration.

There have been Jews resident in Utah since 1848 when Alexander Neibaur, a convert to Mormonism, came to the Zion of his new-found faith. In 1854 Julius Gerson

Brooks and his wife, Isabell, known as "Fanny," came to Utah and decided to stay. They shortly thereafter opened a hat store and bakery and remained to become prominent and respected citizens of the territory. The largest influx, however, were merchants, who helped in supplying the considerable army Albert Sidney Johnston brought to Utah in 1857–58. When the camp was closed Nicholas S. Ransahoff, according to the story, loaned Brigham Young $30,000 to buy the entire supply of pork, a commodity he, for religious reasons, did not wish to deal in. A Salt Lake City directory for 1867 lists the names of thirty-nine Jewish residents, including butcher Charles Popper, merchants Emanuel and Samuel Kahn, the Ransahoffs, and Julius Brooks.

The best known of the group were Samuel, Frederick, and Theodore Auerbach, who had come west in the hope that the surest gold to be gained from the rush would be the profits from supplying the mining camps with food and goods. They had come through Utah in 1859 and later returned to open a store. Their "People's Store" was among the targets of Brigham Young's boycott of "gentile" businesses in his effort to build up the ZCMI system in 1868. Though, as one put it, "for a time this seemed to theaten our existence as merchants," they survived to found a chain of department stores and a dynasty that continues to be important to the state.

A Benevolent Society had been organized in the 1860s and for the next two decades services were held wherever space could be found—in private homes, Independence Hall (the non-Mormon community hall just west of Main Street on Third South), the Mormon Seventies Hall, and a Reorganized Latter Day Saint church. Plagued by division between conservative and reform elements in the community, the reform B'nai Israel Congregation succeeded in 1891 in completing a temple, modeled after the great synagogue in Berlin, which, though no longer used as a

Isaac Herbst and others surveying the site of Clarion, 1911. *Courtesy Robert Alan Goldberg.*

synagogue, still stands on Fourth East between Second and Third South. A conservative group continued to meet in homes and elsewhere until in 1903 they built a synagogue at 355 South Third East as the Congregation Montefiore.

Thus established, Utah's resident Jewish community, including mining magnates Samuel Newhouse and Simon Bamberger, became instrumental in encouraging the founding in 1911 of Clarion—a Jewish farming community intended as a refuge from urban life—near Gunnison in central Utah. The Clarion settlement was part of an international back-to-the-soil movement taking place among Jews at the time, which launched colonies in Argentina, Canada, Israel, and some forty locations in the United States. The idealistic little group of city dwellers from Philadelphia who founded Clarion, the last such colony in the United States, were intimidated by the barren landscape and extreme climate but in other ways found the their new home inspiring. One recalled:

the evenings and nights were exceptionally cold during the winter, but that did not hold back the pioneers from venturing out from their tents. They were well repaid for their courage in more than one way. The sky they beheld was not like anything they ever saw back East. The sky was always clear blue, with never a speck of cloud and studded with myriads of stars and they looked so near and so bright.

Despite the poor soil, problems in completing a vitally needed canal, and internal dissension, the colony endured as an organization until 1916, with some remaining on the soil until the mid–1920s. Though most returned to cities on the East and West coasts, a few, including Maurice Warshaw, founder of Grand Central stores, remained in Utah, joining the older Jewish community in Salt Lake City and making an important contribution to the state.

In several respects the Jewish experience in Utah has been different from that of many of the new pioneers. They came not as laborers but as merchants who quickly established themselves as affluent and influential members of the community. Though Utahns were not devoid of anti-

Semitism, the Mormons, who saw them-selves as either adopted or lineal members of the house of Israel, had high regard and admiration for the Jews. Thus Mormon be-lief and practice, which may have exacer-bated the persecution of other ethnic groups, especially blacks, favored Jews. In fact, the diminished anti-Semitism in Utah may, in a curious way, have encouraged dissension among Utah Jews, who, rela-tively free of external pressures, could af-ford the luxury of addressing directly their internal differences.

The Jews, however, were an exception. Other groups found their lives here not significantly different from those of immi-grants elsewhere in America. In their ef-fort to be free from poverty they bound themselves to labor agents, the company store, and the often indifferent decisions of mine owners and industrialists. All suf-fered the loneliness of being far from home in a strange land where one could not even express to others his feelings in words they could understand. All were victims of prej-udice and discrimination. A few were lynched. Others were terrorized by raids of the Ku Klux Klan. Most organized to protest working conditions and wages only to be locked out of their jobs and see them go to a new immigrant group, pleased to find employment at any cost. At first the new immigrants lived lives apart from the older settlers, isolated in railroad and min-ing camps or in smelter towns. Gradually, however, they began to move to the cities, founding businesses and entering profes-sions — becoming visible members of a new Utah.

I have called them Utah's new pioneers because I think they broke new ground in a very significant way for all of Utah. All but the Jews were the first here to earn their bread not as small farmers, artisans, or shopkeepers, who control their own work-ing conditions, but rather as industrial workers who are paid a wage in return for doing whatever the boss asks them to do. In pioneering this new way of life they suf-fered some of its most egregious injustices and indignities. With admirable courage and resourcefulness they founded organi-zations to help raise wages and reduce the awful toll of industrial accidents. And in the process they helped to make factory work safe and decent — a satisfying way of life for their children and for thousands more of the children of the earlier pio-neers, who no longer could make a living off the land.

The new direction was much like that of American cities from New York to Se-attle and from Chicago to New Orleans. It was very much what the old Fort Douglas commander, Patrick Edward Connor, had hoped for Utah. By 1920 the new Utahns had brought the balance between non-Mormons and Mormons in the state to very nearly fifty-fifty. It might not be too far-fetched to suggest that what one scholar has called the "Americanization" of Utah was ultimately accomplished not so much by the U.S. Congress and the Utah Com-mission as by the thousands of migrant la-borers — Chinese, Italians, Slavs, Greeks, blacks, and others, who came here for jobs and then finally settled in and adopted Utah as their home. Surely the cacophony of peoples of different backgrounds and race jostling one another as they seek to better their lives here is one of the distin-guishing themes in American life. In this sense, Utah was far more American in 1910 than she had been in 1880.

The Organization of Utah Labor

The earliest of the new immigration found employment in three places — rail-road, mine, or smelter. All were dirty, noisy, and dangerous. The $1.50 to $3.00 a day they got for their work seemed like big wages at the time. Yet they earned it and no doubt deserved a great deal more. Certainly they felt that way and early on attempted to organize as a means of con-vincing employers to improve working con-ditions, increase wages, and better the conditions of life in company towns. They combated the indifference of the corporation by uniting into a body with sufficient strength to make itself be heard. For this they were seen as foreign radicals; though, looking back on Utah's past, it is not hard to spot those who really tried to counter the American way of doing things.

America's labor unions stem from two traditions—associations of craftsmen and tradesmen and those of unskilled industrial workers. The first has roots going clear back to the Middle Ages, when all shoemakers, tailors, or masons of a town would band together, partly for social and partly for economic reasons. The economic functions of the associations usually took two forms. First, they agreed on limiting the number of apprentices who would be admitted to full practice in the craft. In this way they kept their services in great enough demand to assure that there would be no costly competition and price-cutting. Second, they set prices and quality standards for their services or products.

This tradition continued in both Europe and America clear up until the early 1800s. It was for the most part a quite gentlemanly affair, run by solid middle-class men who owned and worked in their own businesses, controlling the conditions of their labor and enjoying all the benefits thereof. The notion of a strike or boycott would rarely, if ever, occur to them, and if it did it would be action against their consumers or their suppliers, for they were their own bosses. These usually were local organizations—not having strong links outside of a given town—and the tradition was stronger in Europe than in America.

Such guilds had existed among the Mormons in Nauvoo, involving tailors, smiths, boot and harness makers, coopers, wagon makers, printers, and actors. The first to organize in Utah were musicians and actors. William Pitt, English-born director of the Nauvoo Brass Band, was a leader in founding the Deseret Dramatic Association in 1852. The group helped present dramatic productions, and lobbied for construction of the old Social Hall and the Salt Lake Theatre.

They were originally an unpaid corps of volunteers but began by the middle 1860s to demand a wage for their services. In an 1864 meeting with Brigham Young they complained that "we were all forced to earn our daily bread outside the theatre and yet were giving half our lives to it." According to actress Annie Adams's account of the meeting,

> Brigham tried every means and every plan to settle the matter without putting the home-talent players on salary, but none of the plans suited the actors and grumbling grew louder, with the final result that a salary list was drawn up. No one could say that the salaries were magnificently large, but it comforted us to know we were worth something.

The conditions of labor for actors in Salt Lake City have not improved much beyond that to this day.

Salt Lake's typographers also organized in 1852, the same year the National Typographical Union was formed—America's first continuing national union organization. It was an unusual meeting, as union organizations go, with Brigham Young attending and the proceedings beginning with prayer and the singing of an LDS hymn, "Come All Ye Sons of Zion." This printer's guild was a successor to a similar one in Nauvoo but in 1855 was formally organized into the Typographical Association of Deseret. Among the early members were such notables as George Q. Cannon, William W. Phelps, Brigham Young's brother Phineas Young, Ezra T. Benson, Jedediah M. Grant, Erastus Snow, Orson Pratt, and Wilford Woodruff. At first only Mormons in good standing could belong, but within a year that requirement was dropped.

Apparently the organization was primarily social in purpose. The members marched with representatives of some forty-nine other trades in the 1861 Fourth of July parade, the leaders carrying a scroll proclaiming the marching company to be "The Printers of Deseret." The list of other tradesmen in the parade ran alphabetically from artists to wool carders. Companies of tradesmen continued to be a prominent part of public celebrations in Utah through the 1860s. In an 1869 parade, according to one account, "The Engineers presented some beautiful designs of their handicraft, among which we noticed a miniature locomotive and miniature reapers and movers. The next in order were Tinners, Gunsmiths, Wagon Makers, Tanners and Curriers, Harness makers and Bakers, all with banners and representations of their respective trades."

By this time, relationships between the typographers and the church hierarchy were beginning to cool. The main cause of the rift seems to have been church efforts to keep wages down so local manufacturers could compete with goods soon to be brought to Utah by railroad. Brigham Young was determined to keep Utah's economy independent from that of the nation and felt lower wages would help in the effort. This focus upon wages was critical, because the organizations seem at the time to have been moving away from their earlier social and fraternal functions to concentrate more fully on bread-and-butter issues. In 1868 the typographers affiliated with the National Typographical Union. This was seen by church leaders as a surrender of control over local affairs. By the 1880s non-Mormons had come to dominate the union, and the organization began to support anti-Mormon Liberal party candidates in local politics. The rift had become a breach.

The second type of unions—those of laborers and industrial workers—also goes back to the Middle Ages, at least among miners, who formed *Gewerkschaftern* to represent their interests with companies. The influence of this type of union has been generally more recent than that of the crafts or guilds, as factory and industrial working conditions are themselves recent.

The first to organize workers in the American West were the Knights of Labor. Their campaign of the 1880s did not encourage positive attitudes among the Mormon church leaders toward unions. The Knights of Labor were one of the first workingmen's organizations in America to broaden membership from elite trade and craft workers to industrial workers. Sometime in 1884 the Knights began activities in Utah. One of their principal aims in the West was to exclude Chinese workers who, they reasoned, were lowering wages and taking the jobs of Americans. An unruly demonstration was held in Ogden in August 1885, urging a boycott of Chinese businesses and their expulsion from the city. To this the *Deseret News* responded sharply that whatever the faults of the Chinese, it was unjust to drive them out. The next month a vicious attack upon a Chinese section of Rock Springs, Wyoming, took place, the assailants burning houses and killing several men. It was widely believed the Knights were involved. This convinced church leaders in Utah that violence and mob action were the typical tools of the unions and confirmed their earlier distrust of the organizations.

The Mormons in the meantime had responded in their own way to the ills of industrial society with their cooperative and United Order activities of the late 1860s and early '70s. These were, in effect, efforts to make workers the owners of the means of production. Interestingly, these cooperatives were praised by national leaders of the Knights of Labor as models of how industrial society could justly be organized. Utah chapters of the Knights, however, banned persons who believed in or practiced polygamy from their membership, thus making participation impossible for believing Mormons. Church members were by this time being advised not to affiliate with organizations which had national ties, were secretive in nature, and advocated a confrontational rather than a cooperative relationship between workers and proprietors. Thus, historical circumstances decreed that the organization of industrial unions in Utah would become almost entirely an accomplishment of gentiles and disaffected Mormons.

The timing was not bad. For as the early warm relationship of Mormons to workers' guilds was cooling, a new people was entering Utah. These new pioneers were the first in Utah to experience to any great extent the life of the industrial worker. Consequently, they were the first industrial workers to attempt to unite in efforts to gain an adequate wage and standard of living. The story of labor organization in Utah in the modern industrial labor sense is primarily theirs.

The migrant workers who came to Utah in the late nineteenth and early twentieth centuries from southern and central Europe suffered from a long train of injustices, starting almost from the day they decided to come here. All things considered, it is remarkable that Utah's mines weren't the setting of far more effective and radical union protests than actually occurred. The workers were an extraordinarily patient lot. There were sporadic minor strikes in response to particular grievances and a series of major confrontations, frequently over union recognition: Carbon County coal miners struck in 1901 and 1903–4; the Western Federation of Miners organized the 1912 Bingham Canyon strike; Carbon County coal workers struck again in 1922 and 1933.

Recruitment of workers was often by brokers hired to fill the labor needs of railroad and mining companies. Leonidas G. Skliris was surely the most famous working out of Utah, his advertisements proclaiming him to be "The Reliable Labor Contractor," with a main office at 507 West Second South in Salt Lake and branch offices in New York, St. Paul, Chicago, Kansas City, Denver, San Francisco, and Sacramento.

Agents of these "padrones," as such brokers were called, recruited in the homeland and in U.S. cities where there were large numbers of the new immigrants. Skliris placed so many Greeks in positions in the Mountain West that the 1910 census shows a greater concentration here than anywhere in the United States. And each worker he placed was required to pay an average twenty-dollar fee for his position and sign a contract written in English — to him a foreign language — promising to "irrevocably assign and set over to L. G. Skliris, of the City and County of Salt Lake and State of Utah, the sum of One Dollar (1.00) per month out of any wages earned or which may hereafter be earned by me . . . and I do hereby irrevocably authorize, empower and direct said Railroad Company to deduct said amount and to pay same to L. G. Skliris."

Not only did such padrones exact an unending deduction from each employee's pay, they set up grocery stores, saloons, and other businesses close to working areas where the workers ran up debts that kept them continuously obligated. Greek participation in the 1912 strike at the Bingham mines was gained only with the promise that the striking union would free them from the domination of Skliris. The subsequent strike did not bring recognition to the union, but it did break the power of Skliris.

Once the workers had undertaken and paid for the long, arduous journey from Europe to Utah they found only the most rudimentary accommodations available to them. Railroad crews were divided into "white men's camps" that enjoyed separate railroad cars for sleeping, cooking, and eating, and "foreigners' camps" where one car served all three functions for the same number of men. Some lived initially in shacks built on company land from blasting powder boxes. Eventually the compa-

Burying the dead at Scofield, 1900. G. E. Anderson photo. *Courtesy Utah State Historical Society.*

nies built houses for workers' families, though they often were small, crowded, and inadequate for the families' needs.

Whether in mine, smelter, or railroad crew, the workers found the hours long, the labor strenuous, and sometimes they encountered unfair practices, such as the shortweighing of coal or ore mined. The 1922 Carbon County coal strike began as a protest against shortweighing.

Worse than the long hours of hard labor was insufficient concern for health and safety of the workers on the part of company officials. The reports of state inspectors are filled with tragic stories of death and dismemberment as the result of industrial accidents. In fact, everyday accidents were perhaps in the aggregate as devastating as the great disasters that rocked Utah mines early in the twentieth century.

The first of these was the Scofield explosion of 1900. Two hundred and fifty men were in the Winter Quarters mine near Scofield on May Day when about 10:28 A.M. a gigantic explosion ripped through

the tunnels. The concussion killed 83 men, the gases it produced another 117. Help poured in from all over the state as a massive effort was launched to find and identify the dead, plan for the mass burial, and assist the widows and their families.

An investigative commission cleared the Pleasant Valley Coal Company of any responsibility for the explosion, but many felt if the practice of clearing the mine before firing a charge had been followed, as it was at nearby Castle Gate, the loss of life could have been avoided. A subsequent generation of miners would suffer its own calamity at Castle Gate in 1924 when 172 were killed. The Castle Gate explosion helped bring the mortality rate in Utah mines between 1914 and 1929 to twice the national average.

All things considered, it is remarkable that Utah's mines weren't the setting of

far more effective and radical union protests than actually occurred. It would seem
that loyalty to unions or union ideology
was not as important to Utah workers as
were specific grievances. Had the unions
not competed for the loyalty of the workers, a single, sustained protest might have
led to much earlier, effective improvement
in the conditions of their work. Competition between unions, divided ideologically
and tactically, no doubt helped minimize
the success gained through workers' protests.

The state government played a role as
well, usually in behalf of mine owners. The
state militia was called out in the 1903
Carbon County strike, and deputy sheriffs
helped break the 1912 Bingham strike.
When Governor Mabey in 1922 refused to
call the National Guard on behalf of management, he was severely criticized by company sympathizers.

Also important was the cynical practice
of employers in playing off one group of
immigrants against another. In the 1903–4
Carbon County strike, led by Yugoslavs
and Italians, management rushed Greeks
to the scene to serve as strikebreakers. The
Greeks struck in 1912 against the Bingham
copper mine owners and again in 1922
against Carbon County coal mine owners,
but in both cases Mexican workers were
brought in to break the protest. Sometimes
different factions of the same nationality
were pitted against one another—Cretans
against mainland Greeks, northern Italians
against Sicilians.

The most effective union in organizing
sustained activity among Utah's new immigrants was the United Mine Workers,
founded in 1890 under the leadership of
John Mitchell. One of their most able leaders, Carlo Demolli, came to Utah from Colorado to help organize the 1903 strike
against the Pleasant Valley Coal Company.
Though the company conceded quickly to
many of the workers' demands, the union
failed in its main aim—to gain recognition as the workers' bargaining agent. The

popular Demolli was hidden and protected
from law enforcement officials by the Italian community. The United Mine Workers were also involved in the 1922 strike
against Carbon County's Kenilworth Mining Company, led by union organizer Frank
Bonacci, to protest a cut in wages. Again,
the outcome was undecisive, the company
using strikebreakers to minimize their con-
cessions.

The UMW concentrated mainly on organizing coal miners. Another union, the
Western Federation of Miners, was founded
in 1893 in Butte to represent the metal
mining and extraction workers. The WFM
moved its headquarters to Salt Lake City
in 1898 for a three-year period, but its perhaps undeserved reputation for violence and
radicalism kept it from becoming a major
force in Utah labor. Likewise, the Industrial Workers of the World, or IWW, made
efforts to organize in Utah, particularly in
the 1912 Bingham Canyon strike. Again,
their reputation for violence and radicalism was used against them, and they did
not make significant gains in the territory.

On the whole, Utah workers seem to
have been, like most American workers,
more interested in improving their wages
and working conditions than in reforming
American society. The final test came in
1933, when the National Miner's Union
was pitted against the United Mine Workers in efforts to attract the loyalty of Carbon County coal workers. The struggle had
an ethnic dimension, as Yugoslavian men
and women fought fiercely for the National
Miner's Union against Frank Bonacci and
the United Mine Workers. During the
course of the struggle, however, it was
claimed that the National Miner's Union
had Communist connections, and the
United Mine Workers became at last the
recognized representative of Utah coal
miners.

Similarly, Utah's workers in other industries finally affiliated in large numbers
with unions representing their interests to
employers. Perhaps the largest union in

Utah until recently was the United Steelworkers of America, which in the 1950s absorbed the Mine, Mill, and Smelter Workers Union, successor to the Western Federation of Miners. Other large unions include the American Federation of Government Employees, the Teamsters, the many building trades unions, and the pioneers of Utah's labor organizations—the United Mine Workers and the International Typographical Union. Many of these are affiliated with the giant AFL-CIO. Utah is one of about twenty states to have noncompulsory union membership and is still considered to be one of the strongholds of open shop sentiment in the United States. Though unions in Utah today probably have at least as many Mormon as non-Mormon members, the non-union bias among many Mormon church leaders can be linked to the days when unions barred polygamists from participation and were seen by Mormon leaders as perpetrators of violence and strongholds of gentile influence in Utah.

The one event that continues to link Utah with radical unionism was the conviction and execution in 1915 of IWW member Joe Hill. The case began when John G. Morrison and his son Arling were murdered in their Salt Lake grocery store at Eighth South and West Temple the evening of January 10, 1914. Witnesses claimed the son had wounded one of the assailants, and later that night a Swedish immigrant, Joel Haggelund, also known as Joe Hillstrom or Joe Hill, asked a Salt Lake physician to treat him for a severe gunshot wound. After an investigation he was arrested, convicted, and sentenced to be executed.

Many felt that Hill's being a foreigner and member of a radical union, the IWW, had caused the jury to convict him unfairly. His case became a cause among wide segments of the American public, his poems and songs, some of which he wrote in prison, adding to the sentiment for commutation of his sentence. President Wood-

row Wilson, Samuel Gompers, a head of the American Federation of Labor, and other prominent persons sent Governor William Spry telegrams urging that the sentence be changed to life imprisonment. After much litigation Hill was executed at the state prison in Sugar House on November 15, 1915. The evidence suggests that he may well have been guilty as charged, a question separate from that of whether his trial was conducted fairly. But whether he was or not, the case remains Utah's only enduring connection with radical unionism—one that created a compelling symbol for social protest around the world.

The ordinary workers who spent much of their lives in Utah's mines and smelters were clearly not a radical people. Pioneering as industrial laborers in Utah, they also pioneered in organizing to see that their pay was good and their working places safe. Bread and butter, not the overthrow of capitalism, were their aims. Yet, because of their grit and determination, nearly all of Utah's workers today can count on reasonably safe and pleasant working conditions, compensation for accidents and industrial diseases, comfortable necessities, and a good many of the luxuries of life.

Interestingly, the new pioneers attempted far less in the way of reorganizing society than did the Mormons, with their marriage practices, cooperatives, United Orders, and consensus politics. The Mormons sought no less than the transformation of all of society, making the unions of the new pioneers from eastern and southern Europe seem conservative indeed.

For Further Reading:

Histories

The New Pioneers. The indispensable set of readings on Utah's various peoples is the volume edited by Helen Z. Papanikolas in 1976, *The Peoples of Utah.* Authors of the essays in *The Peoples of Utah* are almost invariably those whose studies published over the years have built up the still too meager body of work we have on the new pioneers. Those of special relevance to this chapter were by Philip F. Notarianni (Italians), Joseph Stipanovich (Yugoslavs), Helen Z. Papanikolas (Greeks and Japanese), Alice Kasai (Japanese), Don C. Conley (Chinese), Vicente V. Mayer (Spanish-speaking people), Ronald G. Coleman (blacks), and Jack Goodman (Jews).

The *Utah Historical Quarterly* has taken upon itself the vital role of being the major — almost the sole — publisher of the history of Utah's new immigration and other ethnic peoples. See especially Joseph Stipanovich, "South Slav Settlements in Utah, 1890–1935," Philip Notarianni, "Italian Fraternal Organization in Utah, 1897–1934" both in the *Utah Historical Quarterly*, spring 1975; Philip Notarianni, "Utah's Ellis Island: The Difficult 'Americanization' of Carbon County," in the *Utah Historical Quarterly*, spring 1979; Margaret K. Brady, "Ethnic Folklore in Utah: New Perspectives," *Utah Historical Quarterly*, winter, 1984; Helen Z. Papanikolas, *Emilia — Emily; Yoryis — George* (1987); "Wrestling with Death: Greek Immigrant Funeral Customs in Utah," *Utah Historical Quarterly*, winter 1984; "Growing Up Greek," *Utah Historical Quarterly*, summer 1980, *Toil and Rage in a New Land: The Greek Immigrants in Utah* (1974,

reprint of *Utah Historical Quarterly*, spring 1970), and "Women in the Mining Communities of Carbon County," in *Carbon County: Eastern Utah's Industrialized Island* (1981); also Edward H. Mayer, "The Evolution of Culture and Tradition in Utah's Mexican–American Community," *Utah Historical Quarterly*, spring 1981; Michael J. Clark, "Improbable Ambassadors: Black Soldiers at Fort Douglas, 1896–99," *Utah Historical Quarterly*, summer 1978; and George Kraus, "Chinese Laborers and the Construction of the Central Pacific," *Utah Historical Quarterly*, winter 1969. The Jewish experience in Utah has been ably studied by Juanita Brooks, *History of the Jews in Utah and Idaho* (1973), and Robert A. Goldberg, *Back to the Soil: The Jewish Farmers of Clarion, Utah, and Their World* (1986). On the Klan see Larry R. Gerlach's *Blazing Crosses in Zion: The Ku Klux Klan in Utah* (1982).

Unions. Early union organization in Utah is covered in J. Kenneth Davies, *Deseret's Sons of Toil: A History of the Worker Movements of Territorial Utah, 1852–1896* (1977); Paul E. Frisch has written a useful and relevant article in "Labor Conflict at Eureka, 1886–97," *Utah Historical Quarterly*, spring 1981. Helen Z. Papanikolas's scholarship includes "Unionism, Communism, and the Great Depression: The Carbon County Coal Strike of 1933," *Utah Historical Quarterly*, summer 1973. Allen Kent

Powell has made labor history in Carbon County his special domain. See his "Tragedy at Scofield," *Utah Historical Quarterly,* spring 1973; "The 'Foreign Element' and the 1903–1904 Carbon County Coal Miners' Strike," *Utah Historical Quarterly,* spring 1975; and *The Next Time We Strike: Labor in Utah's Coal Fields, 1900–1933* (1986).

Eyewitness Accounts

The New Pioneers and Unions: There is a lamentable paucity of published and readily available diaries, memoirs, or other documents created by the new pioneers and their union activities. For that reason both are considered together here. There is a fine collection of such materials in manuscript Special Collections, Marriott Library, University of Utah. They are available to researchers but are not as convenient to the general reader since they cannot be taken out. The rich Utah Ethnic and Minority Oral History Collection, gathered by the Oral History Institute is being transcribed and placed in Special Collections at the University of Utah Library as well. A transcription of an oral history by a Greek immigrant, Angelo Georgedes, prepared by Allen Kent Powell, has been deposited in libraries in Price, the Utah State Historical Society, and the University of Utah. What practically amounts to the memoir of a

mine manager is in the *Utah Historical Quarterly* (fall 1985), "The Peerless Coal Mines," by A. Philip Cederlof. Dr. Eldon Dorman's charming "Recollections of a Coal Camp Doctor" in *Carbon County: Eastern Utah's Industrialized Island* (1981) offers a particularly valuable perspective on coal camp life. Many issues of *Beehive History,* published by the Utah State Historical Society, have visual materials and readable biographies of persons from the new immigration.

One can learn much by contacting those of the new immigration—visiting with them or even making recordings of conversations about their past. Old coal towns, such as Hiawatha near Price, mining ghost towns, other company towns, and the remains of smelters, are still accessible. A thoughtful visit—noting how large the houses are, how the buildings and streets are laid out, what kind of economic or social hierarchy they may reflect, etc., can be worth volumes of readings.

Photograph collections in private families, at public and university libraries, and at the Utah State Historical Society often can take one quickly and vividly into the world of the new pioneers. Especially poignant are photographs taken by George Edward Anderson following the Scofield explosion. Some are printed in Nelson Wadsworth's *Through Camera Eyes* (1975).

Bingham, 1917. Painting by Jonas Lie. *Courtesy University of Utah.*

Eight

Progressive Reform in the Beehive State

As the "new immigration" from southern and eastern Europe streamed into American cities at the end of the last century, people crowded into tenement districts where they suffered an urban poverty far worse than any we could find in Utah today and, perhaps, at any time in the past. Jane Addams, in 1889, moved into Hull House, a run-down mansion in Chicago's Nineteenth Ward, in an attempt to help the poor within their neighborhood. "The streets are inexpressibly dirty," she wrote, "hundreds of houses are unconnected with the street sewer; . . . many houses have no water supply save the faucet in the back yard; there are no fire escapes; the garbage and ashes are placed in wooden boxes and fastened to the street pavements." She recalled

> a little Italian lad of six to whom the problems of food, clothing, and shelter have become so immediate and pressing that, although an imaginative child, he is unable to see life from any other standpoint. . . . He once came to a party at Hull House, and was interested in nothing save a gas stove which he saw in the kitchen. . . . "I will tell my father of this stove," the boy said. "You buy no coal, you need only a match. Anybody will give you a match."

The concerns of such social workers as Jane Addams stimulated a sweeping wave of reform that touched all of America in the first two decades of the twentieth century.

A thorough examination was made of politics, working conditions, food and drug processing, the natural environment, and big business. Hundreds of pieces of legislation were passed to deal with the problems that were found. This "progressive movement," as it was called, touched Utah as well, but different circumstances here gave the movement different meanings and results.

As reformers looked at the ills of the Republic in the early years of the century, they asked themselves, "Where could we have gone wrong? How, in America, could there be acres of slums, rat-infested packinghouses, and a corruption-prone political process?" With a zeal that was avowedly religious, they turned their faith in the new social sciences to the tasks of diagnosing the malady, isolating its causes, and rooting them out.

They noted first that politicians had become corrupted by big business—indeed, had become willing partners in graft, accepting kickbacks from favored contractors

Women's First Aid Team at the Winter Quarters Mine of the Utah Fuel Company, 1917. O. A. Morrow photograph. *Courtesy National Archives, Bureau of Mines (RG 70-G, Neg. #1292).*

and overlooking corporate abuses of all kinds in exchange for personal favors. Inexpensive, mass-circulation magazines were just coming on the market, thanks to improved printing techniques, and several chose to build circulation by printing exposés of the abuses reformers had found.

Lincoln Steffens, for example, printed in *McLure's Magazine* in 1902, an article on corruption in St. Louis city government. In it he described the bribing of the St. Louis city assembly and council by a promoter who stood to reap a handsome profit if he could get a franchise from them to build urban transportation. It cost him only $300,000 to get the needed law passed over the mayor's veto and against the opposition of all the city's newspapers. The next week the promoter sold his franchise to an eastern firm for more than $1,000,000.

"What went on in St. Louis," Steffens claimed, "is going on in most of our cities, towns, and villages." And to a large extent he was right. The California legislature was notorious for being instantly responsive to the Southern Pacific Railroad. Montana government was widely seen as the pawn of the giant mining companies such as Anaconda Copper. Huge ranching firms ran Wyoming to suit themselves.

But what about Utah? Who were the bosses? Where were the political machines that ran Utah? What corporate interests had the state firmly in control? Certainly there were men of wealth and power. Samuel Newhouse, for example, thought he would make a fortune on gold with his Highland Boy mine in Bingham Canyon. The ore contained more copper than gold, however, and Newhouse soon capitalized on the situation by exploring the commercial potential of the reddish-yellow metal and then setting up a smelter in Murray to refine it. As home electrification spread around the world, Utah copper helped supply the need for an inexpensive, efficient conducting wire. Soon there were three copper smelters and one lead smelter in Murray and Midvale.

Another Utah entrepreneur was Daniel C. Jackling, who hit upon the idea of exploiting even the low-grade copper ores in Bingham Canyon with open-pit mining and the refining of huge quantities of the ore. He built mills and smelters at Magna and Arthur, making a fortune by processing vast amounts of the low-grade ore.

Thomas Kearns helped develop the Mayflower properties and the Silver King Mining Company in Park City, becoming a millionaire at thirty-eight in an age when millionaires were rare. The mansion he built on South Temple was renovated as the Governor's Mansion in the late 1970s. There were others; Simon Bamberger built an interurban railroad from Salt Lake to Ogden that was a mainstay of public transportation in Utah for half a century; David Eccles made a fortune in the lumber, util-

Utah entrepreneur and former U. S. Senator Thomas F. Kearns and family in front of their South Temple mansion. *Courtesy Utah State Historical Society.*

ity, and sugar industries; George Hearst took millions from Park City's Ontario mine. The Denver and Rio Grande Railroad ran the Utah Fuel Company, which mined and shipped a good deal of Carbon County's coal production.

Yet none of these men or corporations formed a lasting political alliance that could successfully influence politics to serve mainly their own interests over any extended period of time. The diversity of Utah's economy seemed to minimize the possibility of a single economic interest gaining control. Moreover, most of the big businesses were not long established when the progressive era began. Utah's industrial economy was still young, without set patterns, and with as yet little opportunity for economic alliances to be organized for political ends.

There was, however, one complicating factor in early Utah politics that overrode all other issues. That was the lingering problem of church/state relationships. Utah was young in industrial development during the progressive era but, also important, Utah was young in political development. Not until the 1890s were the two national political parties organized in the territory.

The result was a certain instability in political loyalties that Mormon church leaders were acutely aware of. Working behind the scenes in Utah politics throughout the progressive era was Mormon church president Joseph F. Smith, a nephew of church founder, Joseph Smith. His primary aim was to assure that Utah politics would follow national patterns. This, he felt, was essential to avoid bringing down once again the wrath of Washington upon his church. He discerned that the favor of the majority Republican party was essential and feared a resurgence of the almost instinctive devotion of his followers to the States' Rights principles of the Democrats. There

Senator Kearns introduces Senator Smoot to a less than friendly U. S. Senate. From Allan L. Lovey, *Cartoons by Lovey* (1907). *Courtesy Salt Lake City Public Library.*

had already been a moment of alarm in 1896 when citizens of the brand-new state voted overwhelmingly for Democrat/Populist William Jennings Bryan. But in the next election the staid business-oriented William McKinley squeaked by, reassuring national officials that Utah was integrating into national political patterns. There were good reasons for the disgruntled observations of Mormon Democrat James H. Moyle:

> Joseph F. Smith, throughout his long presidency of the Church, was persistently represented by the underground, rubber-shoed Mormon Republican Party leaders as wanting the Republicans to win, and they encouraged the campaign of underlings in circulating the thought that it was the will of the Lord that they should win or that Utah should be Republican.

Smith's close associate in the effort to Americanize Utah politics was Reed Smoot, a Provo businessman and Mormon apostle who was elected by the Utah legislature to the U.S. Senate in 1902 as a Republican. Non-Mormons in Utah protested that he was unfit to be seated in the Senate. Smoot, they pointed out,

> is one of the self-perpetuating body of fifteen men who, constituting the ruling authorities of the Church of Jesus Christ of Latter-day Saints, or "Mormon" Church, claim, and by their followers are accorded the right to claim, supreme authority, divinely sanctioned, to shape the belief and control the conduct of those under them in all matters whatsoever, civil and religious, temporal and spiritual, and who thus, uniting in themselves authority in church and state, do so excercise the same as to inculcate and encourage a belief in polygamy.

Their protest led to Senate hearings on the question from 1904 to 1906. As is evident from the wording of the protest, the hearings in the Senate Committee on Privileges and Elections centered as much on the political power of the Mormon church as the continued practice of polygamy in Utah. Robert W. Tayler, representing those opposing Smoot's being seated, maintained that "Reed Smoot, by his covenants and obligations is bound to accept and obey [the church prophet's teachings] whether they affect things spiritual or things temporal." Asked by progressive Republican Senator Albert J. Beveridge if objection to Smoot's being seated on those grounds would not mean "that no member of the Mormon Church has a right to hold office," Mr. Tayler replied, "I think that is true."

The committee heard dozens of witnesses, including the tall, aging church president himself. Smith testified under affirmation, but not under oath. In the questioning Tayler made a point of the many business and financial enterprises in Utah on whose boards Smith sat by virtue of his position as president of the Mormon church. Smith was at times evasive.

Rather than affirm that he was a prophet, seer, and revelator, he responded that "I am so sustained and upheld by my people." He maintained that he continued to believe polygamy was a correct principle but did not advocate its practice because of the federal laws against it:

> I understand that we are under injunction by the manifesto not to practice plural marriage. . . . Under that injunction we refrain from teaching it, inculcating it, and advocating it, and out of respect both to the law and to the manifesto of President Woodruff. Senator Beveridge. What I mean is this: Your belief may be one way, which is nobody's business; you, notwithstanding your belief, obey the law of the land? Mr. Smith. Yes sir; that is exactly what I mean.

During the lengthy hearings a number of witnesses testified that polygamous marriages had taken place since 1890 with the knowledge and approval of high church leaders. The majority of the committee voted not to seat Smoot, but, partly because of President Roosevelt's support for the Utah senator, their advice was rejected by the whole Senate. One of the senators, conservative Pennsylvania Republican, Boies Penrose, reportedly concluded that the Mormon was acceptable, being "a polygamist who doesn't polyg." Smith, for his part, set out to make sure that no one among the Mormons "polyged" by issuing, even before the Smoot hearings had concluded, the "Second Manifesto" strongly prohibiting the solemnizing of polygamous marriages anywhere in the world. Two apostles, John W. Taylor and Matthias F. Cowley, were dropped from the quorum for refusing to support Smith's tightened interpretation of Woodruff's Manifesto.

Smoot immediately set about building a strong Republican party in Utah and confirming his Republican loyalty by toeing the party line on national issues such as the tariff. So assiduously did he work at this that he helped make Republican party nominee William Howard Taft in 1912 the victor over the progressive challenge of

Teddy Roosevelt and the Democrat Wood-row Wilson. Only one other state, Vermont, went to Taft.

Smoot successfully developed a political machine called the "Federal Bunch" that elected two of the first three governors of the state, John C. Cutler and William Spry. He helped solidify a tradition that lasted twenty years of there being always one gentile and one Mormon from Utah in the Senate. He succeeded in 1904 in securing the replacement of Senator Thomas Kearns by a less independent lapsed Mormon, George Sutherland, an act that infuriated Kearns and led the *Salt Lake Tribune,* if that were possible, to step up its stridently anti-Mormon editorial policy.

This last action convinced non-Mormon politicians that the Mormon church was in full control of Utah politics. They responded by reviving the old Liberal party which they now called the American party. The coalition of gentile politicians had the strong endorsement of Kearns and his *Salt Lake Tribune.* They controlled Salt Lake

Smoot's magic with Utah legislature replaces Senator Kearns by George Sutherland. From Allan L. Lovey, *Cartoons by Lovey* (1907). *Courtesy Salt Lake City Public Library.*

and Ogden city governments between 1905 and 1911 and though not avidly progressive did effect improvements in the urban transportation system. Defection of the American party members from the Republican party threatened the balance Smoot and Smith had worked so carefully to establish, but after a defeat at the polls in 1911 the American party was disbanded.

In 1916 Utah elected Simon Bamberger to be the first non-Mormon governor since statehood and the second Jewish state governor in the nation. Bamberger was a thoroughgoing progressive, and it was during his administration that most of the important progressive legislation in Utah was passed. Also during Governor Bamberger's administration a resolution was found to perhaps the most delicate of all the political issues the new state had faced. One of the great causes during the progressive era was that of prohibition of alcoholic drinks. The measure was enormously popular in Utah and many LDS church leaders, including apostle Heber J. Grant, publicly urged passage of a state prohibition law.

With that kind of support the measure should have sailed through without difficulty. Yet the Utah legislature sidetracked a statewide prohibition bill in 1909. They did pass a local option bill that year, but Governor Spry allowed it to die through a pocket veto. Two years later the legislature repassed the local option bill, which this time Governor Spry signed. Why was there such tough sledding in Utah for a general prohibition law with such obvious appeal to the great majority of the state's voters?

Though Governor Spry took the heat for initially not supporting prohibition, Senator Smoot was in the background masterminding its defeat. The anti-Smoot forces lampooned "King Smoot," comparing him in a satirical article to Pontius Pilate:

> For he knew that the Prohibites hated William the Spry for that which he had refused to do, to dry up all the land of Utah and to consume the wicked with thirst.
>
> And straightway he called from among the Prohibites the chief centurions thereof and said unto them: "Ye know this wicked thing which William the Spry hath done. Therefore, whom shall I deliver unto you?"
>
> And they cried with a loud voice saying: "William the Spry, deliver him unto us."
>
> And the great king said unto them: "Be it even so."

But more remarkably, Smoot had the support of the church president, Joseph F. Smith, who avoided having to speak out on the issue by finding important church business to attend to in Hawaii. Both were concerned about offending Republican gentile businessmen, such as Fred Kiesel, who opposed prohibition. But, more important, they were afraid the issue might divide the Republican party on Mormon/non-Mormon lines, bringing Smoot to defeat in the process.

Prohibition became law throughout Utah only after the non-Mormon Democratic Governor Simon Bamberger was elected. The 1916 elections that brought Bamberger to power led to a clean sweep for the Democrats—their first significant victory in the state since 1899—and to the decline of the Smoot machine. Smoot himself remained in office, however, until the Democratic sweep of 1932, a powerful and enduring symbol of the stand-pat, big-business-oriented conservatism of the Harding, Coolidge, and Hoover years.

The point is that politics in Utah during the Progressive Era was muddied by the legacy of the territorial days. Reform issues, even those seemingly clear-cut and easy to resolve, sometimes took second place to the need to launch a stable Republican party that would serve as guarantor of a reasonably balanced two-party system. When Brigham F. Grant, Heber J. Grant's half-brother, was appointed to head the police department in 1911, he set out to make sure vice laws on the city books were strictly enforced. His campaign was opposed by those who saw it as Mormon meddling in public morals and was cut short in 1915 when a non-Mormon, William Montague Ferry, was elected mayor. The give-and-take of progressive politics in Utah revolved as much around such local political divisions as around the need to root out whatever graft and corruption there may have been in city hall.

Though Smoot and his allies tended to favor business interests, as did the national party they were so loyal to, there were few cases of businesses offering kickbacks or favors. Moreover, there was important progressive legislation passed under their leadership as there was under that of their opponents. In the game of boss politics and political graft, Utah could not hold a candle to such big-time cities as Chicago, Cleveland, or St. Louis. Nor did big business control the state, as was the case elsewhere. There were, quite simply, relatively few abuses reformers could use to whip up

The old Salt Palace. *Courtesy Utah State Historical Society.*

enthusiasm for a progressive movement in the state.

What about the teeming tenements that moved Jane Addams and others to call for reform? Here again, Utah cities could hardly compete with the big league. Salt Lake city had just passed 50,000 in population in 1900. Ogden had reached 16,000 and Provo was but 6,000. All were still relatively small towns, with a strong agrarian flavor in spite of nearby smelting and mining industries. Extremes in wealth, though evident, did not span nearly the dimensions they did in the great industrial cities.

Important changes in urban life were taking place. The state's first telephone exchange had been installed in Ogden in 1880. Electric power plants were built in the canyons in the 1890s, the competing companies, each with its own distribution system, making downtown Salt Lake streets a spaghetti of wires and poles. The first electricity was direct current, which could carry only low voltages and but a short distance. In 1897, however, Lucien Nunn came

to Utah and set up in Provo Canyon the world's largest alternating current transmission system, delivering 40,000 volts to ore-processing plants in Mercur. His Telluride Institute became an important training center for those involved in producing and marketing electrical power. Eventually, in 1913, some eighteen competing power companies merged into Utah Power and Light, which still supplies most of Utah's electrical needs. Federal surveys during the 1930s found Utah to be one of the most electrified of all the western states, thanks in part to the Mormon village settlement pattern, which minimized the distances over which poles and wires had to be spread to reach the bulk of the farm population.

Streetcars had appeared in 1872, with horses drawing the cars over fourteen miles of track in Salt Lake City. For a dime you could get around most of the downtown area. By 1899 the streetcar system was electrified, extended to a number of suburban areas, and the fare had dropped to seven cents, with free transfers. Ogden opened a rapid-transit system in 1900 and Logan in 1919. These, together with the Orem line and the Utah-Idaho Central Railroad, eventually offered interurban electric railroad passenger service from Payson through the Salt Lake, Ogden, and Cache Valley areas, and north to Preston, Idaho.

As these services were being built and expanded, a new competitor was entering the transportation market—the automobile. The first automobiles were seen in the state around 1900. By 1909 a state law required that all 873 cars and trucks in the state be registered. Most families could not at first afford personal transportation, and the various interurban lines took throngs of weekend visitors to such favorite fun spots as Saltair, built in 1893 on the south shore of the Great Salt Lake; Lagoon, built by Simon Bamberger near Farmington; and Castillo Springs, in Spanish Fork Canyon. The original Salt Palace (at Ninth South, between Main and State, certainly more palatial than the present one) featured a public arena and bicycle racing track which drew large crowds to various activities. Recreation in the towns varied. Those with large immigrant populations held traditional festivals and elaborate celebrations for weddings, national holidays, and feast days. Dancing and brass bands continued to be popular among all groups.

The improved transportation systems made it possible for the cities to expand in size. Whole new suburbs were built in Salt Lake and Ogden. The capital city was about 93,000 in 1910 but grew to 118,000 in 1920 as isolated rural districts, such as Sugar House, became suburban bedroom communities. Ogden grew from 25,500 to 33,000, while Provo gained 1,000 during the decade, from 9,000 to 10,000.

As this range of activities and developments suggests, the early 1900s were prosperous times in Utah. Purebred Hereford cattle and Spanish Merino or French Rambouillet sheep were imported and greatly improved the quality and profits in the livestock industry. In 1914 there were about 240,000 head of cattle in the state and more than 2 million sheep. The practice of grazing the herds in summer mountain pastures proved devastating to the watersheds, as increasing numbers of livestock devoured and trampled the grasses that had stabilized the powdery mountain soil. Spring runoffs caused serious erosion and disastrous floods in many localities until control of grazing was instituted by the United States Forest Service and other public agencies. Stockyards and packing plants were built to fatten and process animals. The first were built in the early 1890s in Salt Lake City. Yards built in Ogden in 1906 grew quickly to become one of the largest meat-processing facilities west of Omaha.

Farmers profited as well from introduction of the sugar beet industry after the first successful factory began production at Lehi in 1891. The product stimulated in turn a local canning industry, which brought Utah to fifth among the states in canned food production. Dairying grew, as cheese processing and the canning of condensed milk gave new portability to the products of the dairymen. Holstein cattle, which produced huge quantities of low butterfat milk, became the favorite among the newly imported purebred strains. Utah farmers also began to enter the poultry business, while continuing to supply tomatoes, other vegetables, and fruits to the canneries.

The mining of both precious metals and of lead and copper remained profitable, and the coal fields of Carbon County continued to produce their vital product. Most homes at the time were heated with coal furnaces. Old-timers remember the days when smoke rising from hundreds of chimneys on cold winter days became so thick "you could step off the bench and walk across the valley on it."

There were abuses that sprung up amidst

all this frenetic activity and growth. The major cities of Salt Lake and Ogden had poorer sections where the problems and perils of urban poverty were obvious. In addition, numerous small company towns housed the burgeoning immigrant population, often in unpleasant and unhealthful circumstances. There was a notable reluctance on the part of the legislature to pass laws regulating railroad rates, which were unfavorabe to Utah shippers. Nor do we see an eagerness to regulate the meatpacking industry. Yet, as historian Thomas G. Alexander has pointed out, the state was quick to adopt a number of progressive reforms.

The lingering influence of Populism—the farmer's protest movement of the '90s—was evident in the state constitution drafted in 1895. It provided for an eight-hour day for public employees, prohibited the labor of women and children in underground mines, and mandated health and safety legislation for industrial workers. Perhaps most significant, it reinstituted women's suffrage in the state, after the vote given in 1870 had been taken away by the Edmunds-Tucker Act. Not until 1920, a quarter of a century later, was the Nineteenth Amendment adopted, giving women in all states the right to vote. The Utah constitution even included a clause that guaranteed equal rights for women.

Concern for mine workers was evident in the first session of the state legislature, which, following recommendations of Governor Heber M. Wells, extended the eight-hour day to mine and smelter workers and specified that no boys under fourteen and no girls or women of any age would be allowed to work in these industries. When a Bingham businessman contested the law, it was upheld by the U.S. Supreme Court in the landmark decision of *Holden vs. Hardy*. The legislature also created a state board for the arbitration of labor disputes and prohibited blacklisting of employees. In the area of political reform, the legislature replaced the widely used party ballot—where ballots were printed and provided by the political parties—with the Australian ballot, where the ballots were printed by a public election commission and supplied only at the polling place under controlled conditions permitting complete privacy in voting.

Other progressive legislation followed, originating from both Republican and Democratic politicians. State Senator Martha Hughes Cannon, likely the first woman to hold the position in the United States, pushed through a law creating a state board of health, with authority over sanitation, water supplies, and other matters affecting public health. Other consumer legislation provided for a state board of bank examiners and a public utilities commission.

A number of laws further regulated the conditions of industrial employment, providing for a minimum wage, stronger mine safety regulations, prohibiting enforced patronizing of company stores and living in company housing, and finally establishing a strict workmen's compensation law. A state industrial commission was provided for under Governor Simon Bamberger in 1917. The same legislature declared unions legal organizations and limited the use of injunctions to break strikes.

In the area of food and drug administration a state dairy and food commission was established in 1903 and laws regulating the practices of veterinarians, physicians, optometrists, and barbers followed. There was strong support in the state for various measures to preserve and care for natural resources. Several commissions were created with the backing of Governor Spry and Senator Smoot to accomplish these aims.

In the area of political reform, the initiative and referendum gave voters the means of originating laws and rejecting laws passed by the legislature. A city commission form of government was pushed through in 1911 by a coalition of Mormons, Evangelical Protestants, and Socialists. Progressive reformers advocated the city commission form of government as a way of insulating city administration from political pressures and assuring a more rational and scientific management of city affairs.

Looking at this record, what can we say about progressivism in Utah? Some have said that Utah was backward and reluctant to enact the reforms progressives around the nation advocated. Others have claimed that Utah was advanced in moving towards progressive reforms. It would seem, however, that Utah was about as progressive as circumstances in the state warranted, but not a lot more. Progressivism was not for Utahns an enthusiasm — leading to uncritical passage of laws for which there was no real need or justification just because they were part of the nationwide progressive package.

The great bulk of progressive legislation in Utah addressed itself to the conditions of industrial work and the treatment of industrial workers by big business. There was an evident need for such legislation, and the state responded to that need. The conditions of urban life were not nearly as dismal as Jane Addams encountered in Chicago, and the incidence of poverty in Utah cities probably lower. There was consequently less sanitation, food and drug, and consumer legislation, though in 1905 the citizens succeeded in closing some of the Murray/Midvale smelters because of air pollution.

Utahns were aware of and concerned about the beauty and the resources offered by the canyons and mountains. They fully supported national action under President Theodore Roosevelt to preserve forest and range lands and to develop water resources. They encouraged the preservation of Natural Bridges, Zion, Rainbow Bridge, and Dinosaurland, as national monuments during the Progressive Era. They did not, however, move as strongly in the direction of political reform.

Interestingly, those reforms that seemed least justifiable in terms of need, such as initiative and referendum, which is rarely used, and the city commission form of government, which is now seen as undemocratic, were passed under new administrations — the American party in city government, and the Democratic party under Governor Bamberger — both anxious to demonstrate their progressive credentials.

For the most part, however, Utah's legislators responded not to the tides of fashion but to demonstrated need, picking and choosing from the progressive catalog measures that would help in dealing with the rapid changes the new century was bringing. Perhaps the most far-reaching accomplishments of the Progressive Era in Utah were responses to peculiar local circumstances — the establishment of a viable two-party system in the state and the integration of Utah's economy into national patterns.

By 1917, when America's entry into World War I brought progressive reform to a screeching halt, Utah would seem to have undergone a remarkable transformation. Just over two decades before, the majority of the state's citizens had been brought to their knees by federal pressure — their religious and economic institutions crushed, their loyalty and morality impugned. Now they were increasingly seen as the most loyal of patriots, the most accomplished of businessmen — the preservers of old-time American virtues. There is cause for suspicion when a 180-degree transformation takes place so quickly. The change, I think, was far more complicated and subtle than the simple Americanization of the Mormon population that is often assumed. Nonetheless, the outward indications of the change were there, and Utah seemed by the end of the Progressive Era at last finally and fully an American state.

For Further Reading:

Histories

Useful studies relating to the present chapter are "Political Patterns of Early Statehood" and "Integration into the National Economy" by Thomas G. Alexander in Richard D. Poll, Thomas G. Alexander, Eugene E. Campbell, and David E. Miller, eds., *Utah's History* (1978). Charles S. Peterson covers some of the period in his lively and informative *Utah: A Bicentennial History* (1977), especially chapter 7. Those matters relating to the Mormon church are skillfully explored by James B. Allen and Glen M. Leonard in *The Story of the Latter-day Saints* (1976), part 4. Thomas G. Alexander and James B. Allen's *Mormons & Gentiles: A History of Salt Lake City* (1984), chapter 6, focuses on events in Salt Lake City. The two earlier general studies of the period, Noble Warrum's *Utah Since Statehood,* 4 vols. (1919–20), and Wayne Stout's *History of Utah, 1896–1929* (1968), are more chronicles than interpretive histories.

There are a good many studies of more specific topics. Economic change is explored in Leonard J. Arrington and Thomas G.

Alexander's *A Dependent Commonwealth: Utah's Economy from Statehood to the Great Depression* (1974); Jan Shipps has charted journal coverage of the career of Reed Smoot in "The Public Image of Reed Smoot, 1902–1932," and James B. Allen has studied his career as "The Great Protectionist, Sen. Reed Smoot of Utah," both in *Utah Historical Quarterly,* fall 1977. Especially helpful is Thomas G. Alexander's "Reed Smoot, the LDS Church, and Progressive Legislation," in *Dialogue: A Journal of Mormon Thought,* spring 1972. Leonard J. Arrington and William Roper wrote *William Spry: Man of Firmness, Governor of Utah* (1971).

On prohibition see Helen Papanikolas, "Bootlegging in Zion: Making and Selling the 'Good Stuff,' " *Utah Historical Quarterly,* summer 1985, and Brent G. Thompson, " 'Standing between Two Fires': Mormons and Prohibition, 1908–1917, *Journal of Mormon History,* 1983; John E. Lamborn and Charles S. Peterson's study one of Utah's earliest anti-pollution campaigns in "The Substance of the Land: Agriculture v. Industry in the Smelter Cases of 1904 and 1906," *Utah Historical Quarterly,* fall 1985; Miriam B. Murphy's useful piece on "Women in the Utah Work Force

from Statehood to World War II" was published in *Utah Historical Quarterly,* spring 1982. John S. McCormick has studied the more sensational aspects of urban life during the Progressive Era in "Red Lights in Zion: Salt Lake City's Stockade, 1908–11," in *Utah Historical Quarterly,* spring 1982. He also examines the activities of Socialist politicians during the era (no connection) in "Hornets in the Hive: Socialists in Early Twentieth-Century Utah," *Utah Historical Quarterly,* summer 1982.

Eyewitness Accounts

A delightful memoir of one family's response to the advent of prohibition is John Farnsworth Lund's "The Night before Doomsday," *Utah Historical Quarterly,* spring 1983. Clyde G. Woolley's memories of bicycle racing at the old Salt Palace are printed in two letters he wrote to his sister, Olive W. Burt, who edited them for publication in the *Utah Historical Quarterly,* spring 1982.

Political events can be seen through the jaundiced eyes of Frank J. Cannon and Harvey J. O'Higgins in *Under the Prophet in Utah: The National Menace of a Political Priestcraft* (1911)

or the roseate view of S. A. Kenner, *Utah As It Is: With a Comprehensive Statement of Utah As It Was* (1904). A more temperate perspective, though through the eyes of a life-long Democrat, is the enormously useful memoir of James Henry Moyle, *Mormon Democrat: The Religious and Political Memoirs of James Henry Moyle,* edited by Gene A. Sessions (1975). Progressive muckrakers saw both good and bad in Utah. See Ray Stannard Baker's "The Vitality of Mormons: A Study of an Irrigated Valley in Utah and Idaho" in *Century Magazine,* June 1904, and Alfred Henry Lewis, "The Viper," series in *Cosmopolitan,* March, April, and May 1911. The four volumes of transcripts from the hearings of the Senate Committee on Privileges and Elections relating to the seating of Senator Smoot are available in larger libraries and make fascinating, if not always lively, reading.

For this period, as for all of the twentieth century, newspaper files and photograph collections, even those in private homes, often take one back quickly to an earlier time. Moreover, there are still a good many grandparents and older neighbors who with proper urging can give one intimate insights into life in Utah during the early decades of the century.

Destination Nowhere, 1941. Maynard Dixon. *Courtesy Brigham Young University Fine Arts Collection, Herald R. Clark Memorial Collection.*

Nine

War, Depression, and War

Geneneral Patrick Edward Connor (promoted from colonel in 1863, after the Battle of Bear River) finished his military career in Wyoming and then returned to live out his retirement in his adopted Utah, where he died in 1892. Had he been able to look out on Salt Lake City in, say, 1916 — twenty years after statehood — he no doubt would have smiled contentedly. To his right the bawling of cattle signaled the location of an active and vigorous meat-packing industry. Straight ahead the steam could be seen rising from the breweries, the pungent smell of hops and yeast filling the evening air. Far off to the left the first scars of open-pit mining at Bingham Canyon were discernible, the smoke of smelters diffusing the evening sun into spectacular shades of pink and orange against the Oquirrhs.

Well to the south of Temple Square a new downtown was burgeoning, the Boston and Newhouse buildings and the Newhouse Hotel marking the center of business and financial dealings in the state. The Cathedral of the Madeleine rose confidently in the foreground. The old St. Mark's Hospital and Holy Cross Hospital stood out in their respective neighborhoods, and St. Ann's Orphanage kept its lonely vigil at Twenty-first South.

No more than 55 percent of Utah's 500,000 people were Mormons, making them less significant numerically than were Catholics in San Francisco. A non-Mormon governor would shortly be taking the reins of state in an era of unprecedented material growth. Within a year Mormon youth would be fighting valiantly alongside other Americans in the battlefields of France. From all outward appearances Connor's vision of Utah had pretty much been realized.

War

The integration of Utah's economy into national patterns, which General Connor had worked so hard to accomplish, could not have come at a more promising time. The national economy was enjoying a healthy boom after the short recession of 1907 when in June 1914 the Austrian Archduke Francis Ferdinand was assassinated at Sarajevo. Within weeks Europe was at war. America, for a time, stayed aloof. A brief slump in the economy followed the outbreak of the war, but within a few months orders for the goods war-torn Europe could not produce began pouring into the United States, further stimulating the economy.

The demand for farm products and metals — the mainstays of the state's economy — was especially great, and by 1916 Utahns were prospering as never before. America's entry into the war in 1917 had further repercussions. Parts of the Brigham Young University campus became a training center for infantrymen bound for France. Fort Douglas took on new life as an officers' training camp. It also served as an internment center for some 300 German nationals who happened to be in the U. S. when we entered the war. American citizens served time there as well — pacifists, Socialists, and other war protestors — summarily imprisoned for criticizing government policy. Public campaigns were mounted to destroy the "Huns" and foster "100 percent Americanism," making it necesssary for German-Americans in Utah as elsewhere to keep a low profile. German Ave-

Utahns celebrate the end of World War I. *Courtesy Utah State Historical Society.*

nue in Salt Lake City was renamed West Kensington.

Civic leaders helped stir the patriotism of the people, enlisting their aid in planting Liberty gardens, subscribing to Liberty Bonds and otherwise contributing to the war effort. The campaign was given an ecumenical cast when Clarence Bamberger and Mormon apostle Heber J. Grant worked together as chairmen of the Liberty Bond drive, raising subscriptions from the state amounting to $72,500 — well over the quota.

More important, a draft was instituted — the first to affect Utahns. Voluntary enlistments and the draft brought nearly 25,000 from the Beehive State into military service during the war. Utah men and women were in many military units, but some were made up almost exclusively of Utah youth. The war took its toll. About 665 Utahns died while in the military, 219 were killed in action and 446 from disease and accidents. The sacrifices to the war effort affirmed that Utahns were loyal to the United

States and convinced many she had integrated fully into the nation.

Depression

The armistice of November 1918 ended the conflict and brought the boys home to parades and celebrations—and to a terrible Spanish flu epidemic so severe that the Salt Lake City health commissioner and the city cemetery had to expand their staffs to care for the sick and bury the dead. The suffering and dislocation of the epidemic seemed to presage the economic gloom that would characterize most of the next two decades.

The end of the war brought a cutback in defense spending, a return of European farms to full production, and in Utah a serious depression. In 1919 the state's total production of gold, silver, copper, lead, and zinc dropped to 54 percent below the 1918 level. The Utah Copper Company began closing down its mills and by 1921 had stopped production entirely. In the Bingham Mine 6,000 men were laid off or transferred to other operations. Arthur, Magna, and Garfield lost more than half their populations.

The closing of the metal mines greatly reduced the demand for coal, electricity and rail transportation, causing cutbacks and layoffs and a general decline in purchasing power. Utah Copper was idle for a full year, until stockpiles of the metal were used up. When it started up again in 1922 the plant ran at only about 40 percent of normal. The whole mining industry experienced a gradual recovery until 1925, then declined until 1928, when a bullish economy brought momentary revival. In 1929 the value of mineral production finally climbed above that of 1917, only to be cut in half the next year by the Great Depression.

On the farms things were even bleaker. The postwar depression had hit the farms somewhat later—during the winter of

Abandoned Kaysville Brick Mill, 1922. Le Conte Stewart etching. *Courtesy Robert O. Davis.*

1920—but the blow was sharper and more lasting than in the mining industries. Wheat that had sold for $3.50 a bushel in 1919 dropped by November 1921 to $.98. Plagued by recurrent drought as well as low prices, farmers in many parts of the state sold their acreages and moved to the cities or out of the state, seeking more secure employment. Most businesses and manufacturing plants likewise suffered as did their employees. The *Deseret News*, just before Christmas 1927, listed forty-four pages of delinquent taxpayers in Salt Lake County.

These conditions launched a great diaspora of native Utahns to other parts of the United States. In 1920 about 95,000 native Utahns lived outside of the state. By 1930 that figure had risen to almost 143,000. At the end of the 1920s 64,000 more people from Utah were living in other states than there were people from other states living in Utah. California, whose delights had always been a great temptation to Utahns, received more than any other state. Next, in order, were Idaho, Nevada,

Oregon, Washington and Wyoming. Several thousand moved to cities on the East Coast or in the Midwest. Many rural towns declined in population, the young people moving away to places where they had a least some hope of getting a start in life. Cozy adobe homes, now neglected, began to crumble back to dust. Houses were boarded up; unpainted barns began to collapse. Rows of poplars died of old age and disease and were not replanted.

Political divisiveness based on religion raised its ugly head again. A faction of Republicans, led by George Wilson and Ernest Bamberger, organized a secret society in 1922, called the Order of Sevens. Determined to reduce Mormon influence in the party, they engineered the nomination of Bamberger over Mormon diplomat J. Reuben Clark, Jr., for U. S. senator. When the Democratic nominee, William H. King, also a Mormon, won, with some crossover Republican votes, they cried foul and proceeded one more time to attempt a revival of the American party. In 1923 they nominated a slate of candidates for offices in Salt Lake City but concentrated on opposing the incumbent mayor, a Mormon, Clarence Neslen. The popular Neslen had strong support from Mormons and non-Mormons who had worked with him in city government. He won easily, while all the American party candidates lost. The rout led to the final demise of the American party effort.

The attempt to revive the American party coincided with an equally abortive attempt to establish the Ku Klux Klan in the state, and the two efforts may have been in some measure intertwined. It is likely that Joseph E. Galigher, an American party candidate for councilman and Henry C. Allen, the party's campaign manager, were Klansman. Important Mormon officials made a point of publicly opposing both the Klan and the American party. Heber J. Grant, who had become church president in 1918, was asked to meet with Klan organizers and pointedly refused to do so. Church leaders

George Albert Smith and Charles W. Nibley openly spoke against the organization. In addition, Grant and the other members of the church's First Presidency publicly announced their support for candidates opposed by the American party. Leaders of the American party and the Klan were justified in feeling their ambitions had been defeated by Mormon church influence in politics.

Beyond the brouhahas of local faction, Utahns commenced a long-standing tradition of following national trends in presidential elections and ignoring them in state elections. They voted strongly for winning Republicans Warren G. Harding in 1920, Calvin Coolidge in 1924, and Herbert Hoover in '28. A member of each party—Reed Smoot (R) and William H. King (D)—represented Utah in the Senate throughout the '20's, but only Republicans were elected to the House of Representatives through 1928 (Don B. Colton and E. O. Leatherwood). After a brief flirtation with a Republican governor, Charles R. Mabey in 1920, Utahns consistently elected Democrats to the office until 1948—two terms each for George H. Dern, Henry H. Blood, and Herbert B. Maw, seeing no apparent contradiction between their preference for Democratic executives at home and Republicans in the White House.

The '20s were made up of much more than politics and hard times, even in depressed Utah. The rest of the nation was enjoying a period of remarkable exuberance and prosperity known as the Jazz Age. If the horns sounded with muted tones in the Beehive State, they nonetheless were audible. Automobiles, buses, and trucks were opening whole new industries, changing blacksmith shops into service stations and causing expensive hard surfaces to be laid down over the dusty roads of the state. Home electrification was making great strides, replacing ice boxes with refrigerators and giving each home, through that magic box, the radio, continuous access to news, music, and product advertisements.

Station KZN opened in Salt Lake City in 1922, offering a full half-hour of programming each evening from 8:00 to 8:30 P.M. By 1925 the call letters had become KSL and on July 15, 1929, the first broadcast of the Tabernacle Choir took place, the beginning of the longest continuous program in American radio.

The popular dances at Saltair, featuring the famous big bands of the day, now began to suffer from the competition of a less involving, but nonetheless absorbing, American passion, the movies. Utahns not only attended the cinema but provided a setting for the making of films. Thanks to the persistent promotional efforts of Kanab's Parry brothers, Whitney, Chauncey, and Gronway (known locally by the unlikely names of "Whit, Chaunce, and Gron"), southern Utah, with its spectacular natural backdrops, became a popular site for motion picture production. The first

The First KSL (then KZN) radio broadcast, May 6, 1922. Heber J. Grant, president of the Mormon church, is speaking into the microphone, with his wife Augusta beside him. To the right of Grant are Salt Lake City Mayor C. Clarence Neslen and George J. Cannon. To the left of Mrs. Grant are George Albert Smith and Nathan O. Fullmer. *Courtesy Special Collections, Marriott Library, University of Utah.*

was in 1922 when cowboy star Tom Mix made the silent film *Deadwood Gulch* near Kanab. The legendary John Wayne got his first big break in show business in *Stagecoach*, filmed in Utah's Navajo country in 1939. The popularity of the movies hastened the closing of the venerable Salt Lake Theatre on October 20, 1928. Despite strong protests, the historic building was razed, to be replaced with a gas station and eventually a telephone office building.

The decade also saw the advent of airline mail and passenger service. The first transcontinental mail flight was in 1920 and by 1925 Salt Lake had become an important stopping place on the transcontinental route. Commercial passenger service began in 1927. The flight across the United States took thirty-two hours, with fifteen stops en route, and cost $404. Passengers had to dress in flying suits, wear goggles, carry parachutes, and bring their own meals, but the Chicago/New York route carried 445 hardy travelers the first year.

Utah was not completely isolated from the bob haircuts and daringly short chemise dresses of the time. And it even looked, as the decade went on, that if the '20s did not exactly roar in the Beehive State at least things were beginning to hum. Then the year the most promising new president since Woodrow Wilson assumed office, disaster struck. Herbert Hoover had been president only seven months when the worst stock market crash in the nation's history presaged a depression of catastrophic depth and duration. Frantic selling of stocks began on October 23. In six days, by the twenty-ninth, all the market gains of 1929 had been lost. By early November the profits of 1928 had eroded. The ensuing months saw the Depression deepen, helping the rest of the nation to understand what Utahns in mining and farming had endured throughout the '20s. But that did nothing to help Utah — in fact it made matters much worse.

Utah's industrial workers and farmers suffered severely — more even than did most Americans. Utah was firmly tied to the international economy through mining and agriculture. In both sectors demand was low all through the '20s and the '30s. Severe drought struck the state in 1931 and again in 1934. The state's high birthrate made it necessary for those who could find jobs to feed and educate a proportionately higher number of youth than in most states, the burden contributing to the general poverty. Annual income per person dropped from $537 in 1929 to $237 in 1933. In 1932 almost 36 percent of the

work force was jobless. A pall of discouragement spread across the state. Senator William H. King's son David wrote a friend that his father felt Utah

> was drying up. The Utah Lake is little more than a mud puddle, (smaller than it has ever been) and rain is falling less and less every year. He said that it was becoming more and more difficult to support the population, and that the people were becoming more discouraged now than ever. . . . Why . . . in the land of plenty, with its huge mountains, rich in mineral resources, with its beautiful orchards, with its prairies, with its cattle and its trees, why should there be such want and destitution?

Most had no satisfying answer to that question. Economists and businessmen generally agreed that depressions were in the main a healthy "wringer" for the economy and that all folks could do was to tighten their belts and wait for the natural order of events to bring about a spontaneous recovery. The best predictions were that the economy would begin to right itself sometime in 1933.

President Herbert Hoover was not among those who advocated a hands-off policy. A man who had risen from humble origins to found an engineering firm with worldwide activities, Hoover used the instruments of government at his command to combat the Depression. He launched a wide-ranging program of public works to provide employment and founded the Reconstruction Finance Corporation to bolster the sagging financial structure and provide relief funds to the states. In the end, though, the gospel of efficiency and his sense of how much direct relief could be given without damaging the character and independence of the people kept him short of measures that would be effective against so great an international calamity. Good engineer that he was, he could not bring himself to spend public funds on make-work projects. Moreover, his solid background of political progressivism had given him a lifelong attachment to efficiency and economy as cardinal principles of government. When the reserve of properly surveyed and engineered dams and highways was built, the limits of justifiable public spending had, in Hoover's mind, been reached.

Hoover was defeated in 1932 by Franklin D. Roosevelt, the well-born governor of New York—a polio victim who had gamely fought his way back into public life. Standing at his inaugural with the aid of heavy leg braces, he assured Americans that they had nothing to fear but fear itself, and then proceeded to "out-Hoover" Hoover, initiating a wide variety of relief and work programs, which under their alphabetical names, the FERA, the PWA, the WPA, and many more, elicited the gratitude of many and contempt of some Americans from Maine to California.

On April 12, 1945, the day of Roosevelt's death I was a young child, my family living in an oil town in central Wyoming. I was visiting friends that evening, listening to their tall gothic wooden radio, with a lighted amber dial that promised Tokyo, Berlin, and London, but was doing good if it brought in Casper. Suddenly funereal music broke in upon Tom Mix and at five-minute intervals the announcer began to inform America, even in remote Wyoming oil towns, that the president of the United States had died. My father was a Republican and I was speechless as every member of that roustabout family, from the father to the smallest child, burst into tears. One of the children turned to the father and asked, "Daddy, who are we goin' to vote for now?"

Such was the impact of Roosevelt on the American people. His New Deal programs were enormously important to Utah. Utah received much more New Deal aid per person than most states because the need was so great. During the blackest days of the Depression 36 percent of Utah's workers were unemployed. Farm income by 1932 had dropped from $69 million to $29 million. The value of mineral production

shrank from $115 million to $23 million. Thirty-two of Utah's 105 banks failed by 1933. Barney L. Flanagan, in his duties as a labor inspector, enforcing rules designed to spread the few jobs available as far as possible had many occasions to see the human consequences of such statistics:

> One day I thought I was doing a man a favor by telling him when his shift ended, that he had completed twenty-eight hours [of a thirty-hour quota] and that he need not come back the next day. I simply did not think it would be worth coming ten miles to work two hours and get ninety-six cents. He didn't say anything at the time. About 8 P.M. the fellow showed up in my backyard. I happened to know that he lived five miles from my home. He asked if he could not come out the next day and get the ninety-six cents to which he was entitled. He told me he had walked all the way from his home and planned on walking back. That's how much he needed the money, and that is what he was willing to do to get it— walk ten miles and work two hours, plus find some way to get another ten miles to work and the same ten miles back.

Helen E. Bunnell of Price remembered that:

> People who depended on work in the mines really had it hard. I didn't know many of them at the time, but I visit with a friend now who lived through those years in Hiawatha. Her husband worked twelve to fourteen hours for four dollars a day. He was glad for one day's work a week. She says there were many times when their cupboard was bare and that if she wrote to her mother, her mother had to send her the stamp. She never had any cash, not even two cents.

The various New Deal programs minimized the suffering Bunnell and Flanagan saw about them, bringing about $289 million into the state's economy between 1933 and 1939—a per capita average of $569. Only eight states of the then forty-eight received more help per person than did Utah.

CCC boys building contour terraces in the
Wasatch Mountains. *Courtesy National Archives,
U. S. Forest Service (RG 95-G, Neg. #308648).*

It is easier, however, to understand the New Deal impact in terms of what the programs actually did. Take, for example, the terraces one sees frequently in Utah mountains, such as those east of Bountiful. One cannot notice them without being impressed with what a monumental labor their building must have been. Most of it was accomplished by young men of the Civilian Conservation Corps—(CCC)—one of the most popular of New Deal programs. The CCC brought several thousand young men to Utah from all parts of the country between September 1933 and 1941. The men were housed in forest camps and were paid a dollar a day, plus food, clothing, and shelter, to work on a wide variety of jobs, such as clearing forest trails, fighting fires, reseeding grasses in eroded areas, and building terraces to check erosion in Utah's mountains. Their work went far toward repairing the damage done to mountain watersheds by overgrazing earlier in the century.

The Work Projects Administration, or WPA, financed a variety of public projects in Utah between 1935 and 1942. WPA workers built dams and canals, did highway construction and maintenance work, and built or renovated dozens of public buildings. They built a new courthouse in Sanpete County, improved the airport in Cache County, and improved and added buildings to the Utah State University and University of Utah campuses. They constructed National Guard armories at Logan, American Fork, Nephi, Mount Pleasant, Fillmore, and Cedar City—all told a neat bag of tricks to pull off while leaning on shovels, as they, according to the opponents of New Deal programs, were supposed to have spent most of their time doing.

WPA administrators recognized, in addition, that artists, musicians, and librarians were unemployed and needed work so they could take care of their families' needs and exercise their talents. A mural in the Price City Hall was painted by Utah artist Lynn Fausett for the WPA. Fausett also supervised the reproduction on canvas of ancient Indian paintings on the walls of Barrier Canyon threatened by oil drilling in the area. The huge canvas, eleven by eighty feet, was lost for many years but is now on display at the Utah Museum of Natural History. The WPA built the Springville Art Museum, the pride of Utah County in 1937. The city, through donations and public programs, has filled it with one of the finest collections of western art in the country.

Though various symphony orchestras had been organized in Utah, almost since the time of white settlement, the present Utah Symphony was launched under a WPA music program begun in 1936. They rehearsed at the Emerson Ward meetinghouse, presenting their first major performance in 1940 at the University of Utah's Kingsbury Hall. They have since become one of America's fine orchestras.

Writers, and even historians, suffer in depressions and the WPA helped them by sponsoring a number of programs with lasting consequences. Many eminent Utah scholars participated in WPA projects, identifying and classifying historical documents, writing guides to the state, and producing other works. Among them were Juanita Brooks and Dale L. Morgan, whose historical writings have become classics. These and other programs left a visible legacy in Utah which we all benefit from today. Add to them the millions of relief dollars that helped the poor put bread on the table and clothe their families, the stimulus their spending gave to local groceries, clothiers, and other businesses, and you can get some idea of the enormous impact the New Deal had in Utah.

Roosevelt's administration tried as well to bring a New Deal to Utah's most tenacious peoples, the Utes, Gosiutes, Southern Paiutes, and Navajo. The Indians were accustomed to poverty and lived largely in rural areas which felt the effects of the Depression less strongly than did those in the cities. The New Deal thus concerned itself more with the cultural than the economic conditions of their lives. Federal policy since the General Allotment Act (or Dawes Act) of 1887 had been dominated by a persistent effort to assimilate Indians fully into white society. To accomplish that the federal government had attempted to break up the reservations, which served as the base for perpetuation of Native American traditions and culture. The White River, Uintah, and Uncompahgre Utes of the Uinta Basin were the special targets in Utah of this policy as the "allotment" of their lands early in the century helped reduce their reservation to less than one-tenth its former size. Others suffered from the attack on their culture as well, with Navajo children being forced against their parents' will to attend government-operated schools and Southern Utes being denied a bid for reservation lands in San Juan County. All of this should have had a familiar ring to Utah's Mormons who, under attack by mainstream America at very nearly the same time, were trading some of their own distinctive institutions for the broader autonomy they hoped to gain through statehood.

In the case of the Indians, the government policies were followed by a reassertion, rather than the intended suppression, of tribal consciousness, despite a continuing decline in numbers. The Sun Dance became an established ritual among Utes and Southern Paiutes, helping to reaffirm Indian identity. The Peyote religion, which reinforced the traditional society, became widespread, evolving by the 1980s into the Native American Church.

These evidences of a reawakening gained impetus when President Roosevelt appointed John Collier to be U. S. Commissioner of Indian Affairs. Collier promoted passage in Congress of the Indian Reorganization Act in 1934, which he said was based upon the "simple principle of treating the Indians as normal human beings

capable of working out a normal adjust-
ment to and a satisfying life within the
framework of American civilization, yet
maintaining the best of their own culture
and racial idiosyncracies." Though it imposed a democratic representative system
of electing tribal councils in place of the
traditional process, which relied on age
and special powers as the criteria for leadership, the act encouraged a reassertion of
the tribe as an appropriate representative
of Indian communities in economic as in
social concerns.

In the 1950s, with a new administration in Washington, government policy re-
verted for a time to that embodied in the
Dawes Act. Utah's Senator Arthur V.
Watkins, chairman of the Senate Indian
Affairs Subcommittee, was a leader among
those in the Eisenhower years who saw the
New Deal Indian Reorganization Act as
an unfortunate aberration. He supported
a return to the old assimilationist policy,
now pressed under the chilling new name
of "termination." The essential aim was to
terminate wherever possible special federal
responsibilities for Indian affairs and to encourage policies that would move Indians
into the broader society. That policy was
dominant through the 1950s. The tribe remained the central unifying institution in
Indian life, however, pressing in the 1950s
and 1960s lawsuits that brought the Utes
nearly $48 million dollars in compensation
for confiscated lands and the Paiutes and
Gosiutes some $7 million. Part of these
funds were used to develop cooperative
tribal industries, which served further to
make the tribe central in the lives of Utah's
Indian peoples.

At the same time, the Indian population in Utah began a remarkable recovery,
reaching above 11,000 in the 1980s, with
growth especially strong among the Navajos in southeastern Utah, who became a
majority in San Juan County. Urban growth
was important as well. By the 1980s the
federal courts, which had normally stopped
short of return of real property were be-

ginning in some instances to countenance
the return of traditional tribal lands. This
development was particularly important to
the smaller bands of Southern Paiutes and
Southern Utes in central and southern Utah
who in refusing to be moved to reservations had been subjected to a variety of ad
hoc, usually marginal, arrangements. Now
they had hopes of being able to own again
their traditional lands and sacred places,
which would serve as a focus for a reawak-
ened sense of control over their own
destiny.

Severe problems remained, as unemploy-
ment, alcoholism, and the debilitating effects of being torn between two cultures
continued to darken the lives of many. The
identity of the Skull Valley and Deep Creek
Gosiute peoples seemed especially threatened as their young took jobs in Tooele or
Grantsville, leaving but a few families on
the reservation. Nonetheless, the prevailing mood seemed optimistic, as evident in
the manifesto of Clifford Jake, an Indian
Peak Southern Paiute, who concluded, "It
don't matter how you talk, what you do,
if you're a Paiute you should be proud of
it. . . . I'm a Paiute Indian and . . . [I've]
always been proud of my heritage. I just
don't want to see it fade away, die in the
shadow." The new pride was primarily their
own accomplishment, gained by a dogged
determination to insist on justice and maintain their identity in spite of the relentless
battering of the white society. But the New
Deal, despite its failings, was one of the
brighter moments in the long, dim record
of federal policy towards Native Americans.

The Depression had long-term effects
as well on the political life of the Beehive
State. Republican Reed Smoot's thirty years
in Washington were ended in 1933, his
seat taken by Elbert D. Thomas, a University of Utah professor of political science.
The Democratic landslide that cost Smoot
his position brought Henry H. Blood to
the governor's chair. Though the *Deseret
News* came out strongly in favor of Alf
Landon over President Roosevelt in 1936,

Marriner S. Eccles with Franklin D. Roosevelt.
Courtesy Marriner S. Eccles Foundation.

and several Mormon church officials, including a counselor in the First Presidency, J. Reuben Clark, Jr., were publicly opposed to the New Deal, the elections of that year gave Roosevelt nearly 70 percent of the vote. Utah voters sent only five Republicans to the state legislature. The New Deal created a base of loyalty to the Democratic party in Utah that was to be of great importance in Utah politics through the 1970s.

A number of Utahns accepted positions in Washington to assist in fighting the Depression under the New Deal. Former Governor George H. Dern was appointed secretary of war under President Roosevelt in 1935. Ogden banker E. G. Bennett helped to set up the Federal Deposit Insurance Corporation in 1933 and 1934. The Utahn of most significant impact in Washington, however, was Marriner S. Eccles, oldest son of the second family of pioneer industrialist David Eccles. Marriner had undertaken management of a portion of his father's estate in 1912 at the age of twenty-two,

building it to an important economic empire in the West, which included at times significant interests in the giant Utah Construction Company, the First Security Corporation, the Sego Milk Company, Utah Power and Light, the Utah-Idaho Central Railroad, Amalgamated Sugar, and others. By clearheaded and bold management he kept all of the First Security Banks open throughout the Great Depression—a remarkable achievement in an area where the rate of bank failure was extremely high.

Secretary of the Treasury Henry Morgenthau, Jr., asked Eccles to work in the Treasury Department in Washington in 1934, which led to Eccles's appointment as chairman of the Federal Reserve Board the next year. Eccles demanded, as a condition of his accepting the job, the president's support for passage of the Banking Act of 1935. That act gave the Federal Reserve Board in Washington stronger powers than it had had before, making possible its control over interest rates and money supply that are so vital to its present-day operations. As chairman Eccles directed his considerable talents to persuading Roosevelt, a fiscal conservative, that a federal compensatory fiscal policy was needed—that government should increase spending when private spending declined during depressions and tax during inflationary periods to keep economic activity on an even keel.

The issue came to a head in 1937–38, when a severe "Roosevelt Recession" struck and a fierce battle to shape future policy broke out within the administration. Eccles, who favored increased spending in a recession, was pitted against his old boss, Secretary of the Treasury Morgenthau, who wanted to balance the budget as a means of bolstering business confidence. Eccles and his supporters won out in this "struggle for the soul of FDR," the president deciding to step up spending in the spring of 1938. The vigorous recovery that fall was attributed by many New Dealers to the renewed spending and did much to make the idea of a compensatory fiscal policy a hallmark of Democratic economic and social action since that time. Eccles was chairman of the system until 1948 and remained a member of the board until 1951, serving as a major shaper of administration taxing and spending policies during the later New Deal. In 1982 the Federal Reserve Building was renamed to honor Eccles for his sixteen years as a major figure in the Federal Reserve System.

There were, in addition to the federal programs, many private efforts to combat the Depression in the Beehive State. One man, Benjamin B. Stringham, organized the Natural Development Association which was in essence an attempt to return to a barter economy, where unemployed persons would work on farms and ranches in exchange for foodstuffs. By the spring of 1933 the program had fifteen units operating in four states, with a total membership of 2,000 families. Other self-help programs were begun to supplement the charitable work of the Salvation Army, the Jewish Relief Fund, the Catholic Women's League, the Protestant Ladies' Aid Society, the Mormon Relief Society, and the Red Cross.

In 1936 the Mormon church initiated its Church Security Program, later called the Welfare Plan, modeling it after the efforts of Pioneer Stake President Harold B. Lee, to develop a cooperative program to help his congregations on Salt Lake City's west side. As the program developed, several church congregations were to become co-owners of a producing cooperative, such as an orchard or row-crop farm, the members serving also as volunteer workers for the labor-intensive operations of the project. The products were shipped to Salt Lake City and redistributed to stock local bishops' storehouses. They were then allocated by the local bishops to the poor within their congregations. The program since the '30s has supplemented federal and local welfare programs in many Mormon areas and contributed greatly to disaster relief, such as after Idaho's Teton Dam flood of 1976.

The combined labors of local, state, federal, and private organizations were not sufficient to banish depression from the land. Full recovery came only after war had broken out once again in Europe. As America entered the war in 1941 the enormous wartime demand for metals and food again brought flush times to the Beehive State. The relief programs, with no more clients, were dismantled and Utahns committed themselves to the patriotic task of pressing the war against fascism.

Another War

The story of Utah's participation in World War II is similar to that of her participation in World War I, with one important exception. The use of aircraft as military carriers and bombers had developed significantly between the wars, and, as, the Pearl Harbor attack dramatically demonstrated, United States coastal areas were now subject to enemy attack. More secure inland bases were needed to store and ship supplies of all kinds for the armed services and to serve as training centers. Utah was chosen as a site for a number of such installations; it was a central place, with an abundant work force, good transportation facilities, and a location approximately equidistant from major ports in Seattle/Portland, San Francisco, and Los Angeles. To assist in the problems of manufacturing, storing, shipping, and repairing vital war materials, the government set up the Clearfield Naval Supply Depot, the Tooele Army Depot, and the Ogden Defense Depot. Supplementing the military installations were the Geneva Steel plant, the Utah Oil Refining Company, and the Kalunite, Inc., plant (to produce aluminum), all set up under government support and subsidy. Training, housing, and caring for troops was accomplished through establishing the Kearns Army Air Base, Wendover Air Force Base, the Bushnell General Hospital (later the Intermountain Indian School in Brigham City), and the expansion of Fort Douglas.

Though local farmers and stockmen resisted the conversion of lands to these uses, state officials generally supported it. Beginning even before the war, with Hill Air Force Base in 1938, the federal projects provided an enormous stimulus to the state's economy. By 1942 nearly 52,000 persons were employed by the war industries in Utah, bringing an influx of workers, enormous pressures on housing and public facilities, and occasional tensions between the more established inhabitants and the residents of the newly built housing projects.

The war affected civilians in numerous ways. Rationing of such commodities as sugar, rubber, and coffee was imposed. Many Utah children remember the excitement of buying the first rubber balloons or Hershey bars to be marketed after a long, dry spell during the war. Domestic automobile production stopped, and good cars were almost as difficult to come by in the Mountain West as tires and anti-freeze. The dislocations of general migration in search of jobs seemed to contribute to higher rates of delinquency, teen pregnancy, and crime.

As young men were taken out of the work force women were encouraged to work in industrial jobs. Historian Ann Chambers has noted a Hill Field publication reporting with pride that "the important part that women are playing in this war is revealed in the data showing approximately 45 percent of all [training] courses have been completed by the fair sex." Yet one worker recalled that "the women were never accepted . . . only as a helper, which meant doing the jobs the men thought were women's jobs and were quite messy to do, but we went along with it." Despite such experiences, a good many women gained a degree of confidence and independence from their war work, and though most seemed happy to return to domestic life after the war, they did not forget it. Their experience may in the long run have given impetus to the nearly universal practice in the late twentieth century of women working outside the home.

Though a number of the bases were dismantled or converted to other uses when the war ended, some, such as Hill Field, the Tooele Depot, and the Dugway Proving Ground, were continued. Utah's economy, with its society, had been transformed. By 1945 almost 28 percent of civilian income came from direct government employment—mostly defense-related. Even in 1978, 20 percent of the state's workers got their paycheck from the government, more than any other sector of the economy. Utah has continued to rank near the top of the states in the proportion of the overall economy related to defense.

Among the more important and enduring effects of the war production effort was the stimulus it gave to Utah's steel industry. The Columbia Steel Company had be-

gun production at their Ironton plant near Springville in 1924. But the opening of the Geneva Works near Orem in 1944 was a major step in the scale of steel production in Utah. The Geneva plant was built to provide an iron supply for the West Coast in case shipping from East Coast mills was hindered by military action. It remained one of Utah's most important employers until 1986.

Utah's distance from the coast was also a factor in the establishment of the Topaz relocation center for Japanese Americans, one of the least justifiable and saddest consequences of the war mentality. In 1942 President Roosevelt succumbed to pressures urging removal of Japanese Americans from the coast, where, it was thought, some might assist their homeland in an all-out crisis. Altogether, more than 110,000 American citizens of Japanese ancestry and resident aliens were moved from the West Coast to "relocation centers" in the interior. Some 8,000 were brought to a site thirteen miles northwest of Delta, where

Children at Topaz. *Courtesy Utah State Historical Society.*

they were kept in virtual confinement for the duration of the war. Toyo Suyemoto Kawakami wrote of her family's arrival there on October 3, 1942.

As we stepped down from the bus . . . a small band of uniformed Boy Scouts stood in the hot sun and played on their brass instruments. . . . [The] camp was a strangely desolate scene of low, black, tar-paper buildings, row on row, through each block. . . . The camp contained forty-two blocks, thirty-five of which were residential. All the blocks looked alike, so that later, weeks after we had settled in, camp residents would occasionally lose their sense of direction at night and wander into a barracks not their own, much to their embarrassment and that of the occupants.

The first sight of our rooms was dismal—no furniture, unfinished walls and ceiling, a two-inch fine layer of dust on the floor and windowsills. We had to sweep out the dust and mop before we could bring our suitcases in. Army cots were delivered that night, giving us something to sit on. Eventually Father made a table and stools of varying heights from scrap lumber.

Topaz finally closed in 1945, most of its residents returning to rebuild their lives in West Coast cities. A number remained to add their numbers to the Japanese American community in Utah.

During the turbulent years from 1917 to 1945, Utah had changed dramatically. The stimulus provided by the First World War seemed to confirm the wisdom of General Connor's effort to integrate the state into national patterns. After the war, however, the world markets for the metals and farm crops Utah produced fell into a dismal slump that lasted two decades. During the 1920s and '30s we paid a heavy price for our recently formed ties to international markets.

The Great Depression revived, for some, long-standing, latent traditions of self-help and cooperative effort. For most, though, it increased dependence upon federal programs and government support. The war years brought whole new industries to Utah and stimulated the economy as never before. With the war's end, Utah was set on a course that in economic matters did not change greatly until the late 1970s. New jobs and prosperity reversed for a time the outmigration of Utahns to surrounding states. The new industries concentrated the population even more along the Wasatch Front. By 1970, 80 percent of the state's population was living in heavily urban areas.

From the war until the late 1970s the defense industry and the increasing world scarcity of mineral and food products put Utah into an advantageous position in the world economy. Growth and prosperity were once more on the ascendent, helping to realize the dream of Patrick Connor. But a dramatic drop in oil prices and the stagnant national and world economy of the '80s again returned Utah to conditions approximating those of the 1920s. A series

of economic setbacks set the tone of the late '80s. There was a long shutdown of Kennecott Copper, with only a partial reopening. Banks and thrift institutions failed in numbers greater than at anytime since the Great Depression, eroding the savings of thousands of Utah families. The Triad Corporation, which had developed the International Center near the Salt Lake City airport and was midway through a massive construction and development project on the downtown's west side, filed for bankruptcy. The piles of girders intended for their new high-rises rusted in chain link enclosures that took up whole city blocks. Desperate to keep afloat, builders and promoters pushed the construction of new malls and office buildings destined to remain largely vacant. Migration to Utah abruptly reversed itself in 1984. For the first time in years more people moved out than in. The announcement in February 1987 by USX, the giant American steel corporation, that the Geneva Steel plant would be "indefinitely idled" seemed to sound the knell for an era.

Clearly, we live in a world so fragile and intricately interrelated that it is impossible to look confidently to sustained good times. Our economy is now subject to decisions and events abroad involving persons who do not consider that their choices might radically transform our way of life in Utah. We might have been more independent and stable today, though no doubt poorer, had Connor's vision been attenuated by that of men with a less materialistic view of what constitutes real wealth and progress. Perhaps the farmers and stockmen who fought in the '40's to keep their lands from becoming the domain of bombers and nerve gas were possessed of a deeper wisdom than was then recognized.

For Further Reading:

Histories

General studies relating to the present chapter are "From War to Depression," by Thomas G. Alexander, "The Great Depression," by John

F. Bluth and Wayne K. Hinton, and "The Impact of World War II," by John E. Christensen, all in Richard D. Poll, Thomas G. Alexander, Eugene E. Campbell, and David E. Miller, eds., *Utah's History* (1978). Charles S. Peterson's *Utah: A Bicentennial History* (1977) also covers important events of the period. S. George Ellsworth's *Utah's Heritage (1972)* remains a valuable and important resource for those wishing to understand the state's past. Thomas G. Alexander and James B. Allen's *Mormons & Gentiles: A History of Salt Lake City* (1984) is especially helpful on politics in Salt Lake City. Noble Warrum's *Utah Since Statehood,* 4 vols. (1919–20) and Wayne Stout's *History of Utah, 1896–1929* (1968) contain valuable sources.

Leonard J. Arrington and Thomas G. Alexander explore economic change in *A Dependent Commonwealth: Utah's Economy from Statehood to the Great Depression* (1974); economic data are also available in J. R. Mahoney's "Measures of Economic Changes in Utah, 1847–1947" *Utah Economic and Business Review*, January 1947, and in all other issues of that most valuable resource, prepared by the University of Utah's Bureau of Economic and Business Research. See also ElRoy Nelson's *Utah Economic Patterns* (1956) and Leonard J. Arrington's *The Changing Economic Structure of the Mountain West, 1850–1950* (1963).

A useful general study of the Depression and the New Deal is Richard Lowitt's *The New Deal and the West* (1984). All of the *Utah Historical Quarterly*, summer 1986, is devoted to studies of the Great Depression in the state. Marriner S. Eccles's role during the crisis of 1937–38 is studied in Dean L. May, *From New Deal to New Economics: The American Liberal Response to the Recession of 1937* (1980). Miriam B. Murphy's useful piece on "Women in the Utah Work Force from Statehood to World War II," was published in *Utah Historical Quarterly*, spring 1982. Ann Chambers's continuing work on "Utah's Rosies" will bring the story of Utah's working women through World War II. Helen Z. Papanikolas's "Unionism, Communism, and the Carbon County Coal Strike of 1933," in the *Utah Historical Quarterly*, summer 1973, provides an important added dimension of understanding to the Utah depression experience. The experiences of Japanese Americans at Topaz and elsewhere are explored in the several essays that make up

Japanese Americans: From Relocation to Redress (1986), edited by Roger Daniels, Sandra C. Taylor, and Harry H. L. Kitano.

Political issues of the period are explored by Frank H. Jonas in "Utah: Sagebrush Democracy," a chapter of *Rocky Mountain Politics* (1940) edited by Thomas C. Donnelly. See also Frank H. Jonas and Garth N. Jones "Utah Presidential Elections 1896–1952" *Utah Historical Quarterly,* October 1956.

Eyewitness Accounts

There are, for this period, as for most of the twentieth century, fewer published and readily available diaries, journals, and reminiscences of eyewitnesses to the past. There is a fine collection of oral histories in manuscript in Special Collections, Marriott Library, University of Utah. They are available to researchers but are not as convenient to the general reader, since they cannot be taken out. The rich Utah Ethnic and Minority Oral History Collection, gathered by the Oral History Institute is being transcribed and placed in Special Collections at the University of Utah Library as well. Brigham Young University's Charles Redd Center for Western Studies has a major oral history collection on family life in the early twentieth century which is of great value.

William Mulder and A. Russell Mortensen have reprinted essays on some aspects of Utah society during the early twentieth century in their *Among the Mormons* (1958). See especially the excerpt from Bernard De Voto's "Ogden: The Underwriters of Salvation," originally printed in Duncan Aikman's anthology, *The Taming of the Frontier* (1925), and Senator Richard Neuberger's characterization of Mormon relief programs during the Depression, "The Saints in the Promised Land," in *Our Promised Land* (1939). Wallace Stegner wrote powerfully of Utah in the '40s in his *Mormon Country* (1942).

James Henry Moyle offers penetrating insights into politics through the New Deal in *Mormon Democrat: The Religious and Political Memoirs of James Henry Moyle*, edited by Gene A. Sessions (1975). Marriner S. Eccles's *Beckoning Frontiers: Public and Personal Recollections* (1951), edited by Sidney Hyman, is one of the best by former New Deal figures and has a good deal of material relating to economic events in Utah during the Great Depression. Barney L. Flanagan's experiences during the Great Depression help in communicating the human impact of the crisis. They are published as "A Labor Inspector During the Great Depression" in the *Utah Historical Quarterly,* summer 1986. Helen D. Bunnell's "Depression Memories," in the same number of *Utah Historical Quarterly,* is also helpful. There are a number of personal memoirs of Japanese Americans during relocation, some from Topaz, in *Japanese Americans: From Relocation to Redress* (1986), edited by Roger Daniels, Sandra C. Taylor, and Harry H. L. Kitano.

For this period, as for all of the twentieth century, newspaper files and photograph collections, even those in private homes, often take one back quickly to an earlier time. Moreover, there are still a good many parents, grandparents and older neighbors who with proper urging can give one intimate insights into life in Utah during the 1920s, '30s, and '40s.

Downtown Salt Lake City, 1987. *Dean L. May photograph.*

Ten

Utah Today: And Tomorrow

Utah country has changed dramatically in its 11,000 or so years of human history. Some changes were inevitable; some, perhaps, could have been avoided; some were desirable, some were not. Whole civilizations have lived here thousands of years and then abruptly disappeared, leaving the land to itself until others wandered in. If there is a single theme running through this saga in the Great Basin it must surely have to do with the interplay between people and this dry, difficult landscape.

We know little more about the earliest—the Paleo-Indians—other than that they successfully hunted huge animals with thrusting spears tipped by beautifully crafted points. The giant mammoth, bison, and sloths that lived in their time eventually became extinct, for reasons that remain unclear, though some have supposed that persistent hunting by the Paleo-Indians may have been a factor. Their successors, the Archaic peoples, as they are called, lived mainly along the edges of lakes and streams, harvesting the rich proteins produced by cattails and other swamp plants. If they were lucky they might catch a duck, snare a rabbit, or even bring down an antelope. But their staples were roots and seeds, and they always came back to the water's edge when they were hungry. They lived principally on whatever grew upon or inhabited the narrow stretches of Utah where land and water meet. As time went on some began to add upland plants to their diet, most notably the pinyon nut, which could be harvested, readily stored, and easily made into meal and cakes. They gradually moved from the water's edge onto the benches and into canyons but still harvested only what nature produced, leaving the land undisturbed. The Anasazi planted corn, squash, and beans, bringing water through ditches to keep the ground moist enough for their crops to grow. They also grew cotton and raised turkeys and dogs. Of all the early peoples, they made the greatest imposition on the landscape. Later groups imitated them to some extent, but the more typical way of the Fremont and of their successors, the Shoshonean peoples, was to return to the water's edge and harvest what was there rather than to bring water to cultivated land. These later peoples continued for the most part to move from place to place, as the seasons dictated, gathering and hunting what a stingy nature provided.

Contact with the Spaniards changed the Indian way of life, broadening the range of their activities, opening up new channels of trade, and bringing to the Ute Indians the horse. Buffalo and other big game were now in their grasp. The Spaniards explored parts of Utah in the 1700s, and some even recommended that colonies be founded, but higher officials chose to settle the highly desirable and contested coastal lands of California, over the less attractive Utah country.

The mountain men never intended to stay. They lived almost as comfortably with the environment as the Indians but had trapped the abundant beaver nearly out of existence by 1835. With the beaver gone the mountain men moved elsewhere, leaving Utes, Paiutes, Gosiutes, Navajo, and Shoshone pretty much alone again for almost a decade.

In 1847 the first of a whole new wave of people arrived on the scene—a people not content to accommodate their lives to the land as they found it. They had, within certain limits, skills and technology sufficient to fit the land to their life-style. They built dams and ditches; settled towns and cities, lining the spaces between them with roads and highways. They dug away whole mountains, pocking the hills with mine shafts.

This brings us to our own time and causes us to ask what our future relationship to the land will be. We have learned in the last century that the mountains and deserts of Utah are not indestructible. Nature is not quick in such a land to heal itself. Sediments churned up by mired wagons on salt flats west of Tooele could still be seen a hundred years later. The wrecks of wagons abandoned in the 1840s caused eddys in the drifting sands that formed mounds still visible in 1986. Within a few years of the first white settlement in Utah, overgrazing had beaten down many native grasses and plants on the mountain ranges and foothills of the Wasatch, leading to a long, difficult battle against erosion and flooding. We have learned that there may be limits to how much water we divert into city pipes, how much sewage we can dump into waterways, how many people the land can sustain.

Yet, how do we define those limits, and, more difficult, how do we impose them? These are matters of politics—who is in charge, who has power in Utah, and how that power is exercised. Those questions themselves have many dimensions. Power is held and used by elected officials in the town, county, and state jurisdictions, but also by federal officials, just as in territorial days. In addition, our economy has become intricately interwoven with a fabric that is worldwide. Events and decisions made thousands of miles away by persons who may never have heard of Utah can hit us with devastating impact. How do we identify such forces and develop a strategy for dealing with them?

Let us first take the area of politics. In 1987 Utah's chief executive was Republican Norman H. Bangerter. Utah's United States senators at the time were Jake Garn and Orrin Hatch, both conservative Republicans. In the U. S. House of Representatives were Republicans Jim Hansen and Howard Nielsen, and the newly elected Wayne Owens, the sole and lonely Democrat among the prominent officeholders of the state. And yet the past record shows, at least on the surface, considerable balance.

From statehood through 1984 Republican governors had been elected eleven times, Democrats twelve. The voting record for governor indicates no long-term trend towards conservative Republicanism in the state. New Deal Democrat Herbert Maw was Utah's governor for two terms from 1940 through '48 following another Democrat, Henry H. Blood. In 1948 he was defeated by the highly controversial, conservative maverick J. Bracken Lee, who also served the two four-year terms Utah voters commonly allot their governors. He was followed by Eisenhower Republican George Dewey Clyde. Republicans then had a long dry spell, as Democrat Calvin L. Rampton was elected to an unprecedented three terms and his heir apparent, Scott M. Matheson, to yet another two. Norman Bangerter was elected in 1984 at a time of economic distress and severe budgetary restraints, which may make it more difficult for him to maintain Utah's two-term gubernatorial tradition. The record is one of reasonable balance, with no clear trend in the direction of favoring one party over another and a tendency not to echo, in the governor's office, the party of the presidential winner.

Twenty-one senatorial races have gone to Republicans since statehood and but twelve to Democrats, though seven of the Republican victors were elected by the state legislature prior to the Seventeenth Amendment and four of the popular elections were to one man — Reed Smoot. The record in the Senate is thus not as unbalanced as the numbers on the face of them would suggest. Utahns have elected Republican congressmen forty-nine times, and Democrats forty, again not a dramatic imbalance.

The state legislature was also quite evenly balanced through 1977, the Senate having a Republican majority in twenty-four sessions, the Democrats in seventeen, with the numbers in one session, 1951, being evenly divided between the two parties. The House was dominated by Republicans twenty-two sessions and Democrats twenty sessions through 1977. Starting in '78, however, overwhelming Republican majorities were elected in both houses, maintaining numbers sufficient to override a governor's veto through 1986. In the 1987 legislature nine of twenty-nine in the State Senate were Democrats, and twenty-seven of seventy-five in the House, showing some erosion in the Republican bastion and making veto overrides far more difficult. Moreover, the election in that year of Democrat Wayne Owens to Congress, the very narrow defeat of Democrat Gunn McKay for that office and the impending demise of the Reagan presidency, which almost certainly gave a boost to Republican party fortunes in the early '80s, all suggested a possible return to the more balanced tradition in Utah politics.

Yet one could infer too much about the golden mean in Utah politics by looking simply at the party label. What does it mean to be a Republican or to be a Democrat? Nationally, we in recent years have thought of Republicans as favoring business expansion — opposing federal expansion, particularly in health and welfare areas, and favoring local autonomy over most matters. Democrats, on the other hand, have been seen as favoring the use of federal funds and powers to mitigate social and welfare problems, being less concerned about growth of the federal bureaucracy and more sympathetic to big labor than to big business. When we look back at recent Democratic governors in Utah, however, they fit the Republican stereotype nearly as well as the Democratic.

Calvin Rampton, three-term governor from 1964 to 1976, often spoke of his most enduring legacy as the bringing of new business, new jobs and prosperity to the state. His hand-picked successor, Scott Matheson, was a corporate lawyer for Union Pacific before entering politics and likewise worked closely with business in encouraging development and economic growth. The fact is that in recent Utah politics there has been very little difference between Democrats and mainstream Republicans on the need for economic expansion and the means of achieving it. All have been boosters — advocating rapid economic growth and eagerly promoting the founding of new business and industries. Their own principal measure of their success has been the degree to which they accomplished a rising level of prosperity.

This fixation may reflect in part a generally more conservative temper in the Mountain states, even among Democrats, who cannot depart far from their constituency without committing political suicide. Certain it is that Scott Matheson is no Tip O'Neill and that Wayne Owens is not (the shrill claims of his opponents in 1986 notwithstanding) an Edward Kennedy. But perhaps the greater part of our local politicians' concern for economic growth comes from their awareness of very pressing and peculiar needs imposed by Utah's high birthrate. Thanks in part to their efforts, income per person more than doubled in the state between 1970 and 1980. But that of the nation grew even faster, relegating us by 1980 to fourth lowest among the fifty states. The magnitude of the problem is indicated by the fact that the Utah population grew by 38 percent during the same period, compared to a national growth rate of 11 percent — all of the new, young Utahns requiring food, clothing, and education provided by the relatively small income-earning part of the population. The Utah growth rate slowed

in the 1980s, as birthrates declined, net inmigration ceased, and the economic picture darkened. The estimated rate of growth from 1980 to 1985 was 12 percent, bringing the total population of the state to about 1.6 million persons. Thus, Utah politicians were business boosters in the 1970s and '80s partly because they were in a desperate race to keep incomes rising as fast as population. In the process they have often been less attentive to concerns about the consequences to our land of unlimited growth.

There are other powers that affect the people of Utah, however, and chief among them is the federal government. Ever since the time government officials met the Mormons in flight across Iowa, offering to help with their migration West by taking 500 of their most able young men into the military, Mormons have been profoundly ambivalent in their attitudes toward Washington. This ambivalence has been reflected in Utah politics through the years. Most of the population was yearning for half a century to throw off the yoke of Washington, which maintained tight control of the territorial government. And while there has been since that time a persistent distrust of Washington's meddling in local matters, there has been at the same time a pronounced eagerness to secure Utah's share of reclamation, defense, and other federally funded projects.

Utah's congressional delegation took great pride in the success of its efforts in the late 1970s to maintain federal funding for the enormously costly Central Utah Project, designed to bring more water into the Wasatch Front and help irrigate new lands in central Utah. But while they were scrapping to salvage the project, a proposition was put on a statewide election ballot to cut off all federal monies by 1980. The proposition was defeated, but it is quite remarkable that it should appear at all in a state where 67 percent of the land is owned by the federal government and six out of every hundred civilian workers

gets his or her paycheck directly from Uncle Sam.

The fact is that the federal government has great power in the state. The blessings of the federal influence have been mixed. Economically there can be no doubt that federal dollars have increased prosperity and stimulated growth. Whether in the building of Flaming Gorge Dam or expanding Hill Field, new jobs were created and new resources made available to the citizens of our state. Moreover, watershed management by the Bureau of Land Management and the Forest Service has helped restore mountain pastures, checking erosion and keeping grazing within limits that the land can tolerate. Flooding has been greatly reduced and waters once lost in the spring runoff are now preserved in numerous small dams and reservoirs. Irrigation and city water supplies have been stabilized, except in time of severe general drought or heavy precipitation. Campgrounds, parks, and recreation areas have been developed and are available to the people at low cost. Lands

Central Utah Project crew, November 30, 1981. The crew had just broken through the 4.2-mile Hades Tunnel, north of Duchesne, and marked the occasion by posing for this photograph by Tom Fridman. *Courtesy U. S. Department of the Interior, Bureau of Reclamation, Upper Colorado Region.*

that might in other circumstances have fallen into the hands of private developers have been preserved for public access and use.

All of this is positive. But there is also a negative side to consider. The growth of federal influence has caused us in many instances to trade autonomy for prosperity. Federal officials not accountable through any direct democratic process to Utah's citizens make decisions that have far-reaching effects. Most often they see their decisions and actions as benevolent and in the best interest of the state. They are, nonetheless, ultimately responsible to Washington and not the statehouse, and if state and national interests conflict, they are bound to look out for the national interest. All of this makes us vulnerable and, to a degree, a subject people.

The Air Force can and does unilaterally decide that Utah's deserts are wastelands and our preferences unimportant compared to their perceptions of the national interest. A proposal was made in the late 1970s to build an MX racetrack basing system that would have had an enormous impact on the quality of life in the Beehive State. The project would have taken from public access vast portions of the states of Nevada and Utah, making the Great Basin a principal target in any nuclear conflict. The decision to build the MX would, no doubt, have brought new jobs and greater prosperity, but the federal government, and not the citizens of Utah, seemed to be deciding whether or not the price to be paid for this new prosperity would be too high. Defense spokespersons held hearings throughout Utah to sound public opinion on the MX, but those who attended came away feeling that such hearings were merely for show and that the decision had already been made, so far as the Defense Department was concerned. Only the strongly worded opposition of the Mormon church First Presidency and the change in Washington to an administration unusually sensitive to Utah's interests prevented the MX from coming to the area.

Another less tangible outside influence in recent decades comes from abroad. The whipsaw course of international economic change has often shaken Utah greatly. From 1847 to 1869 Utah was a relatively independent farming commonwealth. Between 1869 and 1900 the state developed a dual economy, producing precious metals and farm crops for export. By 1900 Utahns were beginning in true classical economic fashion to concentrate their efforts mainly on those products they were able best to produce, industrial metal ores, and to a lesser extent, farm crops. This worked well from 1910 to 1920 and during the war years, when world demand for the state's products was high. But for most of the first half of the century the demand for Utah's goods was low. A bushel of wheat brought only 98 cents in 1921. It was worth $3.77 in 1980. Oil-bearing shale, which is abundant in parts of Utah, was worth nothing in the 1960s when a barrel of crude oil brought $6. When crude went up to $34 in the late 1970s the shale deposits suddenly became a valuable resource of great interest to giant oil companies. But when oil prices dropped in the 1980s, the oil companies abandoned their processing plants and shale oil returned to its traditional status, as one scholar put it, of "having a great future. Which it always will."

World markets have commonly favored industrial and highly developed economies. During the 1970s, we were in a period that favored natural resource economies, especially those like Utah, rich in energy resources such as oil and coal. Moreover, monetary conditions caused gold, silver, and other metal mines, once abandoned, to be reopened under the stimulus of skyrocketing prices. An ounce of gold worth $32 in 1965 was worth twenty-five times that amount in 1980. But changes in the world economic system in the '80s dropped the price of precious metals to a level that made most Utah's mines unprofitable. Again we were buffeted by international economic instability.

That instability makes predictions hazardous. Yet, barring dramatic technological breakthroughs, the long-term trend must lead to shortages in natural resources. As that happens, Utah will experience unparalleled prosperity and growth and, if we do not handle our abundance wisely, severe ecological crisis.

As we make the decisions that will determine our quality of life in Utah for the foreseeable future, we no doubt will have our two founding fathers, Brigham Young and Patrick Connor, tugging at our coattails. Brigham Young stressed the importance of balance in economic growth, so as to maintain self-sufficiency. He recognized that development of precious metal

Patrick E. Connor statue at Fort Douglas. James R. Avati, sculptor. *Dean L. May photograph.*

mining in Utah would bring rapid economic growth and great wealth, but did all he could to discourage what he felt was a shortcut to prosperity. Under his leadership Utahns often deliberately chose the preservation of their way of life over quick wealth. He maintained that natural resources were a trust — to be held for public and not private enrichment.

General Connor was more in step with his times. The founder of Fort Douglas constantly urged development of the mining, industrial, and commercial potential of the territory. He led out by prospecting himself, setting up mining districts, and investing his own wealth in Utah's economy. Part of the benefit of this course, he maintained, would be a great influx of people, a people who would help Utah conform to national patterns in matters of religion, social life, family relations, and economic practices. In many respects he was Utah's

greatest booster, urging that the state dash pell-mell into the pleasures of the gilded age. And he lived to see much of his dream fulfilled.

Between 1869, when the railroad was built, and 1930 the basic pattern of Utah's development looked more and more like that envisioned by General Connor. By 1920 mines and smelters dotted Utah's landscape. Business, commerce, and industry had never been better. Then the lingering depression of the 1920s and '30s set in, and for two decades general hard times prevailed. Poverty seemed to cause more gentiles than Mormons to leave the Beehive State and depressed their birthrate more than it did that of the Mormons. Despite a considerable outmigration of Utah-born, the proportion of Mormons in the state began to rise. The population was 61 percent Mormon by 1940, 65 percent in 1950, 68 percent in 1960, 72 percent in 1970, and just under 70 percent in 1980.

These changes were accompanied by more overt actions on the part of Mormon church leaders to affect the moral climate of the state. In the 1920s they were so shy of open political involvement that they dragged their feet on the prohibition issue so that Utah would not approve too quickly and the action be blamed on church intervention. By the 1970s, however, they were showing a lively interest in a number of political matters that in their view had an important moral dimension. A 1968 liquor-by-the-drink referendum was defeated in Utah after a number of church leaders made speeches opposing it. Church leaders felt the Equal Rights Amendment of the late 1970s could have harmful effects on family stability. They asked church members not only to vote against the amendment but to work to assure its defeat. Many believed that the church's organized opposition helped defeat of the amendment nationally. A church call to Mormon women to attend the 1978 Utah International Women's Year Convention and make their opinions heard resulted in an attendance of 14,000 women, more than twice as many as in any other state. They voted down every national proposal on the ballot.

The Mormon church has likewise become increasingly involved in financial activities within the state. Its support of Salt Lake's ZCMI Center in the late 1970s contributed greatly to the revitalization of the city's upper Main Street area at the expense of the old Boston Building/Newhouse Hotel/Auerbach's district at Fourth South. It likewise contributed materially to the Salt Palace Convention Center, the Symphony Hall, and other downtown revitalization projects. Moreover, as the Mormon church continues to grow, its financial concerns transcend state and even national boundaries.

So, by the end of the 1970s, the Mormons were more evident and influential in the state than perhaps at any time in the twentieth century. This does not mean that the tide in favor of the Connor vision of the state's development had been reversed in favor of that of Brigham Young. Some would contend that Mormons in Utah have, true to Connor's hope, become thoroughly Americanized and show no evidence of the peculiarity they and others thought was so evident in the 1800s. This is a complicated and difficult question, but there is much evidence that the most fundamental of their distinctive traits as a people remain—in fact may be even stronger than at previous times—and that their resemblance to other Americans is superficial.

For example, Salt Lake City probably does not have a higher proportion of Mormons than Boston does Catholics. Yet families moving to Salt Lake City from Boston have been genuinely surprised to find that while in the Bay State one's religion is of no great interest or consequence, in Utah it is a powerful agent of social polarization. Here both Mormons and non-Mormons are prone to quickly stereotyping others after determining the all-important question, "Are they, or aren't they (Mormon)?" Such

concerns simply do not carry the same meaning in Boston.

Again, the quite remarkable International Women's Year Convention in Utah is instructive. Why did not other groups, who feel strongly about the issues being discussed, similarly galvanize their followers into participation? Though the Mormon women's voting on the ballot seemed in many instances undiscriminating and obstructive, one cannot but be awed by the remarkable level of their response to what they perceived to be the wishes of the church leaders.

Similarly, the rallying of Mormons to assist victims of Idaho's Teton Dam disaster in 1976 or the calling up of volunteers to contain the Salt Lake City floods in 1983 represented impressive and in these instances beneficial organizational accomplishments. The peculiar function of even urban congregations or wards as small villages, the evident respect of the church membership for the authority and advice of its leaders, the maintenance of an extensive welfare system of cooperative industries, the great extent to which the Mormons contribute time and money to church enterprises—all these have a ring of familiarity—seeming to confirm the observations of visitors to Utah from the 1850s to the recent past.

The Mormons, one suspects, are still a peculiar people, and the extent of their "Americanization" more apparent than real. Yet, ironically, the hope many of today's Mormons have of Utah's future is one that Patrick Connor would be quite happy with. And many non-Mormons would feel most comfortable in the camp of Brigham Young. That is to say that over time Utahns of all persuasions have been subjected to the pull of both Brigham Young and Patrick Connor. Our history since 1869 has been a fascinating story of tension, not only between but within Utahns. Wanting the material pleasures of life, each is unsure of how much of the pleasant landscape, the rural appeal, the quiet uncrowdedness

Brigham Young statue on Main and South Temple streets. Cyrus Dallin, sculptor. *Dean L. May photograph.*

of Utah he or she is willing to sacrifice to gain those pleasures.

Shall we, Connor-like, pull out all the stops, strike while the iron is hot, and, to the extent that the fickle world and national economies permit, exercise no restraint in our efforts to bring growth and prosperity to Utah? If we do, the experts say we shall have over 2,000,000 people by the year 2000. In the process we will virtually eliminate row-crop agriculture as a livelihood, becoming almost totally dependent on imported foodstuffs. What arable land remains will be taken up for urban and industrial use. In the Salt Lake Valley farmlands decreased by 22 percent between 1970 and 1977, and the state overall had been decreasing its agricultural acreage during the previous decade at a rate one and one-half times the national average. This rate of development is bringing congestion to our highways, overcrowding schools, parks, and other public facilities, and rimming our mountain vistas with condominium and apartment complexes. (It is perhaps symptomatic that the Salt Lake City Council voted in 1980 to annex Emigration Canyon, thus extending city services that will expedite development of the area by real estate firms.)

Or shall we, like Brigham Young, put spiritual priorities above material ones? Shall we consciously seek to preserve the natural beauty, the life-style, and the unique historical legacy of Utah even if this means at times putting the brakes on growth and prosperity? Shall we seek, as Brigham Young did, for a balanced, planned, self-sufficient future, for a future where natural resources, and above all the canyons, are considered a trust, belonging to all the people?

The decision, as we have seen, is not entirely up to us. Federal officials have at times seen use and development of Utah's resources as a high national priority. Impersonal, worldwide economic forces have made it richly rewarding to tear out our coal and other minerals as quickly and cheaply as possible. But we have to believe that in a democratic society the people count for something. While it is quite clear that we Utahns will continue to feel the tug of first Brigham Young and then Patrick Connor, and yield now to one and then to the other, it seems we should look clearly at which persuasion might bring the Utah we would like to live in and then do all we can to chart our course toward the one we choose. We can insist that farms and open spaces be preserved, knowing that we might have to be content with a lower standard of material wealth in order to keep up other standards of quality in our lives. Federal officials have been known to grow in their respect for the people's wishes if they are strongly and persistently made known. We can, by putting our mind to it, gain a greater degree of control over forces that seem to be spinning us off into an uncertain future.

Big Cottonwood Canyon, undated. John Hafen. *Courtesy LDS Museum of Church History and Art.*

Almost every Utahn is familiar with the statue of Brigham Young at the corner of Main Street and South Temple. For decades the standard quip has been that Brigham Young has his back to the temple and his hand outstretched to the bank. And sure enough he does. But those who take pleasure in the image don't understand Brother Brigham very well. Time and again he accomplished in his own life, and in that of his followers, the conscious sacrifice of personal material gain in order to achieve a broader community goal. There has been a small controversy in recent years about the location of the statue. Some have thought it obstructs traffic—standing in the way of our new pace of life.

I believe it might be appropriate to turn it around, so the founding father would face the Temple and the hills beyond— symbols of the spiritual in man and the quality of life he wanted for all Utahns. And the handsome companion statue of our second founding father, General Connor could be moved from Fort Douglas and placed at Brigham's back—looking down Main Street and out across the vigorously expanding Salt Lake Valley. In that position each could contemplate the vision he had of Utah's future. And as we pass, each of us might be brought to contemplate our own wish for Utah's future. The philosopher George Santayana once said that those who forget the past are condemned to repeat it. It was an apt proverb for his time— an age of unbounded optimism and faith in the future. The future does not always look as bright to us now. Yet as we stand beside the statue of Brigham Young today it might occur to us that those who remember the past just might be lucky enough to preserve the best of it.

For Further Reading:

Histories

There are, almost by definition, few histories that interpret persuasively for us the recent past. What histories there are deal primarily with economic and political events more than with the lives of the ordinary people, which have been the emphasis in this volume. A valuable general perspective can be gained from Gerald D. Nash's *The American West in the Twentieth Century: A Short History of an Urban Oasis* (2nd ed., 1977) and *The American West Transformed: The Impact of the Second World War* (1985). A wealth of information on many aspects of life in Utah up to1981 is in *The Atlas of Utah* (1981) published by Weber State College and Brigham Young University. Dennis L. Lythgoe's *Let 'Em Holler: A Political Biography of J. Bracken Lee* (1982) is very useful, giving insights into the politics of small-town government, state government, and Salt Lake City government in Utah between 1935 and 1971. The controversial and puckish Lee was mayor of Price in the '30s, governor of Utah from 1949 to 1953, and later mayor of Salt Lake City. See also Governor Scott M. Matheson's *Out of Balance* (1986) and interviews with Governor Calvin Rampton that appeared in the *Salt Lake Tribune* in November 1984. The original transcripts on which the Rampton articles are based are part of the Everett L. Cooley Oral History Collection, Special Collections, Marriott Library, University of Utah.

An argument for Utah's convergence with the rest of the United States in the twentieth century is in Charles S. Peterson's, "The Americanization of Utah" in *Utah Historical Quarterly*, winter 1976. Frank H. Jonas has published many useful studies of Utah politics. See especially his edited volume, *Politics in the American West* (1969). Pieces in the *Western Political Quarterly* and *Utah Holiday*, the latter more journalistic, can help one to keep abreast of recent political events in the Beehive State.

Leonard J. Arrington and George Jensen have offered a valuable study of economic change in *The Defense Industry of Utah* (1965) as has James L. Clayton in "An Unhallowed Gathering: The Impact of Defense Spending on Utah's Population Growth, 1940–1964," in *Utah Historical Quarterly,* summer 1966. A running record of Utah's economy is in the *Utah Economic and Business Review*, published by the University of Utah's Bureau of Economic and Business Research. See also ElRoy Nelson's *Utah Economic Patterns* (1956) and Leonard J. Arrington's *The Changing Economic Structure of the Mountain West, 1850–1950* (1963).

Useful sources of social data on Utah are Phillip R. Kunz and Merlin B. Brinkerhoff, *Utah in Numbers: Comparisons, Trends, and Descriptions* (1969), and Thomas K. Martin, Tim B. Heaton and Stephen J. Bahr, *Utah in Demographic Perspective* (1986).

Eyewitness Accounts

Again, there are few published memoirs, journals, or other eyewitness accounts available of changes in the recent past. Newspapers and magazines are available on microfilm and provide worthwhile accounts by journalists. Parents and other family members, if encouraged, can often recall how their lives have changed over recent decades, putting one in touch with the major events of our time. Much can be gained by taking time to reflect ourselves on how we live differently than we did five or ten years ago and what has caused the changes we perceive—a sort of do-it-yourself history. We should take the time to record such reflections, as persons like Marriner S. Eccles and James H. Moyle did, contributing them to libraries where they will be available to historians trying to understand the course of our times. Firsthand accounts are printed at times in *Utah Historical Quarterly*, and university libraries usually have oral histories that can be used in the library.

The Utah landscape has been much written about and commented upon. Perhaps the best of the lot is Edward Abbey's compelling portrait of southern Utah and the Arches National Park area in *Desert Solitaire*, still in print and widely available in inexpensive paperback editions. Utah's mountains are lovingly described in four lesser-known volumes published by Claude T. Barnes in the 1950s, each about one season, *The Natural History of a Wasatch Autumn, Winter, Spring, and Summer*. Though hardly a Thoreau, or even an Edward Abbey, there is a quality in Barnes's writing that opens new worlds to us as we hike among the mountains and canyons of Utah. A writer could hardly hope to accomplish more.

To the reader who, perhaps, at this point has completed this book, I could offer no better advice for the moment on further understanding Utah than that taught eloquently by lecture at Harvard. A large, attentive audience had gathered to imbibe the distilled wisdom of the great philosopher. According to the story, "He was about to conclude his remarks when he caught sight of a forsythia beginning to blossom in a patch of muddy snow outside the window. He stopped abruptly, picked up his hat, gloves, and walking stick, and made for the door. There he turned. 'Gentlemen,' he said softly, 'I shall not be able to finish that sentence. I have just discovered that I have an appointment with April.' "

Index